ALL OUT

KEVIN NEWMAN & ALEX NEWMAN

A Father and Son Confront the Hard Truths
That Made Them Better Men

RANDOM HOUSE CANADA

PUBLISHED BY RANDOM HOUSE CANADA

www.penguinrandomhouse.ca

Random House Canada and colophon are registered trademarks.

Library and Archives Canada Cataloguing in Publication

Newman, Kevin, 1959– , author
All out : a father and son confront the hard truths that made
them better men / by Kevin Newman and Alex Newman.

Issued in print and electronic formats.

ISBN 978-0-345-81387-9
eBook ISBN 978-0-345-81389-3

1. Newman, Kevin, 1959– . 2. Newman, Alex, 1986– .
3. Fathers and sons. 4. Gay youth—Family relationships. 5. Parents of gays—Psychology. 6. Television news anchors—Canada—Biography. 7. Television news anchors—United States—Biography. 8. Coming out (Sexual orientation). I. Newman, Alex, 1986– , author II. Title.

HQ759.9145.N48 2015   306.874'2   C2014-906394-6

Text design by CS Richardson
Jacket concept and art direction: Alex Newman
Jacket image: © Jesse Senko/Lisa Bonnici: Artist's Agent

Printed and bound in the United States of America

2 4 6 8 9 7 5 3 1

Penguin
Random House
RANDOM HOUSE CANADA

For the women who made us better men:
Cathy, Erica, Lois and Sheila

CONTENTS

INTRODUCTION
KEVIN

IN 1998, I WAS OFFERED the kind of job most broadcasters dream about: co-host of *Good Morning America*. Ratings had slipped, and ABC's senior executives decided I was just the man to turn the show around. At the time, I was *GMA*'s news anchor, and I had less faith in me than they did. A lot less. I knew I could report stories and anchor a newscast—I'd been doing that for years, in all different time slots. But I wasn't sure I had the unique blend of effervescence, likeability and personal authority it takes to carry a morning show. The host has to seem just as engaged by the winner of a cookie bake-off as by a head of state, and be not only a competent journalist but the kind of performer who can turn on a dime, from silly to sharp to serious. A life-of-the-party personality is a big help, and I didn't have one (still don't). But I did have a mortgage, two kids who'd want to go to university some day and a sense of shame about my own reluctance. What kind of wimp doesn't grab the golden ticket and try to run with it? I took the job.

Change is risky in TV, and ABC made a lot of changes all at once, suddenly jettisoning a seasoned on-air team, fluffing up the program with a lot of recipes and how-to segments, replacing a homey set with a fake chrome Manhattan condo, and then plunking two people who barely knew one another down on its art deco sofa. My co-host, Lisa McRee, and I weren't good at faking a married couple, brother and sister, or the holy grail of morning TV casting: secret lovers. Ours was clearly a shotgun marriage, and knowing that four million viewers were observing every eyebrow twitch and forced smile didn't help us bond. When ratings continued to slide, and then to nosedive rather spectacularly, the powers-that-be at ABC decreed that if I only changed my clothes, my glasses, my hair, my demeanour, my accent and my interview technique, I could be the guy America wanted to wake up with in the morning. Among other things, I was asked to dye my eyelashes (too pale), grow my hair (short isn't sexy) and enroll in Matt Lauer school (yes, really): a show doctor operation where consultants coached me to ape the co-host of *The Today Show*, which was killing us in the ratings. Occasionally I protested when a "tweak" of my manner or appearance seemed particularly idiotic, or when I disagreed with a substantive decision about the direction of the show. But never very forcefully.

Confidence in your own judgement is hard to maintain when every signal you receive is that nothing about you is quite good enough. So for the most part, I followed senior executives' orders. I did everything I could to try to live up to their expectations and become the "quarterback type" they wanted me to be. I was only the third male host in the program's history. I didn't want to be the one who failed.

But I was. Eight months in, Lisa and I were fired, along with the show's executive producer. On my last day, with millions of people watching, all of them knowing I'd been shown the door, I tried to smile broadly when I told viewers that Charlie Gibson and Diane Sawyer would be joining them Monday, "and you know how great they are." I thanked the audience for watching and attempted to sound upbeat when I said I'd been reassigned to other duties within ABC News. The *GMA* franchise—and my chances of future employment—required me to seem to embrace the change. My pride required me not to appear victimized. Somehow I had to project strength though what I really felt was flattened by a potent blend of regret, exhaustion and, most acutely, humiliation.

Luckily, I'd had time to think carefully about what would happen immediately after the red light on top of the camera went off and we were no longer on air. There would be no applause or celebration; everyone knew that leaving was not my choice. No, most likely, a painful, awkward silence would descend on the set. To head that off, I'd arranged two things. First, my wife, Cathy, came to the studio with our kids, Alex and Erica, and they joined me as soon as I signed off. Surrounded by the people I love best in all the world, it was easier for me to keep it together. But I also meant it to be a public declaration: my family would be my new priority. During the preceding tumultuous year, I'd all but abandoned them.

Second, I got a haircut, right then and there on the set. No sooner had we wrapped than the show's hairstylist plugged in an electric clipper, put on a number three guard and commenced shaving. The crew watched, perplexed, not understanding that this, too, was an announcement: I meant to reclaim myself and stop listening to anyone else's opinion about who I should be or what I should look like. I hated how much power the network executives had had over me—and hated myself for giving it to them. Cutting off the long hair they had so carefully focus-group-tested was my declaration of independence. I couldn't deliver a stirring speech about throwing off the shackles of network servitude since I wanted to continue working at the network, after all. So the haircut would have to serve as a metaphor, even if I was the only one who really knew or cared what it meant.

It was also a promise to myself: from here on in, I was going to be my own man.

When I was fired from *GMA*, I knew I had to own my part in the failure or I'd never move past it. Yes, the show had been poorly run. Yes, I'd been the whipping boy for bad management decisions I'd had no say in. But the hard truth was that I'd known from the start that I wasn't right for the job, and I took it anyway. I'd ignored my instincts and wound up trying to pretend to be someone I wasn't.

And throughout, I'd been miserable. Even during the brief time when I'd looked like a success to the rest of the world, I'd felt uneasy. The lesson was simple: unless I was true to myself, I couldn't be happy and I wouldn't succeed.

I knew what I was good at and what kind of work I wanted to do. I might have a second act if I could focus on going in the direction that felt right to me, even when people told me I was heading the wrong way, away from the main chance. I don't want to minimize the difficulty of engineering a comeback. Pride had to be swallowed, dues had to be paid all over again, and the slog was strictly uphill. I took lower-profile gigs and pushed myself to learn new skills and become a better storyteller. Three years on, I'd won two Emmys, turned down a second shot at the big time in New York and relocated to Vancouver to launch a new national newscast. I was where I wanted to be, professionally. I felt successful. Happy.

And then, I faced another sort of reckoning: my son turned seventeen and came out. Cathy and I immediately told Alex we loved him and would always support him, no matter what. Our instinctive reaction was gratitude: thank God our son trusts us with what he feels is the biggest truth about himself. I was also relieved. Alex and Cathy had always been enviably close, but with me he was distant, unreachable—had been for years. Suddenly it all made sense. He'd been harbouring a secret, but now that he'd got it off his chest, he and I would be able to bridge the distance between us.

That's not what happened. The gap actually widened. It turned out that Alex had a list of grievances, all variations on the same theme: I'd tried to make him into someone he wasn't—sporty, popular, a guy's guy—and I'd succeeded in making him feel like a disappointment. To hell with that. He was going to be his own man.

The echoes of my own experience were deafening, but still it was hard for me to accept that I'd done to my son what I'd found unbearable when it was done to me. Sure, I'd had expectations for him—what father doesn't? But mine were benevolent, rooted in my hope that he'd have an easier childhood than I'd had. I hadn't meant to squash him or make him miserable. How could the child I still hugged and kissed hello and goodbye possibly feel I was disappointed in him? Did he not know that I valued and loved him just as he was?

No, he didn't.

The truth, as he pointed out to me, was that I hadn't made my family my top priority, as I'd vowed I would when *GMA* ended. I'd thrown myself into a start-up whose success required my full attention. So when Alex hit his crisis, I didn't have much credit in the bank as far as he was concerned. If I wanted to stand by him now, I had to prove I deserved to, by being willing to see myself through his eyes. The view was not always to my liking. I'd thought of myself as a demonstrative father, affectionate to a fault and emotionally open, but my son's perception was that I'd been largely absent, preoccupied with work and a little intimidating. He'd grown up in awe of my success but ignorant of my failures, certain of my strength but unaware of my vulnerability. From his perspective, I'd chosen work over him, time and again. He didn't know why, or what it had cost me, or even that I felt guilt and grief about what I'd missed. He didn't have the whole picture, in other words, but the shape of the thing was clear: I hadn't been the father I'd hoped to be or even thought I was.

Alex was doing what every young man should, demanding to be heard and insisting on his right to redefine our relationship. This is a dangerous moment if a father refuses to renegotiate the terms of the relationship, but to me, it looked like a second chance. I seized it. I wanted to refashion our bond into something deeper and truer, not just for my own selfish reasons but for my son's sake. He was a teenager, willfully navigating a tricky passage into unfamiliar waters. True, I didn't know the first thing about being gay, but I wanted to help him find his way, if he'd let me. I also wanted to protect him. It seemed to me that life for a gay man would be more difficult and also potentially more dangerous. I feared for his health, his safety, his future happiness. I feared for myself, too; maybe he'd turn toward men who could understand and empathize with him in ways I never could, and I'd lose him altogether.

I was not going to let that happen. But to hold on to my son, I had to change. I wasn't the only one with expectations, as it turned out. It wasn't enough for Alex that I accepted his sexuality; he wanted me to embrace homosexuality in general. This was not easy for me. Though I was all for gay rights, I just wasn't comfortable in a social setting where I was the only straight guy in the room—and my discomfort disappointed me even more deeply than it disappointed my son, not least because I'd always thought of myself as enlightened and tolerant.

In fact, I was average, which is to say, a little schizophrenic when it comes to homosexuality. For instance, though a majority of heterosexual Americans support the idea of same-sex marriage, 56 percent admit they would feel uncomfortable or very uncomfortable attending a same-sex wedding, according to a Harris poll conducted at the end of 2014. Seventy-one percent wouldn't feel comfortable taking a child. More than 40 percent said they would feel uncomfortable or very uncomfortable to learn that a family member was gay. Canadians are more likely to tell pollsters they believe society should be accepting of homosexuality, but I'd be surprised if their personal acceptance was all that different from Americans'.

Certainly my own emotional responses were not always in line with my politics. To become the father my son deserved, I had to re-examine my own core beliefs about masculinity; I had to rethink what it means to be a good father. Redrawing the boundaries of my comfort zone has taken years, and it's changed me, and my relationship with my son, profoundly. Along the way, we mystified, misjudged and irritated each other, as fathers and sons will. We did not always find common ground. But we did find one another.

Alex and I set out to write this book in the hope that we could help gay kids and their families understand each other. A few years ago, in the course of reporting a story, I came across a horrifying statistic: gay kids are twice as likely as straight kids to attempt or commit suicide—and they are eight times more likely to do so if their parents reject them. Alex wound up helping me publicize that story, and the overwhelming response to it galvanized both of us. We felt that if we could prevent even one suicide, we had a responsibility to do so.

But when we started talking about what we'd write, we discovered that our real subject was not sexuality or tolerance. They figured into our own story, but the differences between us could just as easily have involved religion, or politics, or money, or values, or career aspirations, or any of the other issues that cause trouble in families. Our real subject, we soon realized, was fathers and sons, and what they have to learn from one another but frequently do not.

Fathers are supposed to teach their sons how to be men, but many of us do that primarily by laying down expectations of what our sons should accomplish rather than trying to help them figure out who they really are. When they start to figure that out for themselves, they may feel that in order to be themselves, they have to break free or even reject us altogether. Different beliefs and values threaten a relationship when both people don't already know and understand each other well. And fathers and sons often do not understand each other: we don't know the stories we tell ourselves about who we are and how we got that way. Yet these narratives shape how we interact and influence what we think—and feel—about each other. They can keep us apart or, if shared, bring us together.

When he was a teenager, Alex and I loved one another, but we were mysteries to one another, too. I'd never been the active-duty parent who knew where his favourite T-shirt was, when the math homework was due, and why he hated John G.'s guts. The stuff of daily life provides connective tissue; Cathy, as a full-time, at-home mother, had a bond with Alex that was richer, more intimate and nuanced than mine. They knew one another inside out. I tended to swoop in to solve problems and mete out punishments, so there was a black-and-white nature to our interactions. It was more difficult for me to know, and be known by, him.

Only through writing this book have we discovered the many parallels in our experience. For instance, we'd never recognized that by a weird synchronicity, Alex and I went through existential crises at about the same time. Mine was a mid-life crisis while his was the adolescent version, but we'd asked ourselves the same kinds of questions: What does success look like? What do I need to be happy? Am I chasing my own dreams, or the ones I'm supposed to want?

For each of us, the next few years were a crucible, but not one we went through together. Both of us felt full of self-doubt and both of us were hell-bent on keeping that a secret. For my part, it just never occurred to me that Alex could learn something from, or relate to, my identity crisis. Insofar as I thought about it, I believed I was shielding him from adult worries. And okay, full disclosure: I didn't want him to learn about vulnerability from me, only strength. As I've since discovered, he thought he was protecting me, too. He didn't want to disappoint me—he knew I would never understand.

What follows is the story of how we did come to understand one another. It is not an object lesson, or a prescription, or a how-to guide. It is just our story—or, to be more accurate, two stories, because this is as much Alex's book as mine. One of the principles drilled into every journalist is that there are at least two sides to every story, and you'd better consider both if you want to get anywhere close to the truth. So we decided to write our chapters separately, without reading one another's words until the manuscript was complete, because we didn't want our memories and feelings to get jumbled in the telling. At times, the process scared me: What was my son writing? Would I be able to show my face in public once people heard his uncensored version of events?

But now that I have read what we've both written, I'm glad we did it this way. Although I've found it surprisingly painful to revisit old conflicts and unearth new ones, I have a new understanding of myself, my history and my son. We were close before. We are even closer now. This book became the conversation Alex and I should have started years ago.

We hope that it helps you start your own conversation. One thing we now know for sure: it's never too late. We had no idea, when we finally began, just how much we'd each left unsaid, or how important it would be to both of us to say it. And hear it. Understanding one another has helped us become better men.

CHAPTER ONE

FATHERHOOD
KEVIN

LONG BEFORE CATHY BECAME PREGNANT with our first child, she'd thought about what kind of parent she wanted to be. Her own mother was creative, fun, demonstrative and endlessly understanding; Cathy always felt she could tell her mom anything, and wanted her own kids to feel the same about her. In a considered way, she'd thought through some of the day-to-day issues—how to discipline, how much screen time—and how she wanted to handle them.

I'd never really given much thought to becoming a father, or even how having kids might change me. Nothing like that ever came up in conversation with other men, either. There was the occasional mention of which sports we'd play with our kids if we ever had them, but there were no meaningful discussions about fatherhood, nothing like the talks we had about current events and our own careers.

While Cathy was pregnant, my attempts to educate myself were largely focused on her: how to help her through her pregnancy and the birth of our child. In my own father's time, men sat in the waiting room with cigars. My generation was the first to try to shrink that distance, by being present for labour and delivery, but there was little information on what to do afterwards. The child-care books I read, and I read several, had only a few lines specifically targeting fathers; as I recall, they concerned the effects children have on a father's sex life and relationship with his wife. If there was anything specific about a father's relationship and interaction with his children, it must have been extremely brief because I don't remember it. The childbirth classes we attended above a submarine sandwich shop were all about getting ready for labour and delivery, not for the profound changes to our lives afterwards. I learned how to help Cathy breathe through contractions and how I could support her during labour (though I held the cardboard cross-section of a woman's abdomen upside down for most of the demonstrations and fumbled the one quick lesson on swaddling a newborn). By the time Cathy's due date was upon us, I was mostly prepared to be a better husband while she gave birth. Not a father.

Then a day passed, and another, and another, with no sign of the baby's arrival. We'd settled on his name long before, after narrowing our short list down to the one both our families had in common: my Irish great-grandfather was Alexander, and so was Cathy's Scottish great-grandfather. I wanted him to share my first name, John, but to use his middle name, as I always have, and Cathy agreed to the request. Our John Alexander Newman displayed a stubborn streak even before he was born. The overnight bag for Cathy's hospital delivery sat in our bedroom for two full weeks after her due date. His increasing size made it hard for her to breathe, and her stomach became so distended that she could rest a bowl of cereal on it with no fear of a spill. Finally Cathy's doctor ordered her to the hospital so delivery could be induced.

Much of what we had practised in our birthing classes turned out to be useless, as Cathy's labour went from zero to full throttle in a matter of minutes. There would be no gentle guidance and reassurance from me as her labour pains gradually intensified—they were extreme from the get-go and I was pretty much helpless to soothe her. She was surrounded by a mishmash of wires and probes, and Alex's vital signs were being continually monitored. It didn't feel like the birth we had prepared for. It felt like a crisis.

I eventually figured out that Cathy's contractions could be predicted by a spike on one of the monitors, so I would tell her another one was coming and hold her hand as each new wave of pain pounded her. We tried lumbering slowly down the hallway of the maternity ward between contractions, but that didn't help. After seventeen impossibly long hours, Cathy had barely dilated four centimetres, and was beyond exhausted.

And then Alex's vital signs faltered. The medical staff rushed us into a surgical suite for an emergency caesarean section. Cathy was given an epidural for the pain and I was allowed to stay by her head to try to calm her; a white sheet was strung up so neither of us could see the quick work the medical team was performing on the lower half of her body. I held her shoulders, kissed her forehead and fought down my own panic so I'd sound convincing when I assured her everything was going to be okay. I kept checking the doctor's eyes, still visible above her surgical mask, trying to look for any sign of concern, but she appeared very calm and focused.

As the doctor made the initial incision Cathy quietly said, just loud enough for me to hear, "Ow ow ow! Am I supposed to be feeling pain?" I said, much more loudly and forcefully, "She's feeling that!" The doctor barked at the anaesthetist, "Do you think we can get this done without pain?" I felt I'd finally added some value to the proceedings.

What happened next is murky in my mind so many years later. Only flashes of images survive, but what I felt—fear, helplessness—was indelibly imprinted. Alex didn't cry, didn't make a sound after he was born. A team of nurses rushed him, umbilical cord trailing, over to another table. He was terrifyingly blue; something was clearly very wrong. Almost simultaneously, the doctor who was sewing up Cathy's incision yelled, "She's hemorrhaging, put her out." A mask was briskly placed over Cathy's nose and mouth, she lost consciousness immediately, and a male nurse grabbed me by the arm and hustled me out of the room. Every instinct told me to resist, but I was still rational enough to know that I wanted everyone in that room one hundred percent focused on saving my wife and our baby, not quieting a frantic husband.

I don't remember being led into another small room, where it was, or how long it took to get there. I just remember being alone, sitting silent and stoically for the most part, but then, when what seemed like too much time had passed and still no one had come, realizing that Cathy and our baby might be dying. Oh God. Had they already died? A strange blast of sound came out of my mouth, horror made audible.

My wife is the most beautiful woman I've ever met who doesn't know it. She's funny, genuine, playful, and she just radiates kindness. Every guy in the newsroom where we met had wanted to ask her out, even though she was dating someone else. I only worked up the courage because I heard a cameraman announce that he didn't care, he was going to ask if she'd go on a date with him. That same evening, well past midnight, I just happened to drop into the newsroom, knowing Cathy was working an overnight shift, to ask her to go to a play with me. I was elated and slightly shocked when she agreed. Three years on, I still didn't quite believe my luck, and the idea that I might have lost her—or our baby—was impossible to bear.

I don't know how much longer I stayed in that room with the door closed, I just remember being afraid to leave because then I'd be forced to confront what had happened. After awhile— another hour?—I made myself go out into the hallway but I just stood there, frozen and disoriented, until a nurse came over and asked whether I was lost. I told her something terrible had happened while my wife was giving birth. She asked if someone had come to talk to me yet. My heart ached. I didn't want to hear what she would say next.

But what she said was, "Oh my God! We forgot about you. Do you want to see your baby?"

"They're alive?"

"Yes, your wife is fine but she's still asleep. You won't be able to see her for a few hours. Your baby is over here in an incubator."

She led me to Alex, who was sealed inside a clear plastic box, wailing. He had my strange toes, my mouth, and he looked cold, vulnerable and utterly alone. His first hours in the world hadn't

been spent wrapped snugly in a soft blanket, with parents holding him close and kissing his impossibly smooth forehead. He
was naked in the incubator, sensors attached to several places on
his body to monitor his vital signs. There was a piece of paper
taped to the side of the incubator with his Apgar score, which
I knew from our classes was a measure of his robustness at
birth. On a scale of one to ten, my son was a two.

The need I felt to hold him, to claim him, to calm him, was
overwhelming, but there was a cold barrier between us. I asked
the nurse if I could at least put my hands into the green rubber
gloves attached to one of the incubator walls, so I could try to
soothe him. She agreed, and I reached in, taking care not to dis-
turb the web of wires around him, and gently rested my hand on
his stomach, hoping that awareness of another human presence
would comfort him. I started humming a lullaby I had sung to
him before he was born, then I sang it loudly to try to block out
the noise of the room and penetrate the plastic walls surrounding
my child. He seemed to recognize the tune, and my voice, and
stopped crying. He was listening, waiting for more. I felt I was
the only person in the world at that moment able to comfort him,
so I sang and he quickly settled into sleep, which comforted me.
It was the first time that I felt I was truly a father. As I carefully
withdrew my hands from the rubber gloves, I made a silent pledge
to Alex: *I'll never let anything bad happen to you.*

Once Cathy and Alex were well enough to be released from the
hospital, I wanted to play an active role as a parent, but I wasn't
sure exactly how to go about it. Cathy's mother and then mine
took turns helping us out, and they were instant experts while I

was clumsy. The diapers never seemed as tight when I fastened them and the burping was never as effective, either. I acquiesced to their expertise and watched from the sidelines, feeling sheepish. Incompetent.

I was better at other things. A few weeks into his life, Alex's appetite couldn't be completely satisfied by Cathy, so while she rested, I'd settle into the only comfortable chair in our living room and give Alex his only bottle of the day, to try to supercharge his sleep into the six-hour range. It usually worked. We were both exhausted—him from simply existing, me from long hours in network news—and when the bottle was finally empty, he'd instantly fall asleep on my chest. I'd slouch down in the chair to create a more level surface for him, then watch his small body rise and fall gently with my breathing, while his own breathing slowed and he relaxed into a deep, secure sleep. I never wanted those moments to end. My boy with his perfect, smooth skin pressed against the coarse hairs of my chest, needing nothing more than the sound of his father's heartbeat to feel entirely at peace.

On nights like these, cupping Alex's tiny head in my hand, the urge to protect him was strong, almost a hunger. I'm not a particularly combative guy. I've been in one brawl in my life (university, drunk, a friend's honour—the usual stupidity), but I knew I would not hesitate to take on anyone who threatened him. I would do everything in my power to keep him from harm. For me, and I suspect many other fathers, this isn't just macho bravado. The drive to provide protection is in our DNA. It's how we're built.

But some of us think we're also here for *projection*. To map a future for our kids. I'll admit it, I indulged in this myself, though my plans for Alex didn't focus on specific achievements. It was never, "He's going to be a doctor." My dreams revolved around the kind of childhood I wanted for my son and the sort of man I hoped he'd become: confident, worldly, popular—everything I'd longed to be, but wasn't, as a child.

Even at six months of age, though, it was clear that Alex was not the passive type who'd meekly submit to being moulded. Already tightly coiled, he tended to greet the day with his fists clenched. Desperate to crawl and intensely curious, he was quick to laugh and to brood. Or to put it another way, he was already showing signs of being very much his own person.

But that didn't stop me from imposing expectations on him. I hoped that he'd be athletic. I hadn't played team sports growing up, so I'd missed out on the camaraderie, and never learned how to put the team's interest ahead of my own while still physically pushing myself to compete. For boys, playing on a team creates social currency, a fact I became keenly aware of in high school, where I was sometimes called a "fag" because my own interests—politics, history, theatre—weren't sufficiently physical. I resolved to enroll Alex in soccer and baseball and whatever else he was interested in, at the earliest opportunity. He didn't have to be a pro athlete. The idea was just to set him up to succeed socially.

I also wanted to show him the world so he'd feel comfortable in other cultures. I hadn't ventured outside North America until my mid-twenties, when my newsroom sent me to the UK to cover a conference on apartheid. I hadn't felt confident or geared up to make the most of the opportunity; I'd felt overwhelmed and uncertain. Well, that wasn't going to happen to

Alex. I'd take him places and show him things, so he'd grow up feeling like a citizen of the world.

Another thing: my kid wasn't going to feel isolated. Growing up, I'd been shy, with never more than a handful of friends. In high school, things got worse. I was ostracized. I didn't want Alex to experience that depth of loneliness, or anything even close to it. No, he'd be surrounded by friends, a "crew."

And on it went. Of course, this list was a perfect reflection of my own regrets and longings. I didn't want Alex to follow in my footsteps—I wanted him to avoid my missteps. Where I had struggled he would excel; he would have all the things I'd missed out on.

I had a list of expectations for myself, too. Aside from being a good provider and good role model, I would be the sort of father I wished my own father had been: physically affectionate, emotionally connected, a family man. Present, in every way.

My father never worked anywhere but Bell, eventually rising to a senior sales role. He worked hard and travelled a lot when I was a child, but by the time I was a teenager, his work was mostly nine-to-five. He was not absent, in other words, but I never felt I got enough of his attention. Our traditional greeting when I was growing up was a handshake, not a hug. To be fair, my dad was typical of his generation: my friends' fathers weren't showering them with affection or worrying about their emotional needs, either. That wasn't how my dad had been raised. He had an accomplished father, a lawyer with a formal manner, and a politically involved mother with mayoral ambitions, who didn't want him to do anything improper or stand out in a negative way. No wonder he was self-contained.

Our interactions weren't marked by harshness, but distance. Sometimes he took me to hockey games, which I enjoyed, but I don't remember any conversations about what was going on in my life, and I didn't feel he was particularly proud of me. I was a disaster as an athlete and he couldn't hide his disappointment when, as a young boy, I came off the ice at the hockey rink short of breath. I had asthma, which was exacerbated by the cold air at outdoor rinks, and I couldn't last more than a few minutes. But that wasn't all: I was a poor skater and I wasn't an aggressive player. After each game or practice, we barely exchanged a word as I unlaced my skates, and then we'd walk home, usually in silence. I knew I'd let him down, and that his disappointment was about something bigger than hockey. Somehow I'd failed as a son.

My mother, who held a series of administrative jobs, was more demonstrative but also often frustrated by my lack of physical and emotional toughness. I was too sensitive, not competitive enough, though the flip side of this failing was that I was a good kid, eager to please. The worst thing I did on purpose was steal some carrots from a neighbour's garden, at the urging of a friend. But my parents tended to zero in on the one thing I'd done wrong in any situation, and consequently, I felt I was a disappointment to them. Quite possibly they were just ambitious for me, and hoped I'd go far. But what child is aware of his parents' motives?

I grew up in Montreal and then Mississauga, outside Toronto, in a solidly middle-class home with parents who worked to live rather than lived to work. They seemed content with our suburban existence—the streets filled with bike-riding kids, summers at the lake—but to me it seemed like big things were happening elsewhere in the world and we weren't part of them. I felt my family embraced the predictability and comfort of the familiar, the conventional, and didn't really "get" me. I was creative, nerdy, the kind of kid who wore glasses and got excited about elections and watched the news. My dad occasionally watched, too, but for me, network news became a religion, one I knew enough to conceal at school. I would have graduated from a mere outlier to a pariah.

Then, when I was fourteen, a jolting change: my parents divorced. My dad moved out and eventually found a welcoming new wife with children of her own, resurfacing for awkward get-togethers with me and my younger sisters, Kelly and Debbie. Years later, he told me he felt his job as a father had been to get us to the point of self-sufficiency as quickly as possible, but at the time all I felt was abandoned. Shattered, my mom retreated emotionally, to a point where she seemed unreachable. I didn't want to burden her with my own sadness and confusion. On some level I'd known my parents weren't happy together, but their marriage had at least given me a sense of safety and security. That evaporated completely when they split up.

I was miserable. I did fine at school but didn't feel I belonged, there or anywhere else, and my instinct was not to reach out but to pull back. Sometimes the need was so overwhelming that I'd go sit in the broom closet at school, the one place that felt safe because I could shut out the world. But I could never hide for long. Post-divorce, money was very tight at home, so I'd started working after school. I had to step up, not add to my mother's distress.

Over time, my fascination with news and politics helped me

focus more on the outside world, where my own problems were irrelevant. Current events provided a lifeline, one that helped pull me up from depression. The more engaged I became with issues and ideas, the more energized I felt. But being well informed wasn't a bridge to other kids—socially it was the kiss of death, so I downplayed it. I didn't want to be seen as a dweeb or a know-it-all. I wanted to be liked. I started going out for the school plays, and discovered I enjoyed performing. And I liked the attention.

I had the yearnings of an extrovert but was still very much an introvert, as became clear when I ran for president of the student council in grade eleven. I lost, as anyone who'd seen me eating lunch alone in the cafeteria every day could have predicted. Losing didn't feel good. At all. But by putting myself out there, I'd learned that adopting a confident persona actually made me feel a little more confident, inside. Acting "as if," I could build myself up.

After that very public defeat I basically withdrew from school life and shifted my focus to the local McDonald's, where I was a shift manager. The lime green uniform of the day was not particularly helpful in terms of improving my social status, but nevertheless, I thrived in the environment. The kids I worked with came from all over, not just my high school, so they had no preconceived notions about me. I finally found the acceptance I had been craving; I was invited to parties, started going to clubs, learned to relax. I accelerated my studies to graduate ahead of my class, then spent eight months as a full-time McDonald's manager, saving for university and my first car. In the summer of 1978 the regional manager pulled me aside and offered a more senior management position, and the opportunity to attend "Hamburger U" for training in Ohio. He promised me a real future at the company, but I politely declined.

I wanted to break free of everything I knew and reinvent myself as someone who belonged in the big world I saw every night on the news.

My "male" skillset was, at this point, limited. I'd come of age in a female-dominated home—even our two dogs were female—without a male role model actively coaching me through adolescence. I knew how to work hard without complaining about it, but I had no game with women, couldn't hammer a nail in straight and had no sport to call my own. Only the white 1975 Ford Mustang I'd bought with my fast-food earnings gave me any street cred.

University is where I really started learning how to be a man. Most of my roommates had attended all-boys schools, so the environment was high testosterone. Studying their behaviour, I started to understand what it means to be one of the guys. They never targeted me, though I was different in some important ways; they accepted me, protected me when necessary, and built me up. We hung out, worked out, called each other out during raging intellectual debates and usually could be found, at the end of a party, wrestling, drunk, in black T-shirts. I discovered a lifelong passion for weightlifting; I learned the value of loyalty, mental toughness and giving my all in any competition. I had always wanted a brother, and now I had many, and they remain my brothers to this day. I dated two women during those years but I wasn't a great boyfriend. I was more interested in hanging with my friends. On my occasional visits home, I found myself anxious to get back to what I thought of as my real life. I was, for the first time, happy.

I began university interested in law (my parents' first choice, because it seemed safe), entrepreneurship and journalism. But after I helped start a campus radio station and taught myself the basics of broadcasting, editing and reporting, there was only one thing I wanted to do with my life. TV news was the goal. Television was how I'd become interested in news in the first place, drawn in by the power and immediacy of the visuals. But this was the early 1980s, and journalism schools tended to have underwhelming programs for would-be TV reporters. The emphasis, post-Watergate, was still on print journalism. I decided to major in political science, figuring that would help me understand and report what was going on in the world, then apply to radio and TV stations after graduation. My mother fretted that I wasn't competitive enough to be a journalist, and she was right that I didn't have the supreme self-confidence that usually fuels a killer instinct. But I did have the hunger that fuels real drive. I really, really wanted this. To me, reporters had the most interesting job in the world, right on the front lines of history (I may have been just a little idealistic—I didn't foresee that one day I'd find myself on a morning show, feigning interest in sweater-folding techniques).

I was still a news junkie, more hard-core than ever, and one day I sent what amounted to a fan letter to a TV reporter at Global News in Toronto, which somehow wound up in the hands of their PR department, which turned it into a rah-rah item that was picked up by a newspaper, which emboldened me to ask whether I could shadow a Global reporter for a day, which led to my first job in journalism, after I got my degree: editorial assistant at Global. My salary was $9,000 a year—peanuts, even in 1981—and the job involved making good coffee and running around the newsroom handing out Xeroxes of wire copy. There were eight of us doing that, and I quickly realized that nobody who mattered could tell any of us apart. So for the first week, I wore a name tag, which was unspeakably geeky but also meant I got asked to do more things because people knew my name.

After a few months, an aspiring cameraman and I asked to borrow a camera during our time off, and eventually one of our stories—we covered a contest where people competed to write a novel in twenty-four hours—made it to air. About eight months later I was hired as a sports reporter. I was on my way.

I didn't know much about sports, and reporting scores didn't interest me. But I'd been told by more than one mentor that the best news writers come out of sports reporting; to describe each game well, they have to find new ways to write about the emotions, the characters, the drama. I found I liked covering the backstories: blood-doping scandals, the machinations behind trades, things like that. Plus, I had the kind of access to professional athletes and team locker rooms that my father and friends could only dream of. In their eyes, that made me a little special, which was something I'd always wanted to be.

A year or so later, I was promoted to the news division—the big time. I'd worked hard to get there, but didn't feel like a real journalist yet. TV news is all about competition. You're always racing against the clock to get a story, knowing that two or three people at other stations are on the same path and if you make the wrong judgement call, one of them is going to beat you—and the loss will, of course, be public. I was plenty ambitious and didn't want to be beaten, but I wasn't comfortable with the idea of bulldozing over people to get a story. Nor did I even know how to do that.

One of my first assignments was to get a photo of a local guy who'd just been killed in an oil-rig disaster off the coast of Newfoundland. This was pre-internet, so the idea was to go to the dead man's father's home, in Toronto, and ask for a picture we could use in our broadcast. I drove over with a cameraman, feeling like a vulture—a guilty, inept one. I was twenty-three years old. I had no idea what to say to a grieving father. The cameraman shrugged, suggesting, "Just be polite." I knocked on the door and when the guy answered, I said, "I'm really sorry for your loss. Look, you don't have to give me a photo but it's my job to ask if you're willing to." I went back to the car empty-handed. While I was sitting there, trying to figure out how to explain to my boss that I'd failed my first test, a newspaper reporter pulled up, charged up to the door and announced, "I need a photo." *He* sounded like a real journalist: confident and direct, peremptory even. When the dad resisted, the reporter coolly dressed him down, saying he had a moral obligation to fork over a picture of his dead child. The grieving father wound up yelling at him and slamming the door in his face—and, after the reporter peeled off, coming out to my car and handing me a photo of his son. That gave me hope: maybe there was more than one way to succeed in this line of work.

Already, I'd figured out that success in TV news depends on a lot of variables you can't control. Luck. Timing. How people feel about your haircut. The only thing you really can control is how well you prepare, so I over-prepared as a matter of course. To this day I never approach a story or an interview unprepared.

Parenthood was another story. Almost from the start I felt I was winging it, or scrambling to catch up. For me, the first years of fatherhood were a blur of baby toys, packing boxes and new jobs. By the time Alex turned three, we'd lived in four different homes—in Ottawa, then Halifax, then Ottawa again, then Edmonton, where Erica was born in December 1989. We always moved for the same reason: a better job, one with more visibility and opportunity. I was now the sole breadwinner. We had no family money, no savings to speak of, nothing to fall back on. It was up to me, and responsibility for my family's economic well-being fuelled my drive to succeed like nothing else ever had or could.

Cathy had intended to return to her job as a TV reporter once Alex was a year old, but as the time drew near, she realized she wanted to stay home full-time to look after him. She felt a little defensive about her decision; her mother, who took real pride in her own job, seemed disappointed. But I wholeheartedly agreed that this was the best solution for our family and especially for our son, so long as Cathy didn't feel pressured into it. Feminism had supplied a handy framework for analyzing the trade-offs mothers make, whether they return to the work force or stay home full-time with kids, and both of us understood that she was making a significant sacrifice. No matter how much she genuinely wanted to stay home with Alex, she was still giving up her own career aspirations and professional identity, at least temporarily.

And if she decided she wanted to return to broadcasting, there was no guarantee of future employment.

I'd have to assume a heavier financial burden, but that meant I was taking something on, not giving anything up. And frankly, it didn't seem like that big a deal, since working long and hard had always been part of my plan. Having a reason beyond my own advancement just added a bit of nobility to the proceedings, and gave me an even stronger sense of purpose. According to conventional wisdom, I was the direct beneficiary of Cathy's sacrifice since now I had carte blanche to put my career first, ahead of everything else. I felt a little guilty about what looked a whole lot like inequity, not least because I would never have been willing to do what my wife did. My sense of myself as a man was intrinsically connected to working; my sense of myself as a father depended more than anything else on providing for and protecting my family. It just didn't occur to me that by splitting our roles along these traditional lines, I was also making a sacrifice.

I don't think that would have occurred to most men of my generation. The public discourse about work/life balance in the 1980s and 1990s was led by and focused almost exclusively on mothers, and if there was much discussion about the tradeoffs fathers had to make, I didn't hear about it. The assumption seemed to be that "having it all" was easy for men, because women were there to pick up the slack on the home front.

We were now expected to be more involved in childrearing, but the bar was still pretty low. A dad who changed diapers and folded laundry was generally hailed as a hero; a dad who did not generally elicited eye-rolling, not outrage. But the idea that some light housework, a little quality time with the kids and a ten- or eleven-hour day at the office constituted "having it all" was dreamt up by someone who a) didn't like children all that much, and viewed spending time with them as a form of drudgery, and/ or b) viewed work as a non-stop carnival of ego gratification.

It would be more accurate to say that most men had more than women in some respects, but less in others—though the deficit was less tangible and therefore harder to detect. I didn't detect it, anyway, as a young father because I didn't really understand that parenting, like work, could be a source of self-actualization. Even the women who were urging men to step up and help more with child care were pushing that agenda primarily in the interests of gender equality and, oh yeah, meeting children's needs—not our own needs. Stepping up was framed in terms of fairness, duty and responsibility, not personal happiness.

A man was expected to care deeply about his family, of course, but work was where you tested, proved and improved yourself. No wonder no one I knew considered taking paternity leave, even in those rare instances when it was offered.

As it turned out, however, proving myself at work didn't necessarily mean I could support my family all that well. In TV news, the money is substantial only at the very top, and very few people ever get there. I worked hard and climbed the ladder very quickly, but up-and-comers weren't paid the same way they were in law, medicine or banking, and there was always a long line of people who would have been delighted to take my job for half the pay. We lived modestly but even so, Alex often wound up helping Cathy sort through the change jar at the end of the month, counting up the coins to see if there were enough to buy groceries. I didn't go into journalism hoping to get rich, and I always loved the work, though I didn't always love my job. I figured we'd be okay in the long run if I continued to move up.

Moving up was not, however, conducive to hands-on parenting. I couldn't figure out how to say no when the boss called—and knowing that Cathy was taking care of everything on the home front made it that much easier to say yes. Driving to work on the weekends, seeing dads playing with their kids in the park, I did question my priorities. Racing off to the airport, leaving Cathy to hold the fort with two little kids in yet another new city where we didn't know anyone, I wondered about my choices and what the consequences might be. Once, returning home from a particularly lengthy trip when Erica was a toddler, I got an inkling: I walked in the door and she took one look at me and started screaming. She clearly didn't remember who I was. That made me feel horrible, but the next time I was asked to cover a big story, I didn't say no. How could I? Looking out the window of the airplane, I reminded myself I wasn't just doing this for my career. I was doing it for my family.

Still, I suspected that the small, unremarkable, everyday moments I was missing might matter more in the long run. That's when emotional trust develops. For proof, I didn't need to look further than my own home. For the first years of my kids' lives, they were often alone with Cathy, and their us-against-the-world experiences in new cities, trying to find the best parks and figure out which drugstore stayed open late, knit them close. Heading home to them after a trip felt like returning to a cozy nest where I was completely comfortable but also slightly out of synch. I didn't know which cereals Alex and Erica liked or when their favourite TV program was on or how to motivate them to do something they really didn't want to do. Cathy was the one they ran to when they'd scraped a knee or their pride had been injured in some way. I delighted in our children and they must have felt that, but I didn't understand them the way Cathy did. We just didn't have the same kind of connection.

At least, I consoled myself, I was always physically affectionate, hugging and kissing my kids, telling them over and over how much I loved them. And when I was home, I didn't bury myself in the newspaper or lie on the couch watching baseball. I played with them, ate dinner with them, danced around the living room to bad pop music with them. The more we needed money and the more successful I was at work, though, the less I did any of those things because the less I was home.

And so, without ever making a conscious and definitive renunciation, as Cathy had when she quit her job, I did give something up: my aspirations of being a hands-on, involved parent. I couldn't figure out how to be both the man I wanted to be and the father I wanted to be, but I was still hopeful it was possible to be both. Someday. When I'd really proved myself as a journalist and had more time.

CHAPTER TWO

SONHOOD

ALEX

MY EARLIEST MEMORY OF MY DAD, I must have been about three years old, is of him returning from a trip with a toy car. He knew I loved cars, and this one was red, a Ferrari I think. I remember feeling excited about the car and happy to see him, but also a little hesitant and shy, as though he were an uncle coming to visit, not my father. In my mind, our house was my mother's, not his or even really theirs together, because she was the one who was always there. He was away so much when I was really little that he was more of an abstract idea to me than a real person. It probably didn't help that I'd turn on the TV and there he was, real but not quite real.

To explain what my dad was doing when he wasn't home, my mom drew a wordless cartoon for me. Her grandfather and father were both cartoonists, and when I was growing up she drew in the same way that other people write in journals, filling up sketchpads with what she called "scribbles" about our family. In the first panel of this particular cartoon, my mom, my baby sister and I are on our front lawn, waving cheerfully to the plane overhead, while Dad grins back at us from one of the windows. In the next frame, a cameraman is filming my dad, who's interviewing a balding, beaming guy. In the final frame, Dad is pointing authoritatively to the editing monitor, where the balding, beaming talking head fills the screen, while an editor fiddles with knobs and buttons, cutting the clip for public consumption.

That cartoon explains a lot not just about my father's job but about my relationship with my mother. She always built my dad up in my eyes, put a positive spin on things, and taught me to view his work as important and his absences as inevitable; she also always seemed to know exactly what I needed, and was able to provide it in exactly the form I could handle. Her sketchbooks are what I'd save if a fire broke out at my parents' house and I could grab only one thing. They show me who I was and still am to her, and reveal my own history to me in a way photos never have.

I used to think my dad was her muse, because she always draws him looking strong and in control, at the centre of things, even when he's just sitting on the couch reading a book. But looking through her sketchbooks recently I realized I had it wrong. Most often, the central character is me (poor Erica—my mom had much less time to draw once she arrived). There's a polished, whimsical watercolour of various characters from Beatrix Potter books, working together to set up my nursery, then pages and pages documenting my first year: waking, eating, crawling, crying, standing alone for the first time, trying to escape my crib, admiring my brand-new shoes. In most of these cartoons, she's the only other character, the one who hugs and changes me, saves me from potential disasters and is driven slightly crazy by my antics. Then there's me as a toddler, standing on my head on the couch while my mom blearily nurses Erica and watches my dad on TV. And me as a little boy, pushing a toy boat back and forth in the water, completely immersed in an imaginary game. Most of these are line drawings in black ink, but occasionally my mom used colour. In one of her favourites, I'm in a green jacket, brandishing a stick and stomping on an iced-over puddle; Erica is in a pink coat, her back to me, trudging through the snow. Over my head floats a thought bubble, full of stars, rockets and spaceships, while Erica's bubble is filled with horses, butterflies and flowers.

No wonder our mom was the person we both felt most connected to in the world when we were growing up: she really understood us, even knew what we were thinking, and delighted in us. It doesn't get much better than that, for a kid. Her warmth and compassion may also explain, though, why neither of us had much of an ability to roll with the punches when we were younger. At home, we never had to. Our mother was almost endlessly accommodating, even during the preschool phase when I was convinced that every speck of herb or chunk of onion in my food was a bug. Her response was to turn down the lights so I couldn't see what I was eating. We ate in the dark.

But she isn't so sweet that she has no personality. She's sharp, very funny, and musical, always composing a song for someone, even the dog. And she's crazy about birds, forever rescuing hurt ones and nursing them back to health. There was always a bird or two flying around our house when I was little. The one I loved best was a green parakeet, a little terrorist called Flapper who dive-bombed everyone except me and my mom. She taught me to pick him up like an ice cream cone, my hand over his wings, and he'd happily perch on my head or my shoulder.

As happy as I was at home with my mother, I was just that unhappy at school, pretty much right from the start. The first thing I remember about kindergarten in Ottawa is being in a big playroom where a couple of other kids were building a fort out of blocks. I wanted to play, too, but they said, "No, you're not allowed," and started teasing me. I didn't know how to respond other than knock their fort down, so I went with that. Beautiful friendships did not blossom as a result of this incident.

I didn't really know how to interact with other boys, but I was eager to be liked, which made me an easy mark. Another kindergarten memory: I eagerly handed over the dessert in my lunchbox to a kid who promised, in return, to bring me a toy plane the next day. After school I told my mother about this incredible deal I'd made, and when she gently explained that I'd been conned, I freaked. It wasn't just that I wasn't getting the airplane. It was a feeling of grief, almost, like I'd somehow diminished my mother. She'd lovingly packed that dessert for me, and I'd given it away.

We moved just about every year, so there was always change in the air, and she was the one constant: always there, always caring. When my dad started hosting *Midday* and we moved to Toronto, I remember going with her to a store in our neighbourhood one summer day, and staying outside right in front while she shopped, playing at a bright blue water table with boats that had been set up on the sidewalk so the shop didn't get overrun with screaming kids. I played for what felt like a really long time, then went into the store to look for my mom, but couldn't find her. I panicked: Why did she leave me? Then I realized she'd have to go back to her car eventually, so I found my way back to the parking lot, where the car was unlocked, and climbed in. My mom had always been anxious about my safety, so now, all alone in this gigantic world with kidnappers on the loose, I did the obvious thing: hid from them, on the floor. I was that small, the smallest kid in grade one. I curled up, uncomfortable and sweaty, wondering what would happen next. At the same time, of course, my mother had exited the store, looked for me, then panicked and immediately called the police, who were now urging her to check her car. She resisted, certain I'd been snatched by a kidnapper. I wasn't the type of kid who wandered off! I was dependent, not an adventurer. But the police weren't willing to launch a manhunt until she checked her car, and when she did, I remember feeling that she hadn't found me so much as rescued me.

I was the kind of kid who didn't want to get in trouble, the kind who almost hyperventilated when someone suggested breaking a rule. The world outside my home seemed like a dirty, dangerous place, where your only protection lay in following the letter of the law. The playground at school, for instance, was a death trap, as far as I was concerned. There was this one really tall, rickety play structure, and every once in awhile someone would fall off it and get a head injury. I'm not kidding, this actually happened to a friend of mine. Weirdly, there was never any sound. You'd just look over and through the sea of bodies, make out some kid lying motionless on the ground and think, "There goes another one." I avoided the play structure. The concrete covering the rest of the actual playground had buckled, and there was one perilously steep section that would get slicked over with ice in the winter. Kids loved to slide down it, out of sight of the teachers, but the flat area below was riddled with trees, and to me it was a scene of impending carnage, and any minute kids would be crashing into the trees, bleeding, crying. I avoided the hill.

I didn't have to explain any of this to my mother. She knew all of it, just as she knew that my friend Emma* had a crush on me, and one day we got married, with a twist tie from my sandwich bag as a ring, under the big tree on the playground. She knew that my friend Brad had a fish named Oscar with weird, bulging eyes, and his kitchen had an old-fashioned gas stove that you lit with a match, and she knew I was dying to have a bunk bed like his. I told her everything—it must have been exhausting, this stream-of-consciousness pouring out of a second grader—so she knew when anyone picked on me, which seemed to be happening more and more. I'd never been popular, but being teased and taunted was a new development. Half the time I couldn't figure out why it was happening. Once, in grade two, someone called me a lesbian. I had no idea what that was, only that it must be a terrible thing to be. I raced home, near tears, to ask my mother whether I really was a lesbian. She laughed and hugged me, saying, "Oh honey, it's not possible for you to be a lesbian!"

She was very concerned, though, when another kid in my grade started sneaking up on me and grabbing my crotch when no one was looking. She spoke to teachers at the school, the

---

* I've changed my friends' names throughout the book.

other boy's mother and finally, because nothing else had worked, to the crotch-grabber himself. She was a lunchroom supervisor at my school and I remember watching from a distance one day while my mom, possibly the most nurturing individual on the planet, held the bully's wrist and did her best to look stern and scary, telling him to leave me alone. Unfortunately, this inflamed the kid and he redoubled his efforts, but I didn't tell her. I figured she'd done all she could.

I'm sure my dad was also concerned that I was being bullied, but I don't remember talking to him about it, then or later. By that point he was around much more—he was hosting a show in Toronto rather than reporting from the field—but he wasn't part of the texture of my everyday life in the way that my mother was. He was always incredibly busy, reading something or rushing off to the studio, is how I remember it. There was a distance, somehow, an absence of the intimacy I had with my mother, so I was embarrassed to tell him what was going on at school. I didn't want him to think less of me.

My dad was an important person, in the news, in the know. He wasn't full of himself—once when he took us to see the studio where *Midday* was filmed, he forgot his security pass and was falling all over himself apologizing to the guard and explaining that he worked on this show, would it be possible to take his kids in to see the set? It would never occur to him to say, "I'm the host, let me in or I'll get your ass fired." He's the opposite of self-important. But I knew he was important because I could see how much his being on TV impressed teachers and my friends' parents. Kids, too, though I learned not to mention it. On the few occasions I did, my classmates were either blown away by the coolness of having a dad on TV or convinced I was lying. *If he's so famous, how come you're not rich?* It didn't make a lot of sense to me, either. Money was so tight that there wasn't enough for a battery-powered mini-Jeep, like all the cool kids had. If my father was famous, why did I have less than they did?

My dad cast a large shadow, even if he didn't mean to or want to, and I didn't feel comfortable in it. I wanted to be special in my own right. I looked up to him, of course, but not because he was on TV. He just seemed incredibly strong—physically, since he always worked out, and also in the everyday way of having all the answers and knowing what to do in any situation. I wanted him to think I was strong, too.

Admitting that I was being picked on, and that it made me feel horrible, and scared, and angry, was therefore right out of the question. I tried to take care of things myself. My main strategy was avoidance: just steer clear of boys, especially the alpha-male types. I never got the impression that my mother worried about that, though she may well have. But I knew my father did, or at least didn't think it was normal, because he signed me up for one male bonding opportunity after another, including father-son activities that were meant to bring the two of us closer. They didn't. But he persisted, no matter how much I resisted. He'd enroll me in some sport or other, though I was the kind of kid who could be counted on to score against his own team, so I'd hate it and be terrible at it, and he'd respond by signing me up for something else.

I was kind of dreamy, happy to live in my own head, and I just didn't like the physicality and forced bonhomie of group activities. But my dad had been a Scout, and he wanted me to be one, too. He sold it to me as an opportunity to earn cool badges, and told me that one year he'd even built a lean-to out of branches or something, and had been given a special badge for that. I could tell by the sincerity of his enthusiasm that I was supposed to get excited about this prospect, but all I could think was, "What do I need a lean-to for?" Dad was so gung-ho that he even became the leader of my troop, but at meetings I'd run off and hide; he'd find me and coax me back to where the other boys were all busily doing Scout-like things, and I'd burst into tears or refuse to participate. I knew I was embarrassing myself and him, and that made it even worse. After the third or fourth time, I just flat-out refused to go. So, intent on honouring his commitments as a Scout leader, he went alone. He was that kind of father: fiercely moral, a man of his word. Not a quitter.

To be clear, my dad is not some unreconstructed macho idiot. He's aggressive and determined to win when it comes to his career, but he's always been tender and loving with me, Erica and my mom. However, because the activities he signed me up for were so far from my own interests, I could only assume they spelled out his expectations of me: apparently, he wanted a son who scored goals and thrived on rough-and-tumble play. Instead, he had me, an artistic kid who lived in his own imagination and panicked if a ball came anywhere near his face. I was hungry for his approval, but often felt I was letting him down.

I longed for a deeper sense of connection with my dad but couldn't figure out how to create one. I do remember happy times with him, playing cars on the floor and splashing around in the lake at my grandfather's cottage, but his job was usually looming in the background. Or foreground.

I wanted to do something to eclipse it in his eyes, something that would command not only his attention but his pride. I remember the excitement I felt when I got a good grade on a test or drew something particularly inventive, how I'd make my mother swear she would let me show my father myself, then that pent-up anticipation and impatience, waiting for him to walk through the door. When I did something good, my mother's approval was a given. But my dad was around so much less that his approval seemed harder to earn and, perhaps unfairly, became all the more highly prized.

CHAPTER THREE

WORK LIFE
KEVIN

BY 1992, WE'D MOVED BACK to Ottawa for the third time and I was reporting for my third network after Global and CTV. I was part of a cadre of young white guys covering politics and hard news—a golden boys' competition club, not that we ever talked about it in quite that way. The mood was more collegial than cut-throat and I felt valued, like someone the network wanted to invest in and groom. But everyday life was more grey than golden. I routinely worked twelve-hour days, trudging around the corner from the studio every evening to grab a submarine sandwich for dinner and getting home, exhausted but wired, at ten o'clock when the kids had already been asleep for hours. The lifestyle, if you could call it that, was not exactly family friendly.

So when I was asked to audition to replace the male co-host of *Midday*, CBC's hour-long noontime newsmagazine show, I was intrigued. I'd never longed to be an anchor, but it's the only job in TV news with predictable hours. Everything else is shift work.

Most of my fellow travellers on the hard news career track thought I was crazy. To them, *Midday* seemed like a pointless detour; it was a softer show, with lifestyle and entertainment segments as well as news. The pay was also less than I was currently making, and wouldn't go as far in Toronto, where housing—and just about everything else—was more expensive than in Ottawa. But I'd have a lot more time with my family. The trade-off seemed worth it.

The audition process involved filling in for the male co-host, who was moving on to host a show in the evening. I hadn't ever done live television before but weirdly, though the self-critical voice in my head was too loud to ignore altogether, I didn't feel intimidated. I was accustomed to studios and cameras, of course, and my high school theatrical training also helped me feel comfortable. The countdown to a show going live replicated that terror-filled moment before you step onto the stage, but I'd learned back in grade ten that when it's actually time to say something, I don't freeze. Someone once told me, "You know you're doing what you're intended to do if, at the moment of peak stress, your heart rate actually slows." And that's what happened when the cameras started rolling during my audition. My heart stopped racing and I felt focused. Calm. In the zone. It's the same thing some surgeons say happens in the operating room: the mental clutter disappears and they're fully in the moment, concentrating. Fearless.

As it turned out, I had a hitherto undiscovered technical skill. *Midday* frequently relied on a bit of TV trickery, widely used today, called the "double-ender." It's a cost-saving measure producers resort to when an interviewee—a rock star, say—can't come in to the studio, and the show doesn't have the money or resources to film both ends of the interview. Here's what you do: film the rock star staring directly into a camera that's been set up in his home or wherever, and question him via an earpiece that's connected to a phone line. The interviewer on the other end of the phone line isn't filmed, usually because there isn't a studio available, so he can conduct the interview sprawled on his living room couch if he wants. The next day, as the tape of the rock star rolls, the interviewer re-asks the same questions in the studio, so it looks to viewers as though both sides of the conversation were recorded simultaneously. You basically need to act out the interview all over again, using the same words and the same intonation, but making it look as though you're thinking up the questions on the spot. That was the part of the audition I aced: apparently I could fake an interview better than the other three candidates, which was key, because double-enders were the secret sauce of the show.

There was one more hurdle I had to overcome to land the job. I needed the blessing of the show's co-anchor, Valerie Pringle, who'd been very welcoming and warm during my audition. A few weeks later, when it seemed that I was the producers' choice, she asked me to meet her for lunch at an Ottawa hotel. It was a smart move, because if we didn't have an easy rapport over lunch, there was almost no chance we'd develop it under the intensity of television lights. I recognized this for the final interview that it was, and tried to be especially charming and agreeable. I really wanted to work with Valerie, who was the most natural broadcaster in the country. A veteran of live television, she had a gift for making scripted comments sound like offhand, spontaneous remarks. I knew I could learn a lot from her. But she was almost forty and I was thirty-two and looked even younger. Did she really want to school someone who was obviously her junior?

I tried to raise the subject of our age difference in a roundabout way by alluding to the winning formula for co-hosts—pretending to be siblings, or secret lovers—then asking, "So who would we be?" Fortunately Valerie had a great sense of humour, and she burst out laughing. "Certainly not lovers! But great friends would be good." Near the end of the lunch I asked, "Do you think we could do this together?" And her reaction was, "Yeah, um, I think it could work"—not exactly a ringing endorsement, so I thanked her for meeting me and told her that if I turned out not to be the right co-host, no hard feelings. But in truth, by this point, I *really* wanted the job. I wanted the regular hours, the lack of travel and, yes, the higher profile it would give me.

A few days later I was offered the position and promptly resigned as a reporter, giving up the security of a union job in order to work on contract. It's usually the price of hosting a show, and I didn't think twice about paying it. This job didn't just mean I was going to have a life. It solidified my status. The network clearly had big plans for me, and that seemed like security enough.

I began working in Toronto a month later, leaving Cathy yet again to look after our kids and manage the move from Ottawa. I hoped that this would be the last time we'd have to move on my account. We seemed to be entering a new phase of life, one where the future felt secure enough that we bought a house—nothing fancy, just a solid duplex in an area with good schools, but it was still a stretch on my newly reduced salary. I was confident I'd earn more someday, but in the meantime Cathy became a lunchroom supervisor at Alex's new school because it paid twenty-five dollars a day, and I started moonlighting, teaching journalism at a local college.

Looking back on those years, I remember them as a stressful whirl of activity, punctuated with occasional bursts of elation. Though I could usually get home in time for dinner, I was more preoccupied with work than ever. *Midday* was a whole new game and I had to learn the rules.

For the first time, I had to think about books, music and movies—and my own personality. A reporter's job is straightforward: beat other reporters and get the story right, first. But an anchor's job, especially on a softer show, is to make people like you so much that they want to spend a lot of time with you, day after day. It's a whole different job, really, and making the transition required a strange combination of objectivity and navel-gazing. I had to pinpoint my own irritating tics and mannerisms, then eliminate them. And I had to deconstruct my own personality to figure out what was appealing about me, so I could emphasize it.

I had to show more of myself—or more of a carefully curated version of myself, anyway—and at first it felt uncomfortable. The impersonal, dialled-in reporter mode I'd always relied on had provided something like invisible body armour. Asking the questions, usually off-camera, then editing the answers and weaving them into a coherent narrative, I'd been in control, directing the movie rather than acting in it. Now I was sharing the spotlight, and the goal wasn't to grill people or craft a story from shreds of material, but rather to have seamless, intelligent and engaging conversations with famous people. Live.

The difference became clear early on when I interviewed Premier Joe Ghiz, the retiring leader of Prince Edward Island, Canada's smallest province. I had interviewed many politicians in my years as a parliamentary reporter, and success usually depended on a courtroom-style cross-examination: harsh, direct questions intended to elicit straight answers. So with Ghiz I did what I'd always done, focusing on conflicts, failures and controversies during his time in office. It wasn't the gentle swan song farewell he'd been expecting from a show like *Midday*, and by the time my interrogation was winding up, he was clearly angry. In my old job, that would have been a sign that I'd scored a direct hit, so I was feeling pleased with myself until we wrapped and the phone rang. It was Cathy, asking why on earth I'd been so hard on the poor man. The show's producers were wondering the same thing, and soon the switchboard was all lit up with calls from angry viewers (this was back in the day, when viewers couldn't eviscerate you instantly on Twitter). A field reporter doesn't have to worry what the audience thinks about his interviewing technique but, as I quickly learned, an anchor does. Unless you're Bill O'Reilly and it's part of your shtick, attacking guests who come on your show is a good way to ensure viewers hate you. This doesn't mean you can't ask tough questions. You can, but you have to be sure, first, that it's what the audience expects from you with that particular guest.

During my first year, I got better at longer, less scripted-sounding interviews, and found that I was pretty good at talking to authors and panels of experts, but not so good at celebrity interviews. I tried hard to ask unexpected questions, but it's tough to knock celebrities out of their preprogrammed mode and get them to say something new, and I may have found the interaction even less enjoyable than they did.

Certainly that was the case with Joni Mitchell, who came on the show to promote *Turbulent Indigo*, one of the strongest albums of her career. She's an icon, of course, and I wanted the interview to do her justice, so I pored over her lyrics looking for recurring themes I could ask her about and read reviews of her work and even a full-length book about her influence on folk music. I headed into the interview armed with a list of well-researched, intelligent questions, all neatly arranged in a logical order so the interview would flow well—the first clue that I was a newbie. For a conversational interview to flow, you need to listen to the answers and follow up on them, not stick to a list of prefabricated, smarty-pants questions.

The setting for our talk was weirdly dramatic: Mitchell's record label had stuck a table and two stools in the middle of a very large empty room, and on the table was an ashtray with a lit cigarette resting in it, and a glass of what looked like water but smelled a lot like straight vodka. Joni Mitchell herself was in a playful mood. She quickly sized me up, saw that I was nervous as hell and decided to flirt with me in a way that was innocent but also mocking, and exponentially increased my nervousness. That was, I think, her aim. She seemed to be toying with me the way a cat bats a mouse back and forth, and I had no idea how to respond. Remember, she's about twenty years older and infinitely more confident; I still have no game with women, not even women who aren't famous singers who may or may not be tipsy. I felt like Dustin Hoffman at the beginning of *The Graduate*. I didn't know how to take control of the situation and, frankly, I was afraid of her. She was a living legend, and I couldn't read her at all or predict what she might say next.

When the crew finished setting up and the cameras finally started rolling, I read out the questions on my list with a deer-in-the-headlights expression on my face, and didn't react or respond to her answers (most of which were wonderfully reflective and a little combative). Afterwards, I couldn't get out of there fast enough. I was thoroughly embarrassed by my performance when the piece aired the next day, and hoped I'd never have to interview another celebrity.

But I did, and eventually I got a little better at it. By the time William Shatner was booked on *Midday*, I'd learned that actors want to control interviews, and I had a better idea how to prevent that from happening. I thought Shatner was coming on to promote a new credit card he had lent his celebrity to, so I dispensed with that right at the top of the interview by asking, "What do *you* know about credit cards?" That created a moment of humour, and then I quickly appealed to his ego in a way I hoped might also confound him slightly, by steering the conversation around to his "lifelong fascination with innovation." I could tell he was unprepared for my questions because he had to reflect before answering, but he seemed to enjoy being surprised. At the end of the interview he said, "Does the CBC know how good you are at this?"

"That's a question I better not answer," I said, because in truth, I wasn't sure whether I was valued or not. The show's ratings had plateaued, but were holding steady, not falling. I worked well with Tina Srebotnjak, who'd replaced Valerie Pringle when she moved on to another show, and I was getting more comfortable with the unscripted banter that's a staple of every co-hosted show. Being on display, part of the story rather than narrating it, made me feel special.

But it also made me feel vulnerable, though I tried not to let that show. I never forgot that people were watching and judging me. Not only my bosses but a quarter of a million strangers. And my colleagues. And my family. And everyone who had ever known me personally. And people I'd just met on the street. And any enemies I had ever made.

Even after I had the hang of the job and was finding moments of enjoyment in it, I felt queasy after almost every show. It's the same feeling you get the morning after a party where you had too much to drink, but not so much that you don't remember making an ass of yourself. *Oh God, did I really say that?* Sometimes I'd go back and watch the tape to see just how big a fool I'd made of myself, but usually I looked surprisingly normal, self-assured even. Apparently I'd learned how to cover up my awkwardness and uncertainty and brazen it out—an essential skill for anchors, particularly male anchors. Any sign of hesitation or self-doubt is read as weakness, which is the one quality viewers simply won't tolerate in a male host. You're allowed to be emotional, occasionally, and sensitive. But weak? That's the kiss of death. One American news director described the perfect male television host this way: guys have to feel they could have a beer with you and women have to imagine you secretly want to fuck them. It was crude, yes, but there was a kernel of truth in it.

I was obsessed with work, but I was supposed to be. Working long hours and not having much of a life was and still is a badge of honour for men, whether or not they have families. It's a sign that you're successful, important, going places, and I felt I was. I almost never unplugged. It was my job to know what was happening in the world, which was a time-consuming endeavour pre-social media and smartphones. In the nineties, I had to turn on CNN or log on to my clunky home computer to see if there was e-mail from producers or editors. I vividly remember being at Erica's fifth birthday party, surrounded by balloons and cake, and sneaking off to watch the news. I was only fully untethered during the few weeks of vacation I took each year.

I tried to fight the chatter in my head to be present for my children when I was home, which I was much more often than when I'd been a reporter, but I wasn't always successful. I'd be on the floor playing cars, Lego, ponies, but my mind might be some- where else entirely. There was often a hyped-up, antic aspect to our "quality time" because I was trying so hard to make up for lost time and ensure our time together was special and memorable. We'd go tobogganing and I'd fake extravagant wipeouts at the bottom of the hill; at the pool I'd toss the kids around like bean- bags, trying to cram a summer's worth of fun into an afternoon.

As the kids grew, it became clear that Alex needed more from me than Erica did. Even as a very little girl, my daughter was self-possessed and calm, navigating the world with a certain comfort and grace. Making friends seemed easy for her, but for him it was a struggle. Alex was creative and curious about the world, with a sweet and caring soul, but solitary by nature. He just didn't seem to know how to connect with other kids, espe- cially boys. There was often a moment in a play date when Alex would provoke his guest, knock down his sandcastle or take a toy away, and I'd be embarrassed, apologizing for the sudden turn of events. He could be a pot-stirrer but he wasn't a mean kid, so his behaviour was baffling. Maybe he just wanted attention, and couldn't figure out how to attract the good kind.

Unfortunately he was already familiar with the bad kind. Slight and small, Alex was a magnet for bullies, though it took me awhile to realize the severity of the problem. Work consumed so much of my mental real estate that issues with the kids tended not to register until they'd become serious problems. I only really understood what Alex had been experiencing when he was in grade two and Cathy told me another boy had been pushing him around and fondling him. I was horrified. I'm not sure Alex knew how wrong this was—he didn't tell Cathy what was happening right away, and he never mentioned it to me—but I was stunned that a kid his own age was basically molesting him. My tendency in a crisis is to go into fix-it mode, so instead of sitting down with Alex and trying to reach his injured soul, I went straight to the principal's office. Apparently the school suspected that the kid was himself being abused at home. I remember thinking, "Well, that's too bad, but I don't want him anywhere near my son." I tried to build up Alex's confidence, play-wrestling with him and encouraging him to believe he could stand up for himself. Cathy took a different tack, talking to teachers, trying to engage the bully's mother, brokering play dates with the nice kids, supporting Alex emotionally.

Instead of becoming more confident, though, Alex seemed to internalize what was happening to him, then take it out on Erica, who looked up to him and trusted him a little too much. Once when she was sitting on the couch, her braid trailing over the back, he came up behind her and chopped it off with a pair of scissors. (If there was some provocation, it's long since been forgotten by both parties.) He teased her and excluded her in some of the ways he was being teased and excluded.

Yet, in a sense, he seemed to want *not* to belong. He wasn't a shrinking violet. He was proudly, stubbornly self-isolating. I carved out time to try to introduce him to sports, thinking that would help him make friends, but every attempt I made to involve him in soccer, baseball—any sport, actually—ended with Alex going off on his own, either hiding from the crowd or withdrawing into his world of fantasy. For him, a soccer game became an imaginary spaceship battle, not a quest to move the ball toward the other team's net.

Alex needed friends—he needed to know how to get along with other kids. So I decided to sign both of us up for Scouts. I'd been a Scout for a few years at about Alex's age, and I'd liked racking up badges and being a leader of my pack. I thought it would be a fun activity for us to share, and a good way for him to meet other kids. But, as Alex quickly made clear, he did not think Scouts was fun. In fact, he hated everything about it. He'd disliked group activities since he was a toddler, but now he could go on strike more effectively. He'd just refuse to engage, parking himself under a table in a way that seemed designed to attract attention, while the other Scouts diligently tied knots and did crafts. I'd signed up to be a Scout leader, so I had responsibility for helping run our get-togethers, and I was both embarrassed—no parent wants his or her kid to be the one under the table—and unsure how to respond. Did Alex need my support? Should I hunker down under the table with him? Or would it be better for him to be ignored so he'd eventually be forced to join the group? I leaned toward the latter option, believing I was acting in his best long-term interests, but after a few weeks Alex simply refused to go. Would. Not. Go. However, I was the only male Scout leader, the rest were single mothers. I couldn't just bail. So for the rest of the year, I helped other little boys who weren't related to me learn to pitch tents and sell Christmas trees. If Alex was jealous, he wasn't jealous enough to change his mind and come with me.

It took me awhile to recognize that my desire for my son to have an easier childhood than mine was actually making both our lives more difficult. He had no interest in fulfilling the dreams I'd had for him of being a sporty, popular kid. I was dragging him off to activities he rejected with increasing ferocity, and it was hard not to feel frustrated and occasionally angry about it, especially since I was knocking myself out to make time to do this stuff with him.

We had so little time together. Why couldn't we connect? The irony wasn't lost on me: I'd learned to connect just fine with an audience armed with remote controls. With Cathy and Erica, too. The only issue was with my son, the person I felt I should have been able to bond with most effortlessly because we were the same gender, shared the same genes, and I loved him so much. I couldn't figure him out, really, though of course in the rearview mirror, it's so plain. Alex was just a lot like me.

In 1994, with no warning, my career imploded. I learned that after two years, I was being replaced at *Midday* to create an enticing opportunity to retain an up-and-comer who was being courted by another network. He wouldn't be ready to take over for five or six months though, and in the interim, I had to keep his seat warm.

It's not uncommon for hosts to be shuffled off one show and onto another, and at first I hoped that was the plan for me. I wanted to stay at the CBC, preferably in Toronto, where my family had settled in and was happy. But none of the executives at the network would take a meeting with me. Or look me in the eye. No one was talking about a new assignment. The writing was on the wall.

Suddenly I was no longer a golden boy but a thirty-four-year-old who wasn't sure how he was going to hang on to his house. We were struggling to make our mortgage payments as it was. I was still under contract, so I wasn't allowed to go out and beat the bushes for a new job. I had no idea what I was going to do once my contract was up, how I was going to provide for my family. Cathy was comforting, but clearly scared. So I pretended to feel more optimistic than I did, and both of us made sure the kids didn't know what was going on.

This was the end of my starry-eyed idealism about journalism. It felt like losing my religion: profoundly disappointing and dislocating. Until that point, I'd believed loyalty was appreciated, hard work paid off—the universe was essentially orderly and fair, and people tended to get what they deserved. Now I saw that sometimes you did, sometimes you didn't. It was a crapshoot. I'd worked my ass off, but going the extra mile hadn't protected me from being screwed over. I had every bitter, frightened, angry feeling a man has when he loses his job and is forced to take stock.

When I did, the picture wasn't pretty. The truth was, I was

trapped. Now that work seemed pretty pointless, I wanted to be home as much as possible. That's where I felt most fulfilled, and where I felt best about myself. But I was the sole provider. I needed to find another job where I could earn as much or more than I was currently making. Having been out of the job market for years, Cathy couldn't go back to work and earn what I could. Nor could she make up the shortfall that would be created if I took a major step down the ladder. And Erica hadn't even started school—who would look after her if both of us were working?

I knew our financial predicament was my problem to solve. And I also knew that any viable solution would require me to act against my own interests. I couldn't pull closer to Cathy, Alex and Erica, the way I wanted to. I'd have to pull further away and hope like hell that I wouldn't lose the next job, too. If I could find another job, that is. Depleted by anxiety, I lost weight, stopped sleeping. I was consciously, undeniably, unhappy. Seething. Hurt. In pain.

Nevertheless, the face I presented to the world bore no resemblance to my emotional reality. Every day I went on TV and acted as though I didn't have a care in the world. Game face. I knew that if I let my hurt and anger show on camera, it would only make me look bad. I was being paid to perform, not to emote. To act "as if" while somehow making the audience feel that they were seeing and connecting with the real me.

But at times the cognitive dissonance was so extreme, I felt like I was losing it. One morning, sitting on our front steps in Toronto and waiting for Tina, my *Midday* co-host and friend, to give me a lift to the studio, I actually said out loud, though no one was there, "If this is it for me in journalism, I need a sign."

What happened next sounds like an unbelievable plot twist, but trust me, it really did happen. I got to work and there was a message on my dressing room phone: a recruiter for ABC News wanted to talk to me about anchoring *World News Now*, the network's overnight newscast.

I was about to be a failed Canadian broadcaster. Not in a million years would it have occurred to me to apply to an American network, and I never did find out who sent the recruiter my tapes. She didn't know how they'd wound up on her desk, either, but she didn't seem to care. She wanted me to come to New York to interview for the job. I booked a flight immediately. When I got there, six of the top people at ABC News interviewed me, one after another, in an imposing, darkened conference room. It felt like a Star Chamber, because the walls were lined with photos of the network's biggest names—Peter Jennings, Barbara Walters, Ted Koppel, Diane Sawyer, Sam Donaldson, Charlie Gibson—all lit with pinpoint lights, so their eyes appeared to be staring at me. The executives asked me things like "What did we do wrong last night on *World News Tonight*?" and "What kind of stories do you like to report?" I must have answered with no trace of the desperation I felt, because a week later, I was offered the job.

It was like being cut from the minor leagues, then being offered a contract with the Yankees. Even the most ardent supporters of Canadian broadcasting tend to view American network news as the big time, and as a friend of mine put it, getting hired by ABC was the best "fuck you" exit he'd ever heard of.

Nevertheless, I was conflicted. I'd have to move my family

from a place where they were happy; working nights would mean I'd get to see even less of them. Living in the US concerned me, too. It was familiar yet foreign, and I had no idea what it would be like for my kids to grow up there, how it would affect them. But the salary was double what I was making at *Midday*—a surprise, since we'd never discussed money during the interviews—and ABC would also pay for our move. For Cathy and me, the money was a game changer. Even if I'd had another offer in Canada, we knew the pay wouldn't come close.

There was something else, too. Another Canadian, Thalia Assuras, was then the co-anchor of *World News Now*, and while I was in New York for the interview we'd run through a mock-hour to see whether I could pick up on the quirky style of the overnight show. I hadn't known Thalia in Canada, but she couldn't have been more welcoming. I instantly felt comfortable with her, which was lucky because there was a brash, flying-by-the-seat-of-your-pants quality to *WNN*, and I knew I had to be more aggressive and willing to take risks than I had been on *Midday*. So partway through my audition I challenged Thalia to a game of anchor desk hockey, with a "puck" made out of scrunched up paper and our pens for "sticks." I told her I wanted to see if she'd been working in the US too long and had lost the hockey skills that are the birthright of all Canadians. She hadn't. She killed me, the cameramen laughed, and we moved on. But one thing was clear: if I had to work unreasonable hours, live at opposite ends of the day from my family and somehow survive in the big leagues, then at least being part of Thalia's team would be fun. Fun was not something I was having much of at *Midday*.

So I said yes to ABC and then waited to be approved for a visa. During that time I told almost no one about the job offer. I didn't want to jinx it—what if some US immigration official decided not to give me my papers? For two months I continued to host *Midday* and continued to be shunned by the news division management. When my work visa finally arrived, I was so pissed off that I bypassed my bosses altogether and let the president of the CBC at the time, a very nice man, know that I was heading to ABC. My value shot up dramatically with that announcement, because suddenly it was, "What would it take to keep you?"

I exited with my head held high, and the fact that I was heading to the US changed the optics. Now the public narrative wasn't that I'd failed and been replaced, but that I was a rising star who, regrettably for Canada, had been lured to the Big Apple. But the story other people believed didn't change the truth or how I felt about it, which was bruised and full of self-doubt. I'm sure that being let go during a downsizing feels awful, too, but at least you can blame the economy and look around and know that other good people also lost their jobs. This rejection felt personal, and it was. Anchors are evaluated as much on the basis of their likeability as their journalistic ability, and at *Midday* my personality had clearly been found wanting. What made it worse was that I wasn't even sure how, exactly, I was inadequate. Was it one thing? Or everything about me?

Although I'd landed another, even better, job, I now secretly doubted my ability to do it well. And because my raison d'être as a father was to provide for my family, knowing I'd nearly failed them made me doubt myself to a degree I couldn't admit even to Cathy. I didn't want her to doubt me, too. And neither one of us wanted our kids to know how close we'd come to losing everything.

My old colleagues viewed anchoring *World News Now* as a plum job, but I may well have landed it because no American would put up with the hours. They were brutal: each fourteen-hour day began at ten p.m., when we'd dredge up anyone who was still awake to do interviews, then research and write stories before broadcasting from two to four a.m. and again from five to six a.m. At noon, I'd head home and try to get some sleep. It was the quintessential immigrant experience: come to America, the land of opportunity, work like hell and try to get ahead.

For the first six months, I lived in a hotel room so small that only a bed could be wedged into it. There was no space left over for a chair, much less a desk. I'd moved to the US by myself in January 1995, partly so the kids could finish out their school year in Toronto, and partly so I could hedge my bets. I was doubtful that I could make it in New York. The city intimidated me and I felt out of synch with it—which I was, given the strange hours I worked. My hotel was situated like the prow of a ship at the apex of Columbus Avenue, so cars roared past on both sides all day while I was sleeping. Or trying to. I spent most of my waking hours dizzy and vaguely nauseated from sleep deprivation. I lived on deli food, worked out to fill up the empty hours when I wasn't working, tried not to think about how unhappy I was. But once, jogging in Central Park, I broke down and cried. I wanted to go home. I missed my wife, missed my kids, who were growing up without me. But there was no job back home. And my family was depending on me.

I needed to figure out what the problem had been at *Midday* and fix it, so the same thing didn't happen again. I thought about what I was projecting, what my persona was, how to keep people watching in the middle of the night when they were, in all likelihood, trying to fall asleep. Because of the hour, the feel of the show was a little wacky and the job required a slightly tongue-in-cheek approach. It wasn't my natural on-air mode, but I worked on it and even started to enjoy myself.

The team at *World News Now* included some of the most talented producers I've ever met. The challenge of programming a two-hour show every day rested with a staff of about a dozen people, led by Terry Baker and Victor Dorff, who shared the subversive sense of humour that was a hallmark of the show. Victor, in particular, would bend and play with the conventions of television news and encourage us to make fun of them, with straight faces. We were exploring the same territory Jon Stewart later mined so expertly on *The Daily Show*, but at the top and bottom of each hour, we had ten minutes of serious, no-kidding-now news.

It was as if the grown-ups at ABC News had given us the keys to the car so we could take it for a little joyride in the moonlight, the only proviso being that it had to be back in the garage, without a single dent or scratch, in time for *Good Morning America*. We kept up our end of the bargain most of the time, but not always. One night we viciously mocked footage of North Korea's then newly installed leader, the infamous Kim Jong-il, inspecting his troops—unaware that Roone Arledge, the president of ABC News, was meeting with a high-ranking delegation of North Koreans the very next day. Terry and I were called on the carpet;

even dictators, we were told, deserve a modicum of respect. So the next night, we reran the exact same footage, only this time I read out the ridiculously hagiographic and respectful praise the North Korean state media had heaped on these images of their "Glorious Leader." It was the kind of thing you could get away with only at *WNN*, and working there was like being part of a band of late-night pirates who took over the newsroom, and the brand, while everyone else was asleep. I started to have fun, the most fun I'd ever had in television.

When I realized that I'd probably survive at ABC, I went house hunting. Manhattan was out of the question. Too expensive, too urban. I traipsed around towns in Connecticut and New Jersey, looking for the combination everyone who works in New York looks for: the shortest-possible commute, the best public schools and the most affordable yet attractive housing. One weekend Cathy's mother stayed with the kids in Toronto so she could come down alone and we did a blitz, finally settling on a tiny Cape Cod–style house in Summit, New Jersey. It was barely a thousand square feet—exactly what you buy after narrowly avoiding financial ruin, as we had in Toronto. I took a video of our new house for the kids, glossing over the fact that all four of us would share one bathroom. I also filmed the walk to Alex's new school, so he'd have a clearer idea what his life would be like. Cathy and I both talked up the town to the kids: So pretty! So close to exciting New York! The extravagance of my praise for this wonderful new place was roughly proportional to the guilt I felt about uprooting everyone once again.

In the summer of 1995, we moved into what Cathy called our dollhouse. I loved feeling that everyone who mattered most to me in the world was within arm's reach, literally, and also took great comfort from the fact that we were no longer in danger of going under financially. Cathy and I were determined to live not only within our means but beneath them. Even our one big splurge—a mattress, the first good-quality one we'd ever bought—was highly practical. Sleep was now my holy grail, as it is for anyone who works the night shift. A comfortable bed, an ample supply of melatonin, an eyeshade, earplugs, a white-noise machine to drown out the racket the kids made when they got home from school—I had it all, and occasionally could even get five uninterrupted hours of rest.

Every weekend I switched over to a normal schedule, awake during the day and asleep at night, so I could spend time with my family and run around doing errands. But I felt as you would if you flew to Japan and back every week—jet-lagged, exhausted and frequently short-tempered. I was pretty much a zombie. Cathy shouldered most of the burden, and reaped most of the pleasures, of raising the kids. There wasn't much left for us as a couple in those two fleeting days of the weekend before I would return to living on the opposite side of the sun.

All too often, and to my regret, my family got only scraps of attention, because that's all that was left once I'd satisfied my bosses and indulged my own need to recover, physically and emotionally, from my workday. I could be counted on to put a roof over their heads and food on the table, but rarely for spontaneous outings or even relaxed dinner table conversation. When work is a high-energy race to get to the point and close a story, it's hard to flip a switch and change modes at the end of the day. When I got home, I still kept driving toward conclusions and solutions, rushing to get to the point, to get things done.

I felt like I was running up a mountain I couldn't see the top of, and just needed to keep going, as fast as I could. There was no particular destination in mind, just a direction: higher.

But I wasn't blind. I knew I'd become a visitor in my family's life, which, most of the time, seemed to go on smoothly without me. After the *Midday* debacle, I would gladly have stepped out of the limelight and dialled back my career several notches if money grew on trees. The lasting lesson of that experience was that being with my family was a hell of a lot more fulfilling than being in a TV studio. I couldn't act on that knowledge, though, because I now had a job that gave me even less time with them.

From the outside, it might have looked like selfishness, focusing on my career the way I did. But to me, it often felt like self-sacrifice. I was being torn away from the people who made me happiest because I had to support and protect them. The fact that I was the one doing the tearing only made it worse because it meant there was no one else to blame. The person selling my happiness down the river was me.

CHAPTER FOUR

SCHOOL LIFE
ALEX

WHEN MY PARENTS TOLD ME we were moving to the US, my reaction was "Here we go again"—but in an upbeat, not blasé, way. I was excited, not least because New Jersey was close to both New York City, a place that had existed for me only in storybooks, and Pennsylvania, which is where I thought vampires came from. I was in grade two. Geography wasn't a strength.

Also, I just liked moving. I was a little bit sad to leave Emma, the girl I'd "married" under the tree in the schoolyard, but I liked the idea of wiping the slate clean and starting over in a new school. Every time we moved, I believed that in the new place, I'd have a new kind of life, one where people saw that I had some as yet unrecognized magical gift that made me special.

Our first few days in Summit are burned into my memory. Against the hazy blur of early childhood, they stand out with startling clarity, probably because everything felt so strange. Erica, my mom and I flew to Newark on a hot summer day then proceeded to Summit in a hideous, gas-guzzling Chevy Impala my dad had rented. Somehow I knew this car was quintessentially American (my parents must have told me so), and it struck me as an important clue about our new country. Everything was apparently going to be bigger, shinier, gaudier.

Summit, then, was disappointing at first glance: suburban and leafy, not at all cartoonish. The moving truck hadn't arrived yet, and our new house was crawling with workers, who were busy painting and fixing it up. That also felt familiar. To this day, the smell of fresh paint instantly transports me back to childhood. It's the smell of change, of possibility.

When I was little, each new house seemed like a living, breathing thing, with its own personality and secrets. This one seemed luxurious because it wasn't attached to another house, as our house in Toronto had been, and the backyard was big enough for a climbing tree, a picnic table and a big garden with large, flowering bushes. Soon enough, Erica and I discovered that their long, curving branches created weird floral "caves" that made ideal hiding spots.

That's the kind of thing I looked for when I tore through a new house for the first time: cool oddities, hints of menace. The partially finished basement in the Summit house had both. The stairs were the rickety kind with no risers, and I pictured a huge, hairy hand shooting through and grabbing my leg before I could sprint to the middle of the room and pull the cord attached to the light bulb (naturally, this is exactly what I did to Erica as soon as I had the chance). The kitchen had something exotic, a gas stove, and my mother showed us where our kitchen table would go, right in front of the window so we'd overlook the backyard while eating breakfast. I ran upstairs to stake my claim to the best room, but somehow Erica landed the bigger one and I wound up with the bedroom that had a peculiar little alcove. On one side was my closet, and on the other, a door concealing a staircase up to the attic, which my parents sold to me as a bonus play area. Our first night in the house, though, that door started to bother me and I went to sleep staring at it, so if a demon came down from the attic to drag me off into the night, at least I had a chance of seeing it coming. The next morning I launched my campaign for a lock on the outside of the attic door, and when my dad took me to the hardware store, I went for the biggest, most hard-core contraption they had, something you'd see in a New York apartment. He bought a simple sliding lock instead, the kind any self-respecting demon could bust through in a second, but after that I did sleep easier.

My mother took me to check out my new school, which was one of those big, classic, almost art deco–style American schools you see in the movies, with a bunch of cheap portables on the side. Inside it smelled disappointingly like my old school: a small puff of disinfectant from the nurse's office mixed up with the smell of gym shoes and little kids and cheap floor cleaner. The classrooms also looked pretty much the same. Maps on the walls, big alphabet letters strung over the blackboard, a mat on the floor for storytime. Erica was blown away by the coolness of being in a big kids' school and I remember trying to act jaded for her benefit, but I started to feel queasy halfway through the tour and threw up by the side of the school as soon as we left. It was horrifying. I was one of those kids who lived in terror of vomit, mine or anyone else's, and this didn't seem like a good omen.

Later, when my appetite had returned, my father took me out alone for my very first all-American meal. The Summit Diner was in an old streetcar, the waitress was smoking and had mile-long nails and cat-eye glasses, the too-springy booths were covered in fake red leather—every diner stereotype there is. I fell in love with the place when the waitress brought me an enormous plate of spaghetti swimming in thin, watery red sauce. It was spectacularly bland, no rogue specks of vegetables lurking in the sauce, the best thing I'd ever eaten in my life. I thought, "So this is what Mom meant when she said our lives were going to change for the better in Summit."

When school started, though, nothing was better. I was still the same person, and now I had even more trouble fitting in. The other kids were miles ahead; they already knew their multiplication tables. In Toronto, phys ed had been about fun and games—we'd played dodge ball, and rolled around the gym on these things that were like skateboards, only square—but here, we ran around a track. It was regimented. Barbaric, too: when we played softball or soccer or anything involving teams, the two sportiest kids would pick players, one by one, for their teams. It quickly became evident that I had no athletic ability whatsoever, nor was I popular, so I was almost always the last one left. The kids on whichever team got stuck with me would groan in unison.

Strangely, given how much I wanted to fit in, I was uninterested in addressing my athletic deficiencies. I was oversensitive and prone to taking unkind words to heart, but I had strong opinions, one of which was that sports were a joke. I just didn't see the point in trying to kick a ball into a net, and the idea that a grown man would stand on the sidelines blowing a whistle and screaming at kids until he was red in the face struck me as bizarre. But no one outside my family could have guessed that's what I was thinking. I didn't come off as one of those cool, self-contained kids who doesn't care what anyone else thinks. I came off as one of those shy, wimpy guys who's bad at sports.

I was different in other ways, too, that seemed to provoke boys. I didn't like roaming in a pack; I lived in my imagination rather than in the moment; I was happy to sit alone under a tree at recess, playing games with my *Star Wars* spaceships. Initially I had tried to glom on to some of the lower-ranking groups, but when they told me to go away, I did. Maybe it was a standard challenge, just playground banter, and I would have been accepted eventually if I'd stood my ground. But that possibility didn't occur to me until I was an adult. When I was nine and my feelings were hurt, I backed off immediately.

By grade four, I wasn't just being excluded but bullied. I'm not talking about being beaten to a bloody pulp on a daily basis but about being taunted and ostracized regularly, with the occasional shove or punch thrown in to keep me on my toes. Neil was the ringleader, and sometimes he and his buddies would follow me partway home, laughing and yelling stuff like, "Don't run away, we just want to talk to you." My mother didn't let me watch *South Park* so I didn't even understand the terminology of some of their insults, but I didn't need to speak their language to know I was a target, though I couldn't figure out why. I didn't realize that it was fun for Neil and his friends. When challenged, I didn't fight back—I crumbled, which must have made them feel powerful or at least superior. Once, the mother of a boy who was neither an outcast nor an alpha male saw them taunting me and tried to intervene, but she didn't get far. Neil was the kind of kid who talked back to adults, which shocked me, but kind of impressed me, too. He was gutsy and ungovernable.

There was no way I was going to talk to my dad about what was happening, but my mom must have, because I remember him being frustrated that I wasn't standing up for myself. To me, that was a non-starter. If the grown woman who'd tried to make Neil stop hadn't succeeded, what hope did I have?

I viewed my mother as my rock, the one who would protect me from feeling bad even if she couldn't protect me from bullies, and I wanted to be coddled. So I was horrified when, one day, she cheerfully announced that Neil was coming over to play. She explained that once we got to know one another, we'd see we had things in common, maybe even become friends. The idea of asking Neil over to my house sounded truly crazy, on par with suggesting we get a grizzly bear as a pet, and I resisted strenu-ously. As it turned out, my mother was right. It was harder for him to bully me once I'd let him hold my trophy pet (a newt) and he'd checked out my Lego creations. A few play dates did buy peace. For awhile. But there's a randomness to bullying, an ebb and flow that makes it difficult to predict or counteract. Eventually Neil started again, and if he let up, someone else stepped in.

Over the years, the more I was bullied, the harder I tried to avoid boys altogether. I was friendly with a few who weren't in my class, like John, who was younger but lived down the street and had a fleet of battery-powered mini-Jeeps. One day after a heavy downpour that flooded our street and turned it into a giant slip and slide, John and I got out our sleds and made the most of this makeshift fun ride. I was also friends with Adam, the only other Canadian for miles, who went to a different school. We got along fine, but our play dates were brokered by our parents, who'd become friends.

Sometimes all the kids on our street joined together to traipse from backyard to backyard, stomping through bushes and a little creek until someone yelled at us to get out of their yard. For the most part, though, despite having typical male interests—amphibians, model cars, Lego, space travel, games that involved weapons and ear-splitting sound effects—I gravitated toward the girls in our neighbourhood. There was Molly, who lived down the street in a house that was strewn with toys and unopened mail and smelled like old lasagna. Her mother was always lying on the couch, depressed, leaving Molly in charge of her brother, who had developmental disabilities. Molly had a wicked temper, which wasn't all that surprising given her family troubles, but it was still alarming. I have a vivid mental image of her standing in her driveway swinging a shovel around, ranting incoherently and vibrating with fury. I was closer to Kim, the oldest kid on our block and therefore the local sage. She had a tank of snapping turtles and a computer, and lived right across the street. At school, I ate lunch with the girls. They were nicer than the boys, but not exactly angels. My closest friend, Anna, was happy to come to my house to play and to have me over to hers, but she wanted nothing to do with me at school. She'd ignore me when I tried to talk to her, terrified that my lowly status might be contagious.

Erica, by contrast, seemed to be sailing through school with plenty of friends. She didn't lord it over me, and she wasn't even an especially bratty little sister. Before I was in grade four, we'd been close—after each move to a new city, we'd be one another's best friends until we had a choice of other playmates. Our first summer in Summit, we created an entire imaginary town in our backyard. The garden in the far back was the farmland, the hedges lining the driveway were apartment complexes; with chalk, we drew a bank on the side of our house where we collected ivy leaf "money." We mapped the whole place out on a big piece of paper and proudly scrawled "Map of Mendlensburg" across the top in pencil. We spent hours there, bustling around doing errands, riding bikes along the roads we drew with chalk on our driveway and returning to our hedge apartments at the end of a busy day.

But the worse things became for me at school, the more I envied Erica and resented sharing our mother's attention with her. The worse I felt about myself, the more I teased her. I don't think I did anything particularly extreme—we knew more than one family where the kids came close to maiming each other—but Neil probably thought he was just kidding around with me, too. From Erica's perspective, as she has mentioned once or twice over the years, I made her life a living hell. The worst thing I did, probably, was when I told her I was going to perform an amazing trick using her beloved blankie, and she instantly forked it over. She was troubled when I produced a pair of scissors and started hacking the blanket into small pieces, but I promised that when I put them into my magic hat, the blanket would, miraculously, be restored to its original state. Transfixed, she sat on the floor of her bedroom, waiting eagerly for the final reveal. "Ta-da!" I crowed, flipping the hat over. Out tumbled the blanket, still in scraps. She cried for days and never again believed in magic.

Sometimes I teased my sister on purpose so my mother would send me to my room, where I could dump out a bucket of Lego all over the floor and lose myself in my imaginary world. Alone, I felt happy. But eventually my mother caught on that solitary confinement was more reward than punishment for me, and thereafter when she sent me to my room I was under strict orders not to touch a piece of Lego.

My dad was more inclined to tell me off sharply for being unkind. His anger was eerily quiet and calm, and all the more effective for it, but a lot of the time he didn't catch me picking on Erica. Working nights, he was on a different schedule than the rest of us, more a presence in the house than a force in our lives. My mother got us a board game called Don't Wake Daddy, and the catchphrase in our household was "Shhh! Daddy's sleeping." But I doubt he got much sleep because our house was so small that if one person took a shower, everyone else knew it. Around this time my mother drew a cartoon of him that she titled "Floating Fafa." In it, my dad is kind of wafting down the hallway, supposedly awake but so tired he looks like a zombie. It was true to life. One day he was so bleary-eyed that he stumbled across our black poodle sleeping with her paws tucked under her chest, then noticed his own black socks on the floor nearby, and concluded the dog's legs had been severed. "Why isn't there any blood?" he asked, horrified. I don't think my mother has ever laughed so hard in her life.

No kid has any concept what chronic exhaustion feels like, or how it frays your nerves. I just knew that sometimes my dad had a hair-trigger temper. One day, instead of going home after school, I went to Kim's house across the street so she could help me with math. After awhile, we noticed that there were police cars with flashing lights in front of my place, and ambled out to see what was going on, whereupon my dad flew out our door and down the walk, hyperventilating. My mom wasn't home for some reason and he told me he'd been so worried about me, he'd called the police, then thrown up (likely hyperbole, designed to play on my phobia). He was one-quarter relieved to see me, three-quarters pissed off, and that's what registered: his disapproval. He didn't yell at me—the only time he ever really yelled was if Erica or I woke him up when he was trying to sleep—but he sent me to my room. Curt. Disappointed.

I didn't think, "Oh, Dad is sleep-deprived and under a lot of stress, so he snapped," or, "He's feeling like an idiot for calling the police, when I was right across the street the whole time." Much less, "He jumped to the conclusion that I was in danger because the world no longer feels safe to him." What I thought was, "I screwed up in some way that was really important to Dad and I've let him down. Again."

I spent so much time with my mother, on the other hand, that even when I'd done something really bad, like reading my sister's diary, we moved on quickly. She would be mad or disappointed, but then dinner had to be made and homework had to get done and someone needed to walk the dog. Normal life reasserted itself. The bad thing I'd done wasn't a rip in the fabric of our family but a bump in the texture of our day, which would be smoothed down by the subsequent three dozen interactions we had. By the time I went to bed, I'd know that I was fundamentally the same person to her that I'd been that morning, before I misbehaved. She didn't think worse of me.

My father's disapproval loomed much larger in my mind because his style is more clipped than my mother's, and I saw much less of him; I might have to wait until the weekend to spend enough time with him to be sure he'd forgiven me. I looked up to him and wanted to be like him, and I knew he wanted that, too. So every time I did something wrong, I felt I was failing him, not just myself.

When the school told my parents they wanted me to have a reading assessment, I was scared that it would reveal I was stupid and my dad would be upset. I didn't actually believe I was stupid, though I knew I had trouble retaining information I read; I'd decode the words, then forget what they'd said. This hadn't bothered me too much because I didn't like reading to begin with, but I was alarmed when I found out that I needed to go to a special place in another town to be tested. In the waiting room I asked my mom, "Will this hurt?" She assured me it wasn't a medical test, but by this point I was already in pain: worried that I wasn't good enough, that my dad would be fatally disappointed and there was nothing I could do about it. The diagnosis was that I had poor reading comprehension, so I was moved to the front of the classroom and a teacher's aide sat with me during English to make sure I understood what was going on. I wasn't the only one who needed extra help, but all the other kids who did were visibly disabled, and I remember thinking, "There must really be something wrong with me." (And there was, but it hadn't occurred to anyone to test my vision yet.) When stuff like this happened, I knew my mom would love me, regardless. I knew my dad would, too, but I assumed I'd go down another notch in his estimation.

It was becoming a familiar feeling. After the move to Summit, he'd tried again to get me interested in group activities, signing us up for regular father-son gatherings in our neighbourhood. It wasn't a formal group with a name and a uniform, but there were field trips and manly projects. Maybe he figured that in a new environment, I'd get in touch with my inner Scout and be into building birdhouses. But though I now knew better than to sit at the Fisher-Price table weeping at such gatherings, that's still what I felt like doing. We met at the home of a boy who was a hanger-on of Neil and his henchmen, and I didn't trust this kid at all—nor did I appreciate the fact that my dad fit right in and seemed to be enjoying some male bonding time of his own. He was outgoing, knew just what to say and what to do without even thinking about it, but he never came off as arrogant. People took one look at him and liked him. I felt like a ball and chain, dragging him down.

As a boy, so much of my understanding about who my parents were as people—separate from their identity as my mother and father, I mean—came from the stories they told me about themselves when they were my age. Stories about adult life didn't particularly interest me. My father rarely talked about his work, but when he did, I tuned out. My mother's anecdotes about her day were a little more compelling because usually they involved people and places in Summit, but she wasn't much of a gossip, and the dearth of juicy secrets wasn't to my liking.

However, I was always interested in hearing what my parents

had been like as kids, and my mom had a million stories. I knew about the time she'd wandered around her neighbourhood picking flowers from people's gardens, then going door to door trying to sell them. And the time she'd tried to convince a kid he could fly. Once, after she skinned her elbow, she went to school claiming she'd had a skin graft from an elephant, so wide-eyed that some of the kids believed her. Another time, she'd sworn up and down that farts were visible and she'd seen one, a hazy brown bubble, floating across the classroom. I could see the connection between the kid she'd been and the grown-up she became, and it gave me hope for my own future because like her, I had an overactive imagination and a desire for other people to see me as special.

I knew my dad's upbringing must have been stricter than my mom's, because my sets of grandparents were so different. I called my mother's mother Gallo because when I was really little I couldn't say Grandma Lois. When we visited her, we'd get out of the elevator on the eighth floor and she'd be there waiting, arms wide open for a hug, calling out, "Hello, darlings!" Her apartment smelled like books and was cozy but messy; if you opened a closet, things were likely to tumble out on your head. She was the kind of grandmother who doesn't care if you get crumbs on the floor. She'd let you eat on the floor if you wanted. Everything with Gallo was a game, a treat, an adventure, and often there was an educational angle as well. When she was explaining evolution to me and Erica, for instance, she dismantled her couch and created caves out of the cushions so we could all pretend to be cavemen. She read to me, really listened to me and generally made me feel like the most important person in the world. She was like my mother, funny and enthusiastic, minus the anxiety and the passion for order and cleanliness.

Gallo and my grandfather had separated when my mom was a teenager, and I think that had been traumatic for her. He lived in Burlington, on the top floor of an old building with spectacular views of Lake Ontario, in an apartment that was always sunny, like Gallo's. He was a history buff and maps were his passion; he knew the capital of every country in the entire world, or so he boasted. My sister and I spent countless hours playing in his office, pretending to be important advertising executives, like he was. There were stacks of paper, a computer and an array of punch stamps that would make any kid salivate. Generally, there was a feeling of plenty there. Grandpa's wife, Liz, always prepared a feast for our arrival: turkey, ham, chicken, roast beef— the menu seemed endless.

My father's mother was Gamma, and everything in her house was pristine. The carpet was always freshly vacuumed and Erica and I were afraid to walk on it because we knew we'd leave footprints. The furniture verged on being wrapped in plastic. There were more rules, and a sense that if you broke them, it wouldn't be pretty. I don't remember her hugging my dad or saying "I love you," which was weird because in my own family, whenever someone left, even just for a sleepover party, there was a lot of hugging and "Oh my God, I'm going to miss you so much" carrying-on. We were goofy and over-the-top in a way that was clearly foreign to Gamma, who was more buttoned-down. But she was very proud of my dad—of all of us—and always wanted to know what I was up to. I didn't feel that she "got" me the way Gallo did, but I knew she loved me and she always let me play with my dad's old toys: a floor mat with the map of a town on it, and little blocks with windows on them so you could build houses and buildings to line the streets of the town.

My father's actual childhood, though, was a little mysterious to me. He almost never talked about it and oddly, given that his business is storytelling, his memories rarely cohered into linear narratives. It was more like he rifled through a stack of old Polaroids then pulled one out and reluctantly showed it to me, a random moment in time without much context to ground it. There was usually a moral, though. One of the stories I remember was about his tenth birthday, when his grandmother took him out for his one big gift, a chocolate sundae at Dairy Queen. My father didn't view this as a subpar present, the way I did when I first heard the story. He told me how excited he'd been, what a big deal this sundae was for him at the time, and that I should be thankful for everything I had.

But I really had no idea what his life had been like at my age, what he cared about and who his friends were, what kind of a kid he was. I knew he'd always wanted to be a TV reporter, but that didn't help me picture him. He told me he'd been picked on, too, and he rattled off a list of hopelessly nerdy ailments he'd had at my age: asthma, eczema, myopia. I didn't know if he was just saying it to make me feel better. Given how successful and confident he was, it was a little hard to believe he'd ever been anything like me, and no further details that might have convinced me were forthcoming. On those rare occasions when he talked about his childhood, he was an observer in the story, not the main character. He didn't even really figure in his most riveting story. He'd been up at his family's cottage, hanging around with all the kids who summered there, when one of them decided to go swimming after lunch. The kid got into some difficulty and was eventually dragged out of the lake by some parents, but it was too late. He died there on the lawn, choking to death while the other kids watched, horrified. My father said he'd never forget the sound, and when he told this story, he still seemed traumatized.

My grandfather, too, just had a bit part in these stories. I knew, for instance, that when he'd driven my dad and his sisters up to their cottage, along twisting, unpaved roads in a car full of cigarette smoke, he'd had to stop several times on the way because they got carsick. My father knew they were almost at the cottage when he spotted the local ranger tower, and he'd always call out, "Mr. Ranger! Mr. Ranger!" Though the roads had subsequently been paved and the journey was now a lot more pleasant, my sister and I kept up the tradition of calling out "Mr. Ranger!" whenever we went to my grandpa's cottage, one of our favourite places in the world. I remember he had something in his basement that fascinated us: a poster of Wonder Woman, buck-naked. Erica and I would go down there and imitate her pose, snickering.

Our father would never have a poster like that in his basement or anywhere else. He was just completely different. His dad drank beer, watched sports and wasn't a big talker. Comparatively speaking, our dad was a sophisticate, an intellectual, an adventurer and expressive to the point of being flowery. It was hard to see the points of connection between the two of them. At least my dad and I had Lego. Flipping some bricks upside down, he'd shown me how to make a monorail. Then a house. When he expertly snapped a few together and said, "This is the starship

Enterprise," I sensed for the first time that we were similar. Lego gave us common ground: we'd sit together on the floor of my bedroom, building spaceships and waging imaginary battles. He told me he used to make little TV studios out of Lego, so I took it upon myself to do that, too, fashioning a crude anchor desk, cameraman and lighting rig. I hadn't suddenly developed an interest in current events but I did want to make him proud of me. His pride was like a drug, and as soon as I got some, I wanted more.

After we moved to Summit, I never had to count pennies with my mother again. Even to a kid, it was readily apparent that there had been a major change in our financial circumstances. My father gave my mother a diamond necklace, and in 1996 we went on a cruise to Bermuda. Before that, our vacations had always involved interminable car trips, either to my grandfather's cottage or to a very basic, no-frills seaside cabin we rented on Prince Edward Island. The cruise was our first big-time vacation, especially exciting for me because my dad said we'd pretend the boat was a spaceship. I studied the brochures, memorized the deck plans, counted down the days.

Driving down the West Side Highway in Manhattan, spotting this enormous vessel in the harbour, I was totally awestruck. I remember standing in line to board the ship, with my teddy bear Dewey in my backpack, feeling like I was at the gates of paradise. And I was. Erica and I had our own cabin, an interior one down the hall from our parents', who actually had a window where you could see the ocean. We had charge cards we could use to get pop or fries, and there was a play zone where all the kids hung out, plus ice cream every day on the top deck. We'd play with my dad in the pool and the hot tub, and each night we went out for dinner with our parents, but otherwise we had free rein to roam all over the ship. Everything about the experience was unprecedented, including something unusual that happened a few times on the boat: strangers recognized my dad, knew him from TV. Maybe this had happened in Toronto, too, but I was too young to notice. On the cruise, I registered a slight shift in my father, how outgoing and friendly he was, how he kept his public face on all the time.

When we got to Bermuda, my parents rented mopeds and put us on the back to tour the island, which probably wasn't the best idea since Erica always falls asleep in a moving vehicle. My mother had to elbow her constantly to be sure she was awake and wouldn't fall off, and Erica kept mumbling, "My eyes are closed but I'm not asleep, I promise." Bermuda was special to my parents because they'd honeymooned there, and I'd heard stories about the place. For instance, while they'd been playing in the surf, my dad had lost his wedding ring and had been so upset about it that they'd had to buy a new ring for him there. He's romantic, my father. When I was little, he told me that the first time he kissed my mom, fireworks went off and he knew she was The One. That's really how he talks, without a shred of irony or sarcasm; my parents are still visibly in love, and I grew up expecting the same thing would happen to me. One day I'd kiss a girl, have a pyrotechnical flash of insight and we'd live happily ever after.

My parents took us to Tobacco Bay, where my dad and I floated around in inner tubes. It was the first time in a long time that we'd been together so continuously without his work intruding.

Terrible, and criminally expensive, cell reception on the cruise ship likely had something to do with that. My dad pointed to a rock in the ocean and said, "Hey, do you want to jump off that thing together?" No way. It looked like a skyscraper. He didn't pressure me or try to change my mind; he seemed to understand and not judge my reluctance. Both of us lay back in our inner tubes and watched the fish swimming around our feet. At the end of the day we posed for what we came to call a "happy camper" photo: in this beautiful place, all four of us tried to look as miserable as possible. I'm sure the obliging tourist who took this shot thought our family was deeply weird, but we thought it was hysterical, and it's remained a family tradition we've re-enacted on every vacation since.

The trip was cut short by news of an impending hurricane, so we had to leave the island early, but I didn't mind. There was a delicious sense of fear and adventure, and once we set sail, the seas got very rough very quickly. I'd been wearing a seasickness band ever since we left Summit, so I didn't get sick and neither did my mom, but Erica and my dad were very ill. I remember walking back to the room after dinner, the ship was listing and then went over a wave and everybody in the hallway just keeled over. I thought, "This is so cool, we're on a starship and we're being attacked!" My dad was far too ill to play along, but as I fell asleep to the roar of the engines as the ship hurried back to land, I felt like the luckiest kid in the world.

That vacation was one of the happiest times I ever had as a kid but I didn't really connect it to my father's work. I wasn't oblivious or ungrateful; I knew my dad worked very hard, and for that matter, so did my mom. But it didn't occur to me that the price of the trip was my father's absence—if he hadn't been absent so much, we never could have afforded it. His job, to me, was something he did for himself, something that took him away from us. From me.

CHAPTER FIVE

IN PUBLIC
KEVIN

ON A NEWS BROADCAST, the anchor is less a friend than a salesman, peddling content created by other people and trying to frame it in a way that piques interest, provides context and inspires trust. But of course, you're framing and peddling a version of yourself, too, and likeability is still important, just as it is on softer shows. When I joined ABC, an extraordinarily likeable Canadian was anchoring its premier nightly newscast: Peter Jennings. I studied him closely, astonished by how well he connected with his audience and how calmly he could fashion a narrative on the fly. It was even more impressive because his brilliance was entirely self-made. His insecurity about not having finished high school drove him to out-work and out-research everyone around him. Luckily, he took an interest in me and my career (albeit, an interest that was often expressed in the form of pointed but constructive criticism).

In 1997, after a little more than two years anchoring *WNN*, I joined his show, *World News Tonight*, as a correspondent. At first,

I was assigned New York–based stories: plane crashes, severe weather, that kind of thing. It was a fairly normal progression for overnight anchors with reporting skills. The network would try you out on weekends, sending you into the field to see if you could come back with stories good enough to air when viewers were actually awake.

I also began filling in for Elizabeth Vargas, the news anchor on *Good Morning America*, and became the regular co-host of *Good Morning America Sunday*, where I was paired with Willow Bay. At thirty-six, I was an up-and-comer again. At *GMA Sunday* we didn't really cover breaking news, but the one-hour show was more feature-oriented than the longer weekday morning show and also leaned a little more towards news than entertainment. Willow and I were both new to the format and a little uncertain at times, but instead of making us competitive, our similarities helped us work together. It was a good partnership, or so I thought, until, seven months in, a senior executive at ABC News called me into his office and told me I was a drag on the ticket. With a Cheshire cat grin, he announced that my replacement had already been hired. I was stunned, but had the presence of mind to ask, "What does he have that I don't?" The Cheshire cat grin widened. The guy was really enjoying this now. "Star power," he purred. Clearly, I'd never be anchoring anything at ABC again.

Peter, who'd also done poorly on morning TV, took a longer view. He urged me to forget about the anchor thing for the time being and focus instead on developing my skills in the field and bringing back strong stories for the evening newscast. I did, and also tried to forget the executive's verdict on my abilities (it got easier a few months later, when the new guy with star power was bumped from the show—he'd lasted even less time than I had).

After dinner on August 31, 1997, I was watching TV with Cathy and the kids when the phone rang: the network needed an anchor for a breaking news bulletin. Princess Diana had been injured in a car crash in Paris. Peter Jennings had been the first call, but he was at his summer home and didn't think a "celebrity story" merited the long trek back to the city. I was the next call—not because I was in his league, but because I was so far out of it. On Labour Day weekend, when everyone who mattered at ABC seemed to be in the Hamptons, I was the on-call anchor, the junior guy who has to stay home on the off chance that something newsworthy happens. (The on-call system had been put in place the year before, after the bombing during the Summer Olympics in Atlanta; ABC was late on that story because they needed to scrounge up someone—me again, as it turned out—to anchor live coverage.)

Less than an hour later I was in the studio, where that breaking news bulletin morphed into an eight-hour live special report. Once it became clear that the princess had been seriously injured and others in the car had died, the powers-that-be decided to keep us on air. The fact that CBS and NBC got out of the gate even later than we did was likely a factor in the decision; continuous coverage could solidify ABC's lead on the story. Today, first-hand accounts and photos from the crash scene would be trending on Twitter within minutes, but this was pre–social media. Pre–Wi-Fi on every street corner, too. Very few photos were coming across the wire and there wasn't even an ABC correspondent in Paris at the time; all we had was a freelancer, relaying information to us by phone. At some point the producer decided to go ahead and broadcast some of those calls even though we didn't have a video feed or any visuals to accompany them. It was a gutsy decision, and it had the added benefit of helping to fill airtime when there were few confirmed facts to report and we didn't want to speculate.

The tone of the broadcast had to be even, subdued and respectful, or we'd quickly find ourselves in tabloid territory. This wasn't hard news, exactly, but it wasn't completely soft, either. One of the most famous people in the world had been gravely injured while being chased by the paparazzi. The increasingly fuzzy line between respectable and tabloid journalism was itself part of the story.

I hadn't ever had any particular interest in Diana, but a producer once told me to look for the emotional core in every story, and the core of this one wasn't hard for me to locate. It was uncomfortably close to home. Earlier that summer, my sister Kelly had died, completely unexpectedly, not long after giving birth. An undiagnosed brain tumour, we were told. She was thirty-four, vibrant, a proud police officer with everything to live for and then, in a day, gone. I'd raced from New York to be by her bedside after she was admitted to hospital in Toronto, but I didn't get there in time to say goodbye. When I kissed her cheek, it was already cold.

For the first time in my life, I saw my father acting emotional; he was reeling from the shock. So was my mother, who never really got over the heartbreak. Many years later, she confessed to me that she'd come close to committing suicide, had thought about getting into her car and driving into Lake Ontario, but then Kelly's husband, Don, had withdrawn into his grief and she'd needed to look after their daughter, Breanna. Her granddaughter saved her. She had a baby to raise.

In those first days and hours after Kelly's death, there was a lot to do, as there always is when someone dies. My youngest sister, Debbie, who'd been very close to Kelly, possessed a strength I hadn't realized she had, and between us we held our parents up and tried to support Don, who was devastated. I couldn't stop moving, organizing, checking on everyone else . . . but I couldn't seem to cry. If tears seemed imminent I'd rein in my feelings, afraid of losing control. I'd buttoned down my emotions so long and so well since *Midday* that if I started venting, I wasn't sure I'd be able to stop.

I hadn't been a particularly good big brother to Kelly. We were only starting to grow close right before she died, connecting in a new way over her baby and the challenges of parenthood. Most of my memories of my sister dated back to early childhood. Before Debbie was born, Kelly and I had been one another's only playmates during the two weeks we spent at our family's cottage every summer. There were also occasional weekends at home when all the kids in our neighbourhood played as a group, regardless of age, but otherwise I didn't seek her out. As a child, I'd envied the special relationship she had with our mother. When Kelly was three, she was diagnosed with Legg-Calve-Perthes, a disease that affects the hip; she had to wear a brace on her right leg for several years to make sure the bones developed properly. Mom often had to carry her places, and her worry about Kelly was all-consuming. Many years later, my mother told me some of her friends had taken her aside and pointed out that she was so focused on my sister that she was completely ignoring me. It wasn't all in my imagination, apparently. Kelly was delicate, needed protection, and my mother defended her when I did the things big brothers usually do to little sisters: argue, instigate physical tussles and give it back when she started it. I grew up believing that although my mother loved me and Debbie, Kelly was her favourite.

As we moved into our teenage years, Kelly's hip now completely healed, she made friends easily and was naturally athletic, outgoing, good-looking and popular—everything I wished to be, and believed my father wanted me to be, but was not. I mostly ignored her, and have to admit she was nicer to me than I was to her. When I ran for student council president, some friends of another candidate cornered Kelly after school and pushed her down, warning her that if I didn't withdraw from the race, they'd do worse to her. She didn't tell me until the election was almost over because she didn't want me to quit. As I soon as I found out what had happened, I told the other candidate, who dealt with his friends and apologized to her personally. I felt much closer to Kelly after that episode, touched that she'd put her own safety on the line for me.

It was not a surprise when she became a police officer, and she must have been a good one because she was given the honour of a police funeral. One officer stood out at the service. Kelly had said that he had sexually harassed her. That day, he exuded self-righteous piety, strutting around with his dress uniform weighed down by pins and medals. I didn't say anything to him because I knew Kelly wouldn't have wanted me to, but I couldn't believe a guy like that was still alive and my sister was not. The injustice of her death shook me to my core.

Barely a month after my sister's funeral, waiting for news on the Princess of Wales's condition, it wasn't hard for me to summon the appropriately sombre on-air demeanour. Or to maintain an emotional distance from events. It was how I had been coping for weeks.

A live, breaking news report is the highest tightrope walk in television. There's no script in the teleprompter, the story is developing in real time and initial reports are often unreliable. One mistake, or one fact misreported, can ruin your own reputation as well as the credibility of your news organization. You are often alone on centre stage, speaking without a pause, repeating what you know for sure over and over again, weaving in new facts as they're fed to you by producers who are frantically working the phones and scouring the internet—all the while hoping that a brief lull is coming so you get a moment to cough, drink water or maybe even run to the bathroom. It's improv, minus the comedy, and you need to be able to think quickly and craft a storyline on the fly.

Fortunately I had something to say about Diana. I had covered two of her visits to Canada, so I had personal anecdotes few American anchors had. I recalled watching her return to the Royal Yacht *Britannia* after a long day of appearances: her sons ran toward her outstretched arms, and the spontaneous look of joy on their faces and hers told you everything you needed to know about their relationship. I'd also seen how estranged she and Charles were in their joint appearances, how strained and formal their interactions were. Like anyone who'd ever covered the royal family, I knew about the niceties of protocol, what various titles mean—which gave me plenty to riff on when I had no news to report. I'm sure I came across as a royal wonk, but my citizenship came in handy on that particular evening.

I was also fortunate to be in the hands of Jeff Gralnick, one of the most accomplished live-event producers in American television news. In the control room in New York he and a team of producers scrambled to nail down facts and dig up experts I could interview. I'd be speaking extemporaneously about, say, police procedures in Paris when I'd hear Jeff's calm voice in my earpiece: "We've got an expert on high-speed chases"—my cue to steer the narrative in that direction and introduce the guest, whose face would then pop up on the television screen. I'd read his or her name off the screen, hoping I wasn't mispronouncing it, then ad-lib through the interview. Whenever new facts emerged, Jeff e-mailed them to the computer on the anchor desk rather than telling me through the earpiece, so I didn't lose my train of thought while I was speaking.

Interestingly, for someone who puts so much stock in careful preparation, I felt quite calm. I was in the zone and felt I was hitting the right tone, calm and mature. The style of broadcasting was much more intimate and less format-driven than anything I'd done before, and I was very much myself. As a newscaster I tend to show more emotion than most, and I think on that particular evening it gave people comfort. It felt good to be on the leading edge of a major story, even such a sad one, and I was surprised at how light the weight of authority felt on my shoulders.

At several points during the marathon broadcast, the senior VP of News, Bob Murphy, told me I was doing a solid and credible job. That gave me confidence, as did the fact that I understand French, which turned out to be a big advantage. The press conferences in Paris the evening of Diana's death were conducted almost entirely in French, and we were running audio from them live, without a translator. At that hour, even in New York City, it was too hard to find one. At one point, our freelance producer in Paris was holding out a cellphone during a news conference so that I could hear what was being said, and though my French isn't great, I was able to paraphrase, very carefully, what I was absolutely certain I'd understood. "Elle est morte" was one phrase I heard very clearly, and I'd learned in grade school what those words meant, which is why ABC was the first American network to announce the death of Diana, Princess of Wales.

I knew it was a big story, but I underestimated just how big until Barbara Walters called in, long after midnight. One of the network's most powerful stars and a tireless newshound, she wanted in on the story. Barbara had met Diana and interviewed Prince Charles in the past, so we broadcast a phone call with her at an ungodly hour and she was terrific, full of anecdotes and observations. She'd instantly grasped the depth of people's emotional connection to Diana and her story, and knew that many would take the loss personally. I hadn't really understood just how personally until we'd wrapped up the Special Report and I was driving home at about four a.m., wondering why so many lights were still on in so many apartment buildings. Then I realized: people must have been watching TV through the night. Of course, by the time the sun came up, the princess's death was the biggest story in the world, and Peter Jennings and the rest of the A-list at ABC were eager to own it.

But overnight, there had been a stunning turn of events: I was now within striking distance of the A-list myself. A few months before, when I'd been yanked off *GMA Sunday*, I'd been told I had no star power. Now, apparently, I had plenty of it, because the very next weekend, I co-hosted again with Willow. *TV Guide* anointed me the "breakout star of the coverage," and for the first (and last) time, Roone Arledge, then president of ABC News, sent me a note praising my work.

The capriciousness of this reversal of fortune made it difficult to trust. I wasn't being recognized for my portfolio of work. I was being anointed because I'd been in the right place at the right time on the night a princess died. The whole thing was so fluky that I felt I'd better make the most of any opportunities I was offered in case they evaporated as quickly as they'd materialized. There was something else, too. Kelly's death had forced me to re-evaluate my own life. I'd always been cautious, delaying gratification, deferring pleasure. But now I'd been reminded that life was too fragile and the future too uncertain. I needed to live in the now. Cathy heartily agreed. We didn't go crazy, but we relaxed our grip on the family purse strings—a holiday with the kids, a few home renovations—and I began training with weights in earnest, trying to build myself up physically, emotionally and mentally. I had a new mindset: seize the day. So I walked through every door that was now open to me, including the biggest one, at ABC's flagship morning show, *Good Morning America*. I'd been filling in occasionally for news anchor Elizabeth Vargas, but in the fall of 1997, started doing so for weeks at a time. In November, when Elizabeth moved to *20/20*, I formally replaced her on *GMA*.

I wasn't really thinking strategically about where the job might take me or even where I wanted to go. Just trying to break out of the pack had been my focus, and the news anchor position was a big move up, one that gave me a higher profile and more money than I'd ever had. *GMA* didn't have the prestige of an evening news broadcast or newsmagazine show, but it was very important to the network because of the advertising dollars it pulled in. I knew that if I did well there, it would be noticed, especially since ratings were declining and Roone Arledge viewed turning them around as his top priority.

After a long ride as the top morning show, *GMA* had started losing viewers the previous year.

Long-time co-hosts Joan Lunden and Charlie Gibson were blamed for this—conventional wisdom had it that the pairing had gone stale and the co-anchors were too old to attract the right demographic (conveniently forgotten several years later, when an even-older Gibson and Diane Sawyer took over the show). But there was more to it. *GMA* had started to falter when it was moved from ABC's entertainment division over to the news division, where a new raft of producers had hardened up the show and made it more news-oriented. Fans sensed the fun, family feeling they'd come to expect was gone. In the meantime, Katie Couric and Matt Lauer had breathed new life into *Today*. They were a rare pairing, a teasing brother and sister who exuded completely different kinds of energy yet also clicked. Matt knew that Katie was the star, she was very generous to him, and they genuinely seemed to enjoy one another's company—pure magic, on morning television.

By the time I started filling in on the *GMA* news desk in 1997, there was more than a hint of desperation in the air. In an increasingly panicked quest to halt the ratings slide, ABC executives were shuffling or rumoured to be on the verge of shuffling senior production staff as well as on-air talent. Nevertheless, the feeling on the set was collegial and welcoming. Charlie was particularly encouraging, and I quickly developed a good rapport with him and with Joan. They were under the microscope and knew their futures were uncertain, but somehow they performed for the cameras as though nothing at all was wrong. Just about everybody at that level is faking it to some degree, putting their own emotional reality to one side while the cameras are rolling, but Charlie and Joan were particularly good at that: masters of the game face.

In September, when Joan was eased off the show after seventeen years, she exited gracefully, as though it had been her idea. She was replaced by Lisa McRee, who'd co-hosted *GMA Sunday* prior to Willow, and had more recently been a local anchor in California. Thereafter, though Charlie Gibson still occupied the big chair he'd sat in for a decade, the network was essentially openly auditioning men to replace him. One male fill-in after another rotated in and out, which had to be awful for Charlie, not least because executives seemed to be looking for his polar opposite. They wanted a male host who wasn't grounded in news, as he was, and they were casting the net very wide. Alec Baldwin and Greg Kinnear were approached, but they weren't

interested; ESPN sports anchor Dan Patrick was a serious con-
tender, as was broadcaster Tom Bergeron, who went on to host
America's Funniest Home Videos and *Dancing with the Stars*.

With so many different men sitting on the couch beside Lisa
it was challenging for me to develop an on-air rapport with
them or her. It was pretty awkward most mornings when
Charlie wasn't there. I felt very loyal to him and thought his
skills in driving *GMA* had been seriously underestimated by the
management team. I also felt he was being humiliated, and I
didn't want to be part of that, so I didn't try very hard to engage
his potential replacements; mostly, the weathercaster Spencer
Christian and I kept to our corner of the set and had a good
time trying to make each other laugh on camera. That was
something we could contribute to the show, and we worked at
playing off one another. When Charlie returned for a week or
longer, it felt like Dad had moved back into the house, and
everyone relaxed a little. I was more playful, he was very supportive and generous, and my confidence was growing as the
GMA newscaster. I wasn't Peter Jennings and I didn't aspire to
his job. Delivering hard news in a more casual setting was
helping me develop my own broadcast style, one that felt comfortable and unforced. The *GMA* news desk felt like my sweet
spot, and I hoped that whoever replaced Charlie wouldn't ask
management to get rid of me (it happens).

Given the state of flux, I thought it would be wise to try to
prove my value to the franchise. Going beyond the call of duty
seemed like my best shot at longevity. So I pitched an idea: I
could anchor our newscasts from Iraq. This was during the
years-long cat-and-mouse game Saddam Hussein played with

the United Nations after the Gulf War, when he frequently obstructed weapons inspectors who were looking for evidence of weapons of mass destruction. American and British members of the UN weapons inspection team had recently been kicked out of the country, and the government's anti-West stance had hardened into official policy.

I got the idea to broadcast from Iraq while interviewing Tariq Aziz, then deputy prime minister, who told me and *GMA* viewers that Westerners were welcome there. "Anyone is invited to Baghdad!" he declared magnanimously. The next day I decided to call his bluff and apply for a visa, which he pretty much had to grant if he didn't want to look like a liar.

Subsequently, Charlie interviewed Richard Butler, the UN's chief weapons inspector. Afterwards, I cornered Butler, a telegenic Australian, who agreed to let me shadow him in Iraq. Later, in a private briefing at his Manhattan apartment, he gave me the lay of the land and promised to give me extraordinary access. He was a political guy in a highly political organization, and we both knew there was something in it for him: his bosses in New York would see him in action on television every day. It was important to Butler to display his agency's ability to locate and dismantle weapons, as well as Saddam's attempts to block him from doing so: Butler was certain Saddam had weapons of mass destruction hidden somewhere.

ABC agreed to let me broadcast from Iraq, but I had to get to Baghdad without a crew, and meet up with the ABC team already based there. Their schedules were already packed, so I'd have to fit my work in around theirs. And there would be a lot of work: along with anchoring the news on *GMA*, I'd have to provide an in-depth field report every day—without the help of a dedicated producer.

It was a major test of my ability to deliver in a hot zone. I'd never travelled in the Arab world before, never tried to report in a place where Westerners are considered the enemy. But I was hungry for adventure and wanted to burnish my credentials as a serious journalist, too. This was a big story, and an important one. If Iraq was concealing weapons of mass destruction, the military and geopolitical implications would be profound. (As it turned out, of course, the implications were profound even though no hidden WMD were found before the United States invaded in 2003—or after.)

I flew to Amman, Jordan, carrying a small duffle bag filled with a week's supply of canned tuna and protein bars. I'd been warned that the hotel ABC used would sometimes refuse to serve Westerners, so I should bring my own food, just in case. This was the same establishment that, famously, had a welcome mat with an image of former president George H.W. Bush, so people could wipe their shoes on his face as they entered the hotel.

At the Amman airport I was met by the driver ABC News had hired to take me to Baghdad. After the Gulf War, Iraq had been divided into two no-fly zones patrolled by American and British aircraft, so the overland route was the only way in for civilians. The driver told me to get in the back seat of his Suburban, and be ready to hide on the floor under a blanket whenever we approached a checkpoint. The vehicle's windows were tinted, but there was still a very real risk of discovery. I am not a small man who can be easily concealed.

The driver, however, ensured that no one would inspect the SUV too closely: at each military checkpoint, he quietly slipped what looked like a gram of cocaine into the lead soldier's palm. I never saw the driver snort anything, but it was clear to me he was high on something for the entire trip—he was gunned and gunning it, and played the same Arabic song over and over. And over. For the entire sixteen-hour drive. Fortunately, the road through the desert was well-paved and incredibly straight; Saddam made sure his army had good highways. Also fortunate: I'd brought a Walkman, so I turned it up as loud as it would go to try to drown out the driver's never-ending tape loop. My own cassette tapes had the most upbeat, poppy music I could get my hands on, because I'd suspected I might need something to take the edge off my fear. But though my heart raced at every check-point, I was determined to keep moving forward. I didn't allow myself to think about what might happen if I was discovered. I just took it one stretch of dusty highway at a time, and between checkpoints, tried to catch some sleep.

We arrived in Baghdad the next morning, driving past the giant statue of Saddam that would be toppled after the American invasion in 2003. After checking into the hotel I met up with the ABC News crew and producer who were already there. They cautioned me not to discuss anything important in the hotel, including where we were going and when, because all the rooms were bugged; we communicated by passing notes. I got to work preparing a report for the next day's broadcast and linked up with Richard Butler, who was already in the Iraqi capital. A colourful and divisive figure, he was eager to pressure Saddam's regime to comply with weapons inspections and thought the presence of

American television cameras might help. I expected the Iraqi authorities to protest, maybe even order me out of the country, once my reports started airing in the US. But either they weren't as organized as I thought or Tariq Aziz wanted to be seen as a man of his word (or perhaps, like too many Americans, the Iraqis were no longer watching *GMA*). At any rate, I was able to report fairly freely for a week.

Butler showed me the UN lab where his team tested for evidence of chemical weapons and let us tag along for an actual inspection, so our cameras could capture how tense these visits to various factories and facilities around the country often became. But I also reported on everyday life in the capital, where the sweeping financial and trade embargo imposed by the UN created endless shortages. The military officers and soldiers we saw on the streets looked well-fed, and many were even overweight. Women and children, however, tended to be thin, and they, not men, were the ones openly begging for money. Wild currency fluctuations meant that the cost of a loaf of bread varied from one day to the next; re-pricing goods was a daily chore for merchants. Some had very little to sell. Very few fresh vegetables and fruits were available in the market where we filmed, yet books were everywhere.

The people in the market were warm, but no one wanted to talk on camera. I didn't press too hard. I knew that openly criticizing Saddam and his government could lead to jail and torture, and I learned from a few murmured asides that informants were everywhere. One older man stared pointedly at an innocuous-looking guy hovering nearby to alert me to the local spy, who curried favour with the authorities by reporting on his neighbours. Saddam's regime was clearly brutally efficient, but the whispered conversations I had at the market also confirmed what I had read: Iraq's society was unusually literate and, at that time, women held about as many of the professional positions as men did, and everyone was taught some English. The *GMA* switchboard was probably busy after I reported that America's sworn enemy had created one of the most-admired and egalitarian education systems in the Arab world.

One day, travelling around Baghdad with the film crew and a driver who had been assigned to us by ABC News, we stopped at a red light and a young soldier with an automatic weapon rushed up from behind our Toyota Land Cruiser, yelling. It was hot, so my window was open, and before I had time to react, the barrel of a gun was inside the car, aimed at me. Turning my head ever so slightly, I saw the guy's agitated expression and glassy eyes. He was just a kid, and clearly high.

You never really know how you're going to react in a crisis, and I surprised myself. The thought that went through my head was "no fear," and I kept my eyes fixed on him. I felt strangely calm. Our driver was yelling at the guy in Arabic, and then I saw an older soldier move into position behind the kid and start questioning the driver. It didn't sound like pleasantries were being exchanged. I wasn't quite so calm anymore. I knew this could be the moment I died. But then the young soldier withdrew his weapon, on the order of the older one, I guess, and waved us on. After a high-adrenaline moment like that, I expected to have a delayed emotional reaction, but I didn't. I just breathed a sigh of relief and we got back to work.

The news desk of a morning show is sometimes a way station where a journalist is groomed to become a co-host, so my name also surfaced on TV columnists' lists of Charlie's possible replacements. But I liked being news anchor. News has always been my comfort zone, and there was travel, recognition, the opportunity to report—and, for the first time in years, the certainty of knowing I was doing my job well. I was allowed to bring in a very talented producer I'd known in Canada, Fiona Conway, and I had a lot of confidence in the way we were covering news. For morning television, the hours weren't even that bad: a four a.m. wake-up, two hours later than the hosts. I'd filled in for Charlie a couple of times when he was away, and thought his job wasn't a good fit for me. My personality just isn't big enough. I'm good at interjecting, but I'm not a great raconteur. I can help ground a conversation and I've got something to add to it, but I'm not a bon vivant.

So in December 1997, I went to David Westin, the president of ABC News, and said, "I don't know if I'm even really in the running, but you should take my name off the list. I'm not host material, but I hope you'll keep me around as news anchor." Westin was new in his job, and seemed to be in my corner. After I'd anchored the breaking news coverage of Princess Diana's death, he told a reporter, "I was not surprised, but Kevin's performance opened the eyes of a great many people."

He thanked me for being honest and I felt hugely relieved because he seemed inclined not to fire me. Shortly after that I pulled Tom Bergeron aside in our dressing rooms. He was always gracious and fun to work with, and we'd developed good on-air chemistry built on mutual respect. I wanted to keep it that way, and be sure he knew I'd withdrawn from whatever race was under way. He remembers the conversation, too, and telling me "whoever gets it inherits a poisoned chalice." Though I didn't find this out for years, Tom had actually already signed a contract to replace Charlie. It just hadn't been announced yet because ABC wanted to give him a few months filling in first, so the audience gradually got used to him.

In January 1998, I went off to Cuba to cover Pope John Paul II's visit, part of a team that included Peter Jennings, Roone Arledge and the network's main political correspondent, Cokie Roberts. It was the first time a pope had ever been to Cuba, and the first time since Fidel Castro took power in 1959 that American networks had been given the green light from the US State Department to bypass the ban on American travel to Cuba.

The ban meant that most Americans had no idea how Cubans really lived, so I got there in advance of the Pope's visit and stayed for a week, putting together features on everyday life. I like stories where you get to shine a light on people who wouldn't normally be noticed or heard, and I got to do a bunch of them that week. I interviewed a farmer who owned land where cement remnants of the missile silos from the Cuban Missile Crisis still stood; he was pissed that the Russians hadn't cleaned up after themselves properly. The old man immortalized by Hemingway in *The Old Man and the Sea* was, remarkably enough, sitting on his porch, smoking a huge cigar; he seemed a little stoned on the smoke when he spoke to me. I also followed an average family for a day, just showing what their lives were like and asking basic questions, one of which was, "What do you think my life is like in America?" The mother said something like, "I imagine a beautiful home, well-dressed children. And I also imagine you have no time for them and don't understand what motivates them or why they do things. I imagine you don't have a moment of calm."

That stopped me dead in my tracks because she was right.

I never strived for mega-success, which may have something to do with why I didn't achieve it. My biggest leap up, to co-hosting *GMA*, was mostly the result of a series of decisions made by others. I was just the last man standing. My path to becoming the third male host in the program's history began the night before the Pope was to arrive in Cuba, when news executives learned the identity of the previously unnamed White House intern who'd been rumoured to have had an affair with President Bill Clinton. The senior executive team of ABC News was in Cuba, and they wanted to break the Monica Lewinsky story on *GMA* at seven a.m. the next day. It didn't make sense for me to do it, because I was in Cuba, too. So suddenly Lisa McRee, who was still new to the job, and Tom Bergeron, who was sitting in for Charlie and months away from officially taking over, were in front of a major news bullet. Neither of them had network political reporting experience and they were breaking the biggest political story of the decade. I wasn't in New York so I don't know how it all went down, but I heard later in the afternoon that senior executives were unhappy with the broadcast. All I know for certain is that after that broadcast, things changed dramatically for me.

In a 2013 TV interview conducted for his induction into the Emmy Hall of Fame, Tom Bergeron explained that he was asked, after the Lewinsky scandal broke, whether he would allow me to co-host with Lisa the next time Charlie was off. Since he'd been promised Charlie's job, he had the right to refuse. But he didn't. In fact, he was all for it, for reasons I was completely unaware of for years. Apparently, Tom had signed his contract thinking that Elizabeth Vargas was going to replace Joan Lunden. He had good chemistry with Elizabeth but, he said, such a bad connection with Lisa McRee that viewers at home probably felt "wind chill" coming from their TV sets. Once Lisa was named Joan's replacement, Tom wanted out of his contract because he believed the pairing would never work. If he could somehow get the network to cut him loose, he'd get a handsome farewell package; if he walked away of his own accord, he'd leave empty handed. So he actively wanted me to succeed where he had not. If I did and the network bumped him out of the job he'd already been promised, that would trigger the penalty clause in his contract and he'd exit with a whack of cash. The next time Charlie was off the show, then, Lisa and I wound up as co-hosts. I had no clue what was going on behind the scenes, either the machinations or the motives. I just viewed it as a pat on the head from the network, a gold star of sorts for my work in Cuba. Lisa and I had a good week together. It helped that I was feeling relaxed and confident because of the positive reviews I was getting. Plus, as far as I knew, I was happily out of the running for co-host.

Until one night about a week later, when David Westin called me at home out of the blue and offered me the co-host job. It was his first big decision as ABC News president, so you'd think he'd weigh it carefully. But there was an impromptu feeling to the call, and I remember thinking, "This is a big job to be offered over the phone." What came out of my mouth was, "Are you sure

you really want a Canadian saying, 'Good morning, America'?"
To me, it seemed potentially problematic. But his answer was
quintessentially New York: he wanted the best person to say,
"Good morning, America," and he thought that was me.

I hung up the phone, turned to Cathy, and said, "Uh-oh. He
just offered me the job." She looked stricken and said, "Oh no."
It was the biggest job I'd ever been offered, but my gut instinct,
and hers, was that I should just politely say no and hope they
didn't boot me off the show altogether. I was quite comfortable
at *GMA*—on the news desk. But I didn't think I had what it
takes to carry the whole show. And between the way the show
was being run and the strength of the competition at *Today*, the
deck seemed to be stacked against *GMA*. I also didn't really
know Lisa. Chemistry is everything in morning television, and it
takes time to develop. We didn't know yet whether we had any.

My agent, Richard Leibner, heard me out but cautioned me
not to turn down the job right away. "This is your chance to
set your family up for the rest of their lives," he pointed out. We
were still living in our little house in New Jersey, all sharing
the same bathroom, and I'd been worrying whether there would
be enough money when the time came for the kids to go to university. I let myself start to think about the difference real money
could make in their lives. And mine and Cathy's, too. Carrying
debt, even a small mortgage, wore on me. After *Midday*, I was
perennially braced for financial disaster. How good it would
feel to stop worrying about money, to live debt-free, to know I'd
been a good provider. As soon as I began focusing more on the
potential rewards than the risks, I became more sanguine about
my prospects. Maybe I *could* do this. Maybe the show just needed

a fresh face. Surely they were doing audience research the week
Lisa and I co-hosted—presumably people liked us together, or
they never would've offered me the job. Maybe viewers would
like us even more once we'd had time to develop a rhythm. Maybe
Westin saw something in me that I didn't know was there.

The more money that was dangled in front of me, the more
I second-guessed my gut reaction. Cathy, supportive as always,
said she would back whatever decision I made. But I was deeply
torn. Surely they wouldn't pay me that much money unless they
really believed I could do the job. I reached out to Charlie. I
didn't trust ABC News management to tell him I'd been offered
his job, and I'm not sure they had. He was, as always, gracious
and encouraging, telling me—and others—that he felt I was the
right choice for the show, which gave me some confidence. So
I told my agent that if he could get the network to guarantee the
same salary for three years, regardless of how long I lasted as
co-host, I'd sign a contract. He did, and I did, and on that day
Richard gave me one of the best pieces of advice I've ever
received. He urged me to pretend to myself that I wasn't making
the amount of money I was actually going to make, and to
change nothing about our lifestyle. His message was, "Pay down
debt, bank your savings and don't start living large, because you
never know what will happen."

I'm glad I listened to him. And Tom Bergeron was very glad
I signed: he used his windfall to buy a luxury New Hampshire
vacation home, which, I learned years later, he named McRee
Manor.

With Alex, ca. 1987 in Ottawa.

— LITTLE MAN TAKES FIRST STEPS C. OCT. 17th/87 11 mos.

Cathy has always drawn cartoons of our family. Here are Alex's first steps.

"DANCEY, DANCEY ALEX"

Alex quickly supplanted me as Cathy's muse.

Dec. '87 - Alex feeds
self all alone!

Alex's and Erica's imaginary worlds—Cathy knew both our kids inside out.

With CBC *Midday* co-host Tina Srebotnjak and producer Eva Czigler on a ferry ride to Salt Spring Island, BC, in 1993.

Interviewing William Shatner on *Midday* in 1994.

Sitting in for Peter Jennings at ABC's *World News Tonight*.

Good Morning America's first three male hosts. David Hartman brought the baton; Charlie Gibson then passed it on to me.

With co-anchor Lisa McRee the weekend before our debut on *Good Morning America* in May 1998. We didn't feel as upbeat as we looked on the billboard—the show *was in serious troubl*e before we even started.

Robin Williams cracking us up on *Good Morning America*.

With Alex at the 1998 shuttle launch at Cape Canaveral.

Erica watching the post-show haircut on my final day as co-host of *Good Morning America*.

With Alex and Erica in 2001, after we moved to Vancouver, hoping for a more normal family life.

Alex and his inspiring Lego creations.

Family portrait the day after Alex came out to us in 2004. We thought it was important to proceed with the long-scheduled shoot.

Alex marching in his first Pride parade in Vancouver in 2005

We came to the parade to cheer Alex on.

It wasn't the run-of-the-mill procession we'd been expecting.

Happy campers: on every vacation, we take a group shot trying to look as miserable as possible. Here we are in Lake Louise in 2004.

Cathy buying condoms with Alex.

Cathy rented *Queer as Folk* to watch with Alex, not knowing just how raw and explicit the HBO series was.

Alex with his boyfriend on the raft at our cottage, 2005.

Tearing across the lake so my father wouldn't hear through the cottage grapevine that Alex's PDA had involved a boy, not a girl.

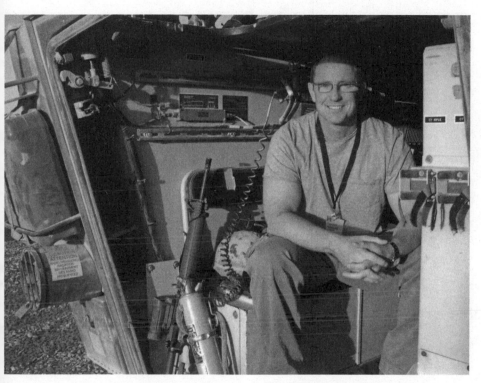

In a light armored vehicle, reporting from Afghanistan in 2005.

Five years after launch, *Global National* was Canada's most-watched newscast.

CHAPTER SIX

IN PRIVATE
ALEX

MY PARENTS WERE NOT FORMAL or strict, like some parents in Summit were. Most of my friends' parents wanted me to call them "Mr." and "Mrs." My parents invited other kids to call them by their first names. When it was just the four of us, we were big on nicknames, and we all had several. Dad's name for Mom was "Piz," for reasons no one remembers, and all of us called her Milla because she has a scar on her stomach that looks like a millipede. Dad was Dadoo, Doon, Faja; Erica was Tweenie and Smee; and I was Gemhead and Schmoo. At the dinner table, Erica and I weren't lectured about current events, the way you might imagine because of my father's job, nor was there a belief that children should be seen and not heard. Both my parents really wanted to know what we'd been up to, and dinner table conversation revolved around our lives—silly things that had happened in the neighbourhood, assignments at school—not theirs.

I knew kids who weren't allowed to play in their own living rooms, and whose parents' bedrooms were off limits. But our parents' bed was a gathering point, the place where Erica and I watched TV until Dad groaned, "Guys, I need to go to sleep." Our parents genuinely liked hanging out with us. My dad and I rode bikes and fooled around with computers together; for Christmas one year he gave me a stop-motion camera, then taught me to film and edit little animated movies set in the cities I'd built out of Lego. My mom did arts and crafts with me and, because she loved animals, encouraged me to have the kinds of pets other mothers wouldn't allow: newts, hamsters, mice, birds. Aside from our dog, my dad couldn't have cared less about animals. A bird held the same appeal for him as a rock, though he was intrigued by one piece of rodent paraphernalia: my hamster exercised on a wheel housed inside a miniature Volkswagen Beetle, which he could drive all over the house. Even my father found that funny.

But he was closer to Erica than to me, or so I felt. She was younger and cuter, and liked to do typical little-girl things: play with Barbies, dance around the house in a sparkly outfit and so on. He "got" her in a way he didn't get me, because I didn't like to do typical little-boy things. I was good at the same kind of stuff my mother was: drawing, playing the piano, being alone.

I often seemed to end up on the wrong side of the gender divide. I wound up in the virtually all-girl choir at school, for example, because on the day instruments were assigned in junior band, I wanted to play saxophone. So did all the other boys. The teacher let each of us try out the sax but by the time it was my turn, the mouthpiece was slimy with other kids' spit and I was quite reluctant to put it in my own mouth. "You don't seem to have the knack for sax, try the trombone," the teacher suggested.

My arms were a little too short to extend the slide fully, though, which explains why, in grade six, I found myself singing in the choir along with one other thoroughly mortified boy.

Fortunately, his mother wouldn't let him quit so long as there was still another male warbling away, and Frank and I bonded over our misery and became friends. He was the first boy I ever met who was at all like me: quiet and rule abiding, interested in computers and art. Different. Other kids were dying to be popular; we were dying to get more Pokémon cards.

It was a revelation, having a boy as a friend, because I'd reached the point of actively disliking boys, and not just because they bullied me. I hated the dirt-under-the-fingernails aspect of boys, their in-your-face aggression and yeehaw humour and the way they always seemed to take things one step too far. I'd tried to pretend that I was good with all that when my mother had forced me to hang out with Neil, my most committed bully, but his older brother was kind of crazy and one day he came after us with a nail gun. He was chasing us, yelling, "I'm going to shoot you in the head with this," whereupon my toughness evaporated and self-preservation took over. I was pleading for my life, until I noticed Neil was unperturbed. He knew this was just guy talk.

I hated guy talk. The issue for me wasn't embellishment—I was all for adding colourful details and flourishes to my own stories—but the way guys exaggerated in only one direction, to make themselves seem bigger and badder. The language they spoke was too limited to express certain key truths, like the fact that I worried I'd cry if someone punched me in the face, and sometimes felt sick with shame after teasing my sister and calling her names. Either there was something totally fake about guy talk and the way boys interacted, or I was a freak: the only boy who ever felt scared or weak or not good enough.

Shortly after we took the cruise to Bermuda, a tree in our backyard had been hit by lightning, and one day I came home from school to find that a basketball hoop had been installed where the tree had once stood. My dad was adjusting the net, clearly excited. I was not. I'd never had the slightest interest in basketball. He said, "Let's play!" I threw a few balls, they didn't go anywhere near the basket, and gave up. My dad urged me to keep trying. "You can make a basket, you'll see, it just takes practice! Oh. Well, almost . . . Try getting closer, that's it! Oh. Well, good try," etc. I was deplorable. We played for about ten minutes, during which time I failed to make a single basket, then never again. It was like the swimming lessons, soccer, baseball, any sport you care to mention—my dad was always optimistic that he'd finally hit on the thing that would be my athletic breakthrough, and he inevitably wound up disappointed and trying not to show it.

I felt bad too. The hoop had been sunk into cement, so it was now a permanent feature of our property, and my father had clearly had visions of us happily whiling away the summer evenings playing basketball. Later, I'm not sure if it was days or weeks, I climbed up the pole and tied a string to the hoop, then built a cable out of Lego so I could run a little trolley car on it, all the way to the house. I was proud of the way I'd repurposed the hoop and my dad agreed that the contraption I'd built was cool. Then the hoop fell into disrepair, bees built a nest in the net, and basketball was never spoken of again. However, my memory of that brief episode is crystal clear, nearly twenty years later. I'm sure that's how things went down.

My father is equally sure it's not. In his crystal-clear memory, basketball is something we liked to do together, along with Lego and watching *Star Trek*. He's not claiming we were out there every night shooting hoops until the light failed, but as he remembers it, we did play "21" frequently enough for me to develop a decent shot. I wasn't so bad after all. He remembers these games just as vividly as I remember that they never occurred. How can two people experience the same events yet interpret and remember them completely differently? How can you ever know what the truth is? These were questions I started to ask myself the year I was eleven, and playing or not playing basketball in my backyard. I wasn't sophisticated enough to articulate my existential musings with any precision, of course, but I did grasp that reality was a slippery concept. My imaginary world, for instance, often seemed a lot more plausible and logical to me than the real world did. In the real world, I started to realize that year, things were not always as real or true as they seemed.

In Summit, you knew everyone's mom by sight, even the ones who had jobs outside the home, but a lot of the fathers worked in the city, like mine did, and just weren't around the school all that much. You could know a kid for two years and have no clue who his dad was.

But everyone knew what my dad looked like, because he was famous. He wasn't Brad Pitt. Photographers weren't camped out on our front lawn. But his face was plastered all over buses in New York, and kids at school would say, "Hey, I saw your dad on

TV!" To me that was no big deal. He'd been on TV my whole life. He'd never been all that famous before, though.

The first time I realized that his job as host of *GMA* was different than other jobs he'd had, and somehow made our family special, at least to other people, was during our photo shoot for *People*. My mother sometimes read the magazine, so I knew that everyone in it was a star or royalty, and that when one of their photographers came to our house to shoot me and Erica running through the sprinkler, it was a big deal. During the shoot I had a sense of pride, but that was nothing compared to what I felt a few weeks later when, standing in the checkout line at the supermarket with my mother, I finally saw the magazine for the first time. The cast of *Seinfeld* was on the cover, and inside, in a section titled "Happy," there was the article about my dad's new job, along with huge photos of him on the set and one of our whole family in Erica's bedroom, watching her play the violin. My dad looked a little apologetic and embarrassed, my mother looked like she was about to say something sarcastic, and I was sitting on the floor grinning from ear to ear, as though listening to my eight-year-old sister scrape away at a string instrument was my idea of heaven. It was, in other words, the most contrived photograph imaginable, but I was blown away to see it so close to Jerry Seinfeld's. I eagerly scanned the pages, looking for my own name, and there it was. According to the article I'd urged my dad to take the *GMA* job: "'Dad, you're the guy that takes challenges,' Alex said. 'If you don't take a challenge, you won't be happy.'"

I showed my mom, crowing, "Look! It's us!" She turned five shades of pink and shushed me. My mother is a modest person and being the focus of attention in the grocery store made her visibly uncomfortable.

I liked attention but I wanted it for my own achievements. Being known as the "son of" didn't make me feel important. Quite the opposite: it emphasized that the only noteworthy thing about me was my dad. It was around this time that I decided I was going to be a scientist—so different from my father that we couldn't be compared, but still a profession he valued and admired, so he'd be proud of me. Especially after I won the Nobel.

I was proud of my dad and proud that he merited a big article in *People*. But I hadn't understood what it would feel like to share him with America, and it didn't take long for me to realize I didn't like it. One weekend, we all went to the Short Hills mall, just up the road from Summit. It's the quintessential upscale American shrine to retail: acres of polished stone and glass, high-end brand names all over the place. But we weren't there to go to Neiman Marcus or Saks. My parents didn't throw money around. I knew somehow that my dad was making more of it, though the only evidence was that he'd bought a new car. Nothing else at home had changed. I didn't get a bigger allowance—just enough to buy a few Pokémon cards and French fries once a week at the school cafeteria—and both my parents were still basically counting down the minutes until they could cut me off altogether. It was always clear that Erica and I would be getting after-school jobs just as soon as there was no chance that my parents could be jailed for violating child labour laws. They wanted us to know the value of a dollar, and in keeping with that theme, we were at the mall to window-shop, mostly.

Dad took me into computer and tech stores to look at all the cool new gadgets I could save up to buy, and Mom took Erica into those girlie tween shops that are crammed with pink clothes to see what piece of glittery plastic jewellery she could get with her allowance. All of us met up again at the food court, which was the height of elegance as far as I was concerned because you could get strawberry-flavoured Italian soda, my favourite. My mother showed us her new cardigan while my sister twirled a cheap bracelet around her wrist. It was a moment of low-key, pure family harmony. And then someone recognized my father.

As soon as that happened, the dynamic shifted, always. It was as though a switch had been flipped in both my parents. My dad was suddenly captivated by his fans, and even my mother, who normally had zero tolerance for phoniness, would pull a Nancy Reagan, smiling adoringly at my father and keeping her mouth shut. Erica and I didn't become invisible—quite the contrary: we were now under the microscope, or that's how it felt, anyway. This particular fan interaction dragged on, because we were trapped at the table, eating. Dad couldn't shake off the small group gathering around us the way he could when we were on the move, walking around town. As kids will, my sister and I got bored and started acting up, trying to win back our parents' attention. Our mother snapped at us quietly to behave, and the sting of her curtness did settle us down.

After the fans left, though, our family outing was over. The day had been ruined—not by the strangers who interrupted us, apparently, but by me and my sister. Dad's disapproval, so much scarier than Mom's reprimand in the moment, hung in the air for hours afterwards. It's difficult to explain because I don't remember him ever berating us or being harshly punitive, but both Erica and I feared his disapproval. Nothing made us feel smaller.

Dad had already explained how easy it would be for someone to damage his public image. But I didn't get it. If millions of Americans watched him, how could the opinion of a few mall walkers in New Jersey matter so much? And what about my opinion? It was frustrating that at a moment's notice, his attention could be ripped away from me by complete strangers. I wanted him to be as responsive to me as he was to them (it never occurred to me until I reread this paragraph that he might have been acting). There was also something confusing and unsettling about how familiar their behaviour was with my dad. They called him by his first name and acted as if they knew him as well as I did. I guess they thought they did, because he was in their living rooms every morning and he wasn't an actor, pretending to be a character. He was a journalist, just being himself.

Only, he wasn't. The guy on TV looked and sounded like my dad, and he sometimes mentioned me and my sister and my mom on the show, but he was not the same person who lived in our house. The Kevin Newman on television was more upbeat and lively. Happier, more outgoing, leading this big life where he chatted enthusiastically with VIPs and movie stars. The Kevin Newman in my own living room was more preoccupied and less engaged. Drowsier and more irritable. After dinner, he got up from the table and started studying for interviews and writing his questions and notes for the next day. Unlike other fathers, who put their kids to bed, he was asleep before we were, at eight o'clock. His friends weren't VIPs but guys he'd gone to university with, and other dads in our neighbourhood. If there was anything glamorous about his existence, I didn't see it.

My father was, in a way, two completely different people. On TV, he was supremely confident, no chinks in his armour. At home, he was softer, more sentimental. When he took me to see *Titanic* he cried at the end, after the old lady tossed her necklace into the ocean. His own grandmother had died not long before, and I guess the woman in the movie reminded him of her. Another thing: on air, he seemed relaxed, but I knew him to be a workhorse, intense and focused. Sometimes the idling engine of the car that came to take him to the studio in the middle of the night would wake me, and I'd peek out the little window over my bed to watch him leave. Even at two a.m., his nose was buried in notes, cramming for the show.

By the time I came downstairs for breakfast, there he was on the small screen in our kitchen, casually talking to the world. *Good Morning America* was almost always on while my sister and I got ready for school, but my mother was the only one really paying attention. Erica was extremely attentive the day one of her favourite boy bands was on the show, but otherwise, both of us tended to tune out. It was nothing personal. If our dad had been a carpenter, we wouldn't have wanted to sit around and watch him do carpentry, either. Eventually, too, we would surely have noticed that his public face was different from his private face, that he was more patient with customers than he was at home, or more jokey with suppliers, or whatever. But one big difference about having a father who's a public figure is that those kinds of discrepancies are much more obvious, and you pick up on them much sooner. I'm guessing that I started to think about my dad as a person—separate from his role as my father, I mean—much earlier than most kids do. I understood, for instance, that the world saw him very differently than I did. People expected him to live grandly, in a mansion on the right side of the tracks in Summit. Railway tracks really did divide our town; on one side, the kids got into trouble all the time at school, and on the other, they wore preppy clothes and lived in sprawling homes with well-groomed lawns and ultra-religious parents. That's how people thought we lived, too, but our house was essentially a nicely done-up starter home on a modest street at the far edge of an affluent neighbourhood, close enough to the railway tracks that the dishes in the kitchen sometimes rattled slightly when a train went by.

GMA had a "fix-it" segment where they'd go into people's houses to do minor repairs to teach viewers how they were done, and one time they came to our place to fix a leak in the ceiling. Our house was so small that my mom ran out of surfaces for the trays of submarine sandwiches and fruit she laid out for the crew. The cameramen were apparently in a state of shock: "Kevin Newman lives *here*?" Both my parents found this story hilarious and satisfying, but I liked it less than they did. I sometimes worried that people looked at me the same way: "*You're* Kevin Newman's kid?" Yet another reason why, if someone didn't already know, I wasn't about to volunteer what my dad did for a living.

Some aspects of my dad's public image were important to him, too important to laugh about. It mattered to him that people knew he was down-to-earth, for instance, and he truly was. The first few years we lived in Summit, there was no direct train access to Manhattan. I remember he had to take a bus, maybe two buses, then transfer to the train in another town. This was the kind of thing my dad would never complain about. He just did it. Only now does it occur to me what a huge hassle this must have been, especially given the hours he worked. And he did it so that the rest of us could live in a nice little town with decent schools.

He also cared about being respected as a journalist. He'd talk about anchors he respected, how many Emmys they'd won, the big stories they'd broken. He very rarely talked about his own work but how it was received and how he was perceived was clearly important to him. Erica still talks about the time in 1998 when she was in a dance recital where all the fathers got together to do a little number, some goofy thing where they all wore tutus. My dad told her he couldn't participate—what if someone at "Page Six" got hold of a picture of him in a tutu? Erica was crushed. She didn't understand why someone at "Page Six" would care about her recital, or why our dad would even care about "Page Six." What was "Page Six," anyway? I didn't really know, either, but I did know that even if my dad hadn't been co-host of *GMA*, he wouldn't have wanted to put on a tutu. That was girl stuff, and he was a man. I'm not sure if he ever said anything like that to me quite so baldly, but I knew for a fact that that was how he felt.

I was home from school, sick, a lot that year—so often that even I began to think I was faking it, until the doctor discovered I had mono—and sometimes I'd go with my mom to the train station to pick my dad up after work. A few hours before, he'd have been on TV, animated and enthusiastic, but when he got off the train from New York, he was grey and drawn. I didn't know why. My mother only told me that he was working really hard, but that didn't have much explanatory power. My father had told me many times that he'd always dreamed of being a TV journalist, never wanted to do anything else. And I knew he loved work more than anything. Now he had this big job on TV, his dream had come true, everyone at the mall fawned over him—why didn't he look happy?

I understood what was happening a little better after I appeared on *GMA* myself. I didn't go into New York that often, so it was exciting to head in very early with my mother, especially near the holidays, when the bright lights, big city appeal of the place is strongest. *GMA* was doing a segment on making Christmas cookies, and a bunch of kids, mostly the children of the show's staff and crew, had been rounded up for it. I'd been in the studio before to visit my dad after work and, once, thrillingly, to hold a baby lion that had appeared on the show. It was cute and heavy and as I recall, a baby bottle was stuffed in its mouth the whole time it was in my arms. But the place seemed different to me when I knew I was going on TV myself. For the first time I was aware how massive the stage was and how many people were running around. I'd never really noticed the tremendous buzz and hum of important activity, or how the tension broke and the mood shifted suddenly during each commercial break. I started to get nervous, waiting to go on. I didn't know what I was supposed to do. "Relax," someone told me. "Just have fun."

Next all the kids were hustled over to a kitchen area to sit on stools behind a high countertop covered with balls of dough and plates of green, red and silver sparkles and decorations. I knew enough to shut up when I heard the countdown, "Five, four, three . . ." then there was silence, a light went on atop the camera, and here was my father, cheery and highly caffeinated. *On.* So on, in fact, that he seemed more like a guy impersonating my father than my actual father. He was talking to the cooking expert, sounding all excited about these cookies, which I knew for sure he was not, and the cooking expert was trilling, "Place your thumb in the middle of the cookie" but I must not have done it right because next thing I knew, she'd grabbed my thumb and was squishing it into a ball of dough. We weren't really there to make cookies, I suddenly realized, but to *act* like we were making cookies. I hadn't understood this for some reason, though it must have been explained to me, and was at a complete loss as to how to behave. Maybe I was supposed to do what my dad was doing, amp up my personality somehow, but I didn't know how. Instead, I just sat there with a ball of cookie dough stuck on my thumb. I registered that my father introduced me on air, which made me feel special later, that he'd been proud enough of me to say my name, and then the segment was over and everyone was asking whether I'd had fun and my father was hugging me, saying, "Good job!" I didn't know what he was talking about. The experience had been a flash of action, over in a second, and I'd just sat there, stunned.

Afterwards we looked at the store windows, elaborately decorated for Christmas, and went to Central Park, where I climbed up on a giant rock and wondered how my dad, who now seemed exactly like my dad again, did it. How did he turn himself on and off like that? It seemed like having a superpower, on a par with being able to make yourself invisible, and I wished I had it, too. Not to be a TV star but to make the bullies stop, to make kids like me.

Yet this magical ability my father had made me wary, too. I felt like I didn't know what was real about him anymore, and that made me look at him differently. More critically. I still loved him, still looked up to him, still wanted his approval. But instead of focusing on the ways I was disappointing him, I started focusing on the ways he was disappointing me. He didn't know me well enough to know I'd never like basketball. And he didn't know how bad it felt to share him with the world, and feel that there was almost nothing left for me.

CHAPTER SEVEN

BEING A SOMEBODY
KEVIN

TRADITION DICTATES that when a long-time host leaves a morning show, there's an on-air goodbye party, complete with pre-taped tributes from the president, rock stars and other luminaries. The official story is usually that the host is delighted to be free at last to pursue "special projects." Usually, however, there's nothing at all voluntary about the departure and the host is quietly seething about having been pushed aside.

On May 1, 1998, Charlie Gibson's last day hosting *Good Morning America*, I was braced to feel awkward, but he handled the situation with uncommon grace. Charlie, who'd gone out of his way to welcome me both publicly and privately, played the part of the affable retiree perfectly. And maybe he really was happy to be getting the hell out of there. He knew better than just about anyone what was going on behind the scenes and why *GMA* was floundering. I imagine his wife, Arlene, was euphoric; she knew how much the show and the early shift had taken out of her husband, particularly the past few years. Charlie had endured the very public tryouts of men auditioning to replace him without any promises in terms of his own future at the network. Throughout, our producers had been experimenting with different formats, inventing new segments and rejigging the show to try to play to the strengths of the fill-ins. Unsurprisingly, *GMA* had lost its consistency and became uncomfortable to watch, which no doubt accelerated the ratings decline.

But the impression the producers sought to create in his final show was that Charlie was entrusting the keys to a happy kingdom to his handpicked heir. To add credibility to this dynastic scenario, David Hartman, the show's original anchor, returned for the send-off. He had some unfinished business, he announced when the three of us sat down to do our segment and the cameras started rolling: he'd never formally passed the baton when Charlie had replaced him eleven years earlier. With a flourish, David produced a conductor's baton and handed it to Charlie, saying he should have done it a lot sooner. Charlie laughed and said a few words, then held it out to me. I hesitated for a moment. I'm not a big believer in mystical signs, but just for an instant, that baton didn't look like an inanimate object—it looked like a living thing, crackling with sinister energy. It really did seem to be a poisoned chalice, as Tom Bergeron had said. In that moment, I knew I'd made a mistake. A big one. But there was no turning back. Smiling weakly, I took the baton and, after David and Charlie presented me with gifts and assured me that I was going to love hosting *GMA*, I looked at the camera and mumbled, "I don't know how it's going to work out." But I already had a pretty good idea: not well.

The path to morning glory is littered with casualties: Ann

Curry, Deborah Norville, Peter Jennings, even Walter Cronkite. Some really talented, charismatic people have bombed in the time slot, so of course I was concerned that I didn't have what it took. My only hope, I decided, was to be myself: resolutely normal and relatively low-key. Maybe the fact that I didn't have an outsized, glitzy personality would be a plus. After all, the core audience for morning television isn't New Yorkers with attitude, it's Middle Americans who take a dim view of affectation. I'd signed my contract telling myself, "Convince someone in Nebraska that you're an okay guy, and maybe you have a shot."

But once the publicity machine of American stardom cranked up and millions of dollars were being invested in promoting me, I no longer felt like myself. I was still me, of course, but now there was another me: a supersized, airbrushed version who beamed from the sides of buses. I won't lie. It was heady and exciting, this first taste of real fame. *People* magazine ran a glowing article; people inside ABC who'd never even noticed me before now knew my name. All of that felt good. But it also felt fake. The gulf between the projection of the man I was supposed to be, and who I really was, had started to feel unbridgeable even before Charlie passed me the baton.

On the weekend before my debut, Lisa McRee and I were at an event in Times Square, standing below a massive billboard that showed the two of us laughing as though we were having the time of our lives. We were meant to bring that same ebullient spirit to the event, but Lisa was wearing sunglasses to hide her eyes—she missed her husband, who was still in L.A., and had been up most of the night crying—and I felt I was staring down the barrel of a gun. She was sad, I was scared, but somehow we had to impersonate the radiantly confident people up on that bill-board—and we had to be able to do it not just once, to get through the event, but for two full hours every weekday morning for the foreseeable future. The surreal nature of the challenge really hit me then: I was supposed to convince people that the über-confident, carefree, Photoshopped guy on the billboard was the real me.

Probably all on-air personalities at the highest level of American network television feel this pressure. Some deal with it by drinking, taking drugs and/or behaving badly, but many cope by immersing themselves in work to the exclusion of all else, so that over time, the distinction between the public self and the private reality erodes. They become more and more like their public personas, developing a TV sheen that becomes part of who they are, even when they're home alone eating a sandwich. The most successful anchors at ABC News had it: the carefully modulated voice, the perfect posture, the social graces to move through any event. They conducted themselves at all times as if they were being photographed (and often, they were).

I didn't have that sheen—and didn't want to acquire it, either. Sure, I wanted to succeed, but even more than that I wanted to be the sort of person who could interview Nelson Mandela in the morning and still be genuinely interested in helping my kids with their homework in the evening. It may not sound like much of an aspiration, but I wanted to be a nice guy. Unchanged by recognition. The sort of man Cathy would still respect, and who would set a good example for our kids. I didn't want to become a celebrity asshole.

As it turned out, I didn't have to struggle long to stay grounded. There's no other option when you don't achieve liftoff.

I don't know why, given the hour and the fact that young kids are often watching, the audience for morning television seems to want to see a spark of flirtation or sexual coyness between the hosts. But they do. Co-hosts don't have to be best friends off-camera, but they do need to know and trust one another well enough that when the camera's on, they can play off one another. Regis and Kathie Lee, for instance, rarely spent time together off the set, but they were puckish and playful once the cameras were rolling.

It was a big problem, then, that when I became co-host of *GMA*, Lisa McRee and I barely knew each other. Right from the start, we were under tremendous pressure to deliver a miracle, so there was no time for long, get-to-know-you talks, which might have revealed that Tom Bergeron and Lisa had had, in his words, "zero chemistry," and that's why I'd been offered the job. If I'd known that, I think I would have insisted that Lisa and I work together, consciously, on our on-air chemistry. It's strange, given that misfire, that the powers-that-be at ABC didn't plan for a longer transition to be certain that we clicked. But they seemed to be in panic mode.

Essentially, they wanted Lisa and me to conduct ourselves on air as though we were on the verge of an affair, when in fact both of us felt vulnerable and defensive—a combination, it turns out, that isn't conducive to charming on-air banter. The bonding experience that had been planned for us—an ambitious road trip across the US, where we'd broadcast from different cities—never happened. ABC's technicians went on strike and the roadshow, which had already been announced with some fanfare, was abruptly cancelled. *Today* had beaten us to the punch anyway, with its first-ever, wildly popular "Where in the World Is Matt Lauer?" week, which wrapped up on Charlie's last day and helped ensure an even more daunting ratings lead by May 4, my first day as co-host.

Viewers who did tune in discovered that over the weekend, not just the male co-host but virtually everything else about *Good Morning America* had changed. The show was suddenly very soft, with lots of peppy lifestyle segments. The old set, a lavish country-style home, had been replaced with one that resembled a swanky Manhattan penthouse, so Lisa and I came off as the wealthy city couple everyone hates, not the friendly Midwestern folks next door. We were both relative unknowns, so this first negative impression was especially damaging. Early on in that first show, Lisa reached out and put her hand on my shoulder, the traditional visual cue establishing in viewers' minds that she approved of the decision to hire me. We had a pretty good patter going as we gamely tried to show off our too-slick set, but then struggled to settle into the rhythm of an entirely new format. It felt forced. How could it not? Everything was brand new, including me. And I knew that more than four million people were watching.

To have fun with the person you're sharing that scary place with, you need to have mutual trust. It gives you the comfort to reach out and you become more engaged and more engaging. I'd had that kind of relationship with other co-anchors, and I'm sure Lisa had, too, but we did not have it with one another. At first I thought we were just experiencing some initial awkwardness and we'd grow out of it, but we never really evolved as colleagues. I had a lot of respect for her ability as a broadcaster, and she had the kind of energy and enthusiasm that are so important in morning television, but we just couldn't seem to connect on air. We came from different worlds—she'd grown up in a wealthy Texan family, whereas mine was suburban, Canadian, middle class—and aside from being ambitious, we didn't have much common ground. A lot of co-workers just don't click on a personal level; easy camaraderie, where you feel a colleague elevates your game and brings out the best in you, is rare. But co-hosts should have that, or something close, and Lisa and I did not, as television critics immediately noticed. You could almost hear the knives being sharpened. Our honeymoon as an on-air couple lasted barely three weeks before people started saying our relationship was in trouble.

As the negative reviews gained momentum, Spencer Christian, the show's long-time weatherman, was purged, severing the final on-air link to the show's past. I liked Spencer and we did have strong rapport, but quite apart from that I thought it was a terrible idea to make another big personnel change when viewers were still struggling to get used to me and Lisa. I raised my concerns with the show's producers, but was told the decision had been made upstairs and they were powerless to reverse it. Too much change was being forced on the audience, and long-time loyalists were reeling from culture shock.

So was I, for different reasons. Morning television is an upside-down world, a fact I'd never really had to come to grips with when I was just reading the news on *GMA*. In most TV news operations, the day begins with an ideas session, but morning shows begin with a performance of ideas that were cooked up the previous day. It was like a rocket: wake up in the middle of the night, shower, start cramming for interviews in the car on the way to the studio and then, once the cameras were on, struggle past exhaustion to try to have the kinds of fun, vibrant, high-energy conversations you'd have at a party at ten p.m., after a few glasses of wine. The pace of morning TV is so relentless that even when you're dealing with fluff you have to be extremely focused. During commercial breaks you multitask like crazy—study your notes for the next interview because you won't be able to look at them on air, figure out the staging for the next segment, set up the camera angles—all while trying to listen to the chatter in your earpiece.

The chief architect of a morning show is the executive producer, the content chooser-in-chief who determines the show's tone, focus and template. Shelley Lewis, our executive producer, had been handpicked by Lisa, and had decided the path to success was to build the show around her strengths, just as *Today* was built around Katie Couric's. But Lisa's interests—relationship trends and helpful how-tos, both perfectly appropriate for a morning show—weren't the same as Katie's. They weren't the same as mine, either.

Preparation is my self-protection mechanism, but overpreparation made it difficult to relax into light back-and-forths about summer fashions and home décor. Some people find those kinds of segments easy, but for me they were hard going, and I know it showed. I just could not master the correct, breezy tone. Some hosts have a genius for small talk even on subjects they couldn't care less about, but I'm not one of them. My attempts were clumsy and laboured, and given how soft and light the show's new template was, this was a real problem.

I'm most at ease when the subject matter is news related, or when I can have a conversation with someone thoughtful, where it's possible to ask unexpected questions. This happens pretty frequently in longer-format interviews, but most *GMA* interviews lasted four minutes and were all about a rapid-fire and entertaining exchange focused on a celebrity's new book, movie or album. Celebrities are heavily scripted and trained to stay on-message, and we had so little time that it was very hard to get much else out of them.

We often couldn't land the big stars because Lisa and I were unknowns and didn't have the kind of personal connections and reputations that often help seal the deal. But when "big names" were coming on the program, I'd usually argue for more time. I rarely won. Only a huge star could command eight minutes, even though the longer interviews tended to go much better and I'm sure they were more interesting for viewers, too. I felt good about the segment I did with Tom Hanks about the power of then new cyber relationships; he was promoting *You've Got Mail*, his 1998 hit. Talking about impending motherhood with a very pregnant Jada Pinkett Smith also went well. Robin Williams got more than his allotted few minutes because he brazenly stole time from the show, riffing in his inimitable fashion, knowing that only the most tone-deaf producer would cut him off. But thought-provoking conversations weren't a staple of the new *GMA*. No matter how interesting or entertaining the guest was, I'd hear "wrap" in my earpiece after three and a half minutes, and I'd wind things up so we could barrel off to whatever had been slotted next. Adherence to the template was absolute, as though it had been engraved on a stone tablet and any deviations from it would invite the apocalypse. A successful show was deemed to be one that stuck to the pre-set time limits and crammed in everything the producers had planned. Spontaneity was punished with increasingly urgent reminders—"wrap," "wrap!" "WRAP!"—in our earpieces.

On *Today*, the format had plenty of padding throughout, to encourage kibitzing between Katie and Matt, and over time this casual riffing had become what viewers enjoyed most. On our show, the only time allotted for unscripted chit-chat was during an affiliate break at five minutes to every hour, when Lisa, Spencer, Antonio Mora, our new newscaster, and I would sit down and just talk. That five-minute segment was sometimes the strongest on the show, but many stations cut to local news and didn't carry it.

Any chance that chemistry would develop between me and Lisa was squashed, but the two of us never openly acknowledged the problem and talked about it, much less tried to address it by socializing outside the office. She was living alone in Manhattan, flying to the west coast to see her husband whenever possible, and I was living in suburban New Jersey with a family I barely saw; logistically, it would have been tricky. But Lisa didn't seem open to the idea, either. The gossip columns had us feuding on the set, but we weren't. We just worked in isolation, barely communicating off-camera. An impartial executive producer might have been able to force a change, but Shelley was Lisa's hire and from my perspective, not approachable. She never once asked me, "How are you doing?" or proposed a remedy for the chemistry shortage. Of course, like me and Lisa, she was fighting for her life, professionally speaking, and undoubtedly had a few other things on her mind. Sometimes, extreme pressure encourages cohesion and solidarity. This was not one of those times.

The remedy proposed by senior network executives was that I needed to be more like Matt Lauer. Presumably, if I could do that, it would ignite our on-air relationship and all our problems would be solved. For all I know, they were urging Lisa to be more like Katie Couric; we've never compared notes. Now, Matt was—is—extremely good at what he does. He's also generous-spirited. He sent me a really kind and encouraging note when I started hosting *GMA*, and was always collegial and friendly when I bumped into him. So I liked him as a person but I came to hate the sound of his name because I heard it so often. Eventually a senior executive packed me off to Matt Lauer school: after our show wrapped for the day and I was thoroughly exhausted, I was confined to a room with some show doctors to watch hours of his interviews on *Today*. According to the show doctors, even Matt had needed training to become Mattish. Apparently they'd worked with him to develop a three-beat interview technique—get the smile, hit them hard, then leave it soft—and they wanted me to perfect it, too. They would run tapes of my interviews, pointing out how they didn't fit the Matt mould, and then instruct me to refashion them on the spot into three-beat interviews.

Critics said I seemed "smart" and "affable," but that's not enough to carry a morning show, as was also noted. On a personality-driven show, a relatively quiet personality is not a plus, as I was all too aware. I wanted to get better at the job. My tendency after every show was to focus on all the things I'd done wrong, and I was definitely open to constructive criticism and guidance. What new host wouldn't be? But I was being coached to get further away from my real self. "Just copy the guy on the show that's doing well" isn't constructive criticism. It's destructive. The not-so-subtle subtext is, "We don't value anything about you as a journalist." This was particularly alarming because it was my journalistic skills, not my looks or connections or knack for witty repartee, that had got me the job in the first place. Finally I balked and told the executive I was through with show doctors. I was becoming dangerously distracted during interviews, more focused on trying to channel Matt than on interacting with the person right in front of me. The whole experience really shook my confidence—not just in myself, but in my managers. What were they thinking? We couldn't possibly take on the market-leading show by creating a pale imitation of it. Our only hope was to do something entirely different and try to change the game.

Quickly.

Three months after my debut, the decline of *GMA* was the talk of the town. Someone inside ABC was leaking to the papers, and almost every day "Page Six" ran an item about some gaffe I'd made or gleeful gossip about our ratings, which were tanking to unprecedented depths. There was ongoing speculation about who'd replace me, and when. It got so bad that even Jeff Zucker, who ran *Today*, felt moved to express sympathy. "I was here at a time when we got a lot of unfortunate press and a lot of unfortunate rumours swirling around us," he said, reminding reporters of the debacle when Deborah Norville replaced Jane Pauley. "I know how hard that is to live through. I feel sympathy for people who have to have a bomb squad open their newspapers every day."

A bomb squad would have been helpful. Security guards, too. The whispering and snickering, whether around the water cooler or in the papers—I hated it, but tried to act unfazed. At home, Cathy tried to support me, pointing out that it wasn't all my fault, and that despite everything there had still been some good interviews and good shows. Intellectually I knew she was right, but it didn't make much difference to how I felt, which was humiliated.

Especially after being told to "man up" by the executive who'd hired me, in the first and only face-to-face meeting he ever arranged with us while Lisa and I co-hosted. Bizarrely, though our ratings were in free-fall and *GMA* was the most important revenue-generator in the news division, we had almost no contact with or coaching from senior executives. It was as though no one wanted to get his hands dirty trying to fix the problem, for fear we'd take him down with us.

Four months in, David Westin finally summoned me and Lisa to his office. He looked at me and barked, "You've got to be more like a quarterback. Tougher, stronger, more masculine." Then he looked at her and said, "And you have to do your homework, know what you're talking about." I think she was as shocked and embarrassed as I was. We'd thought of ourselves as journalists, but clearly he viewed us as character actors. Or maybe caricatures. Lisa was from Texas, so she'd been cast as the head cheerleader, and I had broad shoulders, so I'd been cast as captain of the football team. But that wasn't who I was. I'd been hired because I can think on my feet, not because I was buff or

hearty or all-American. Westin concluded by telling us we needed
to work together as a team and he wanted to see the changes by
tomorrow morning.

Stunned, Lisa and I retreated to our offices to try to shake it
off, and then met with the senior producers for a soul-searching
session that lasted well into the day. We talked as a group about
how we could create a better show and what we needed to make
it work. I remember asking for a looser template, more time for
both of us to show our personalities and work on developing some
on-air rapport. Westin's dressing-down had forced us together,
but expecting two green hosts to rescue a failing show and vindi-
cate his first major decisions as news president was naive. The
problems with the show went much deeper than us.

And, as I admitted in this meeting, work wasn't the only place
I was facing a huge challenge. I came clean with the team about
what was going on at home.

After suffering from fatigue and a tingling sensation in her head
for many months, Cathy had seen several neurologists and had
had a number of MRIs. All showed the same thing: six small,
white patches in her brain. The doctors didn't agree on what
these abnormalities meant. Some said they were consistent with
multiple sclerosis, but others were less convinced that an MRI
could provide a definitive diagnosis of the disease. Finally, a few
months after I took over as host, Cathy got an appointment with
a New York neurologist who was touted as the top guy in the
field. He reviewed the MRIs and snapped, "You have MS. No
question." He had the bedside manner of an ill-tempered robot.
When Cathy began to cry, he asked, with something close to a

sneer in his voice, "Why are you crying? At least you know now." It was the closest I've ever come to throttling someone in my life. I said, "You've just told her something devastating. Of course she's upset!" He shrugged. "She might need a cane soon, and maybe a wheelchair in ten years. That's not so bad." Then he sprinted off to do something else, leaving us alone in his office, in shock.

My protective instincts were surging, but I had no idea what to say. How could I ease the news that her life, and our family's life, was about to change, and not for the better? I couldn't. Platitudes would only minimize what Cathy was feeling—and what I was feeling, too, which was very scared and very sad. I could hold her, try to comfort her, grieve with her, let her know I'd walk this difficult path with her and love her, always. But I couldn't give her hope. I didn't know enough about the disease yet to know that there was even any hope to give.

Somehow, we pulled ourselves together and left the hospital. I had a photo shoot for a *TV Guide* profile, which was the last thing I wanted to do at that moment. Cathy headed back to Summit on her own (it must have been an awful and lonely trip) and I got a cab to the photo studio in Chelsea Piers in Lower Manhattan. People fussed over my clothes, my hair, the lighting—all that fluffing and good cheer seemed almost obscene, given what had just happened. I was there but not there, detached and unable to fake the hearty buoyancy the photographer required. I couldn't stop thinking about Cathy, how frightened and anxious she felt. And how anxious I felt for her—and for myself and our kids. Cathy was the linchpin of our family. She took care of all of us, made us feel good about ourselves, and deeply loved and appreciated. She knew me better than anyone in the world, and loved me anyway. The idea of this beautiful, energetic, loving woman confined to a wheelchair was unbearable. But we'd have to bear it. Cathy and I both figured that her experience would mirror that of her close childhood friend, who'd been immobilized by a severe attack of MS shortly after our wedding. We didn't know yet that the progression and severity of the disease is different for each individual.

The photo that was taken that day for *TV Guide* shows me leaning against a wall looking diffident and sad. The photographer probably thought the problem was my less than brilliant career, but the crestfallen expression on my face was that of a man who's just been told that the love of his life is about to be ravaged by a cruel degenerative disease.

It takes time for the pace of MS to reveal itself, so neither of us knew how quickly it would disrupt her daily life. But already, her life had been disrupted by anxiety. If Cathy's fingers tingled, she didn't know if she'd just worn them out on the computer, or if this was the announcement of an MS attack. She became hyper-aware, trying to figure out which physical sensations were benign and which might be symptomatic of the disease. Only one thing was certain: she felt awful. Every day she had to inject herself with a medication that made her nauseous, and she was tired all the time.

Worrying about Cathy's health and the impact it would have on our family added an undercurrent of despair to my life. The only positive thing I can say about this terrible time is that her illness helped me keep my troubles at work in perspective, and also kept me thinking about the present and the future rather than dwelling on the past. I researched the disease, finding out everything I could, and was heartened to learn that Cathy's case was apparently quite mild, and she might not develop severe, life-altering symptoms for many years. Nevertheless, looking around our small home, I realized it wasn't wheelchair friendly, so I got in the habit of looking out for bungalows that would be more suitable.

We told the kids about the diagnosis but we sugar-coated any discussion of the long-term toll the disease might take. I wanted to take care of Cathy but it was hard to do that effectively when I was getting up at two a.m. every day. In the afternoons, though, we switched places in one small way: I became her sleep guardian, looking after the kids whenever I could so that she could nap and build her strength. We hoped that might slow the progression of the disease. We didn't tell many people what was going on because she didn't want to be pitied, so I often had to come up with excuses for friends and people at the kids' schools as to why she was suddenly unavailable. I also turned down some last-minute assignments for *GMA*, declining to chase big stars to try to land the kind of interviews that might have helped the show gain traction. Initially I didn't explain why I was saying no, and producers may have had the impression that I wasn't willing to work hard enough. After all, people like Diane Sawyer and Barbara Walters would do anything, at any time, to beat the competition and land an interview. Before Cathy got sick, I was the same way. But now my instinct was to try to do my job to the best of my ability, then head home to care for my family.

Our private struggle didn't stay that way for long. Shortly after I told *GMA* senior staff about Cathy's diagnosis, there was a story about it in the television gossip section of *USA Today*, which was picked up across North America. Suddenly everyone in two countries knew. I can only assume that someone in that brainstorming session leaked the information. Who knows what the motive was, but it was a cruel violation of Cathy's privacy. Thereafter, wherever she went, people were polite but pitying, as though she had just months to live; at school, our children faced questions and suddenly they had new worries and concerns about their mother. Their private lives were now public, too.

And I needed an even better game face. I was now "the *GMA* host with a sick wife," yukking it up on the set while my family suffered. The predicament I was in felt both bizarre and very wrong: I was embattled at work and going through something terrible at home, but still merrily chirping "Good morning, America!" when the cameras rolled. Very few people could understand just how difficult this was, but Connie Chung did, and she reached out to me, sending a lovely note letting me know that a good friend of hers had MS and was doing really well. She went on to write, "You know, Kevin, doing that kind of program (two hours live) works best when you have close to an 'I don't care' state of mind. You are very good. Go out there with a confident state of mind." I didn't really believe that I had much reason to be confident, but her note meant the world to me. It showed me that other people in my profession could empathize with what I was going through, and at least one of them was rooting for me.

In every man's life there are times that test and define your toughness. This was mine. I had to hold my family, my career and myself together, and not let anyone who didn't know me well even sense my vulnerability. It took me awhile, but I found that place, that toughness, and have called on it many times since.

Cathy and I found a way forward, too. The routine of daily life is good in that way—pick up the kids, pitch ideas at the story meeting—and the rhythms are so well-known that you can maintain them even when you feel numb. But the worry was insidious, weaving its way into our daily lives. How much longer would she be whole?

When I'd agreed to host *GMA*, I'd known I'd be working around the clock for at least the first couple of years. But I'd underestimated, hugely, the distance the job would put between me and my family. We still lived modestly, in the same house, and the neighbours didn't treat me any differently. But the gulf between how I actually felt, and the strength and confidence I was trying to project, was getting wider every day. My career was exploding in a uniquely public fashion; the hurt and embarrassment were so deep, and the effort I needed to make in order to deny my own emotional reality was so strenuous, that I had very little left for my family. Even when I was present, part of me wasn't really there.

I saw an opportunity to make it up to Alex, at least, when the first American to orbit Earth, John Glenn, was given the chance to do so again on the space shuttle *Discovery*. Alex and I shared a passion for space and science fiction, and *GMA* had plans to broadcast Glenn's October 1998 launch live from Cape Canaveral. I asked for a pass so Alex could join me in Florida, and the producers readily agreed. We shared a flight down, and on arrival the lead producer had arranged a surprise: we stopped en route to the Cape at the studios of Nickelodeon TV—Alex's favourite station—for a VIP tour. He got to watch shows being filmed and dip his hand in the famous green slime before climbing into a limousine and heading for the tiny spit of land where rocket ships have been launched since the dawn of the space age. We were both kids that day, climbing into simulators, gasping in awe at the size of the Saturn rockets lining the road.

The next day, with a Shuttle simulator right behind us, I was joined by two of the original Mercury Seven astronauts, the guys with the "right stuff," Scott Carpenter and Wally Schirra, for *GMA*'s coverage. I was able to call on a depth of knowledge I'd been accumulating since I was Alex's age, but something even more important happened that day. Those guys I shared the stage with had been my boyhood heroes, and Alex was there to be introduced to them. How many men get to introduce their son to their own heroes? Especially astronauts?

That bright moment couldn't last, though. On my return to New York I reached out to Charlie Gibson, the only other person I knew who might understand the price *GMA* extracted from a father and husband. He had raised a marvellous family not far from where we lived in New Jersey, and had had his own rough start at *Good Morning America*. The senior producer of the broadcast at that time had confided in me that Charlie had been a regular visitor in his office, uncertain about whether he was really a good fit for the format. The producer had advised him to give it time and try to relax, act more like himself—wonderfully supportive advice that was exactly the opposite of what I was hearing from my own managers.

Charlie is a good listener, and over lunch he offered a few

suggestions about how I might improve my on-air performance. When we got to the family pressures that come along with a big job where you clock in in the middle of the night, he admitted his wife had shouldered most of the burden of raising their children, as Cathy was doing with ours. I hadn't talked to many people about her diagnosis, which had been splashed across the papers the previous week, but I did tell Charlie I was ready to give up on *GMA*, since every part of me just wanted to be home to take care of my wife and children. I left the lunch feeling better that I'd been able to be completely honest with someone who truly understood the show's problems. But my burdens were still with me.

As the ratings slide continued, the attempts to make me over became more desperate. My personality, my hair, my glasses, my clothes, the way I spoke—everything about my appearance needed to be changed, apparently.

It got to the point of absurdity. One of the senior producers decided my eyes needed to "pop" behind my glasses, and suggested I get my eyelashes dyed. I did, stupidly, at one of those cheap estheticians you find on every block in Manhattan. They used jet-black dye, so I came out looking like a boyish hooker. Cathy and I had to go out for a business dinner that evening and at one point I noticed she was staring at me with a look of horror on her face. "The dye started to bleed partway through dinner, and you looked like Iggy Pop," she told me on the way home. I walked into work the next morning, self-conscious as hell, marched up to the producer and asked her how my eyes looked. She thought it was a huge improvement.

The most senior executive in charge of *GMA* at the time invested a little more generously in my physical transformation.

A company was commissioned to adjust my look in dozens of ways on paper, as though I were a paper doll: different hairstyles, different glasses, no glasses, all different colours of suits and ties. About thirty "Kevins" were then trotted out for a focus group, which critiqued them all before settling on "Optimal Kevin," who had longer hair with a well-defined part, no glasses or less obtrusive ones, and a penchant for blue suits and green ties.

I was also being told that my accent and word choices were suboptimal. Early in my tenure at ABC News I had had elocution lessons with a speech coach on Manhattan's East Side, the go-to linguist for Canadians at the network who needed to learn how to say "White House" without the telltale northern inflection. I'd sit on the couch in the speech coach's well-appointed apartment, and we'd practise saying "ahww" together for minutes at a time. I had to hold my index finger and thumb at opposite corners of my mouth to experience the feel and look of an American "ou," not just its sound. Americans opened their mouths wider than Canadians, and the sound that came out was a little more nasal. I'd learned how to say "out" and "about" instead of "oot" and "aboot." And I'd learned that whereas a Canadian emphasizes the first syllable of the word "adult," an American puts the stress on the second syllable.

Still, I made some blunders that only a Canadian would make. Some everyday Canadian words—"eavestrough," "toboggan"—aren't common in the US, a fact I learned the hard way when I unwittingly used them, instead of "gutters" and "sled," on *GMA*. And I had trouble getting worked up about baseball, a game that arouses less interest in Canada than, say, hockey. My lack of baseball knowledge was considered a deep and troubling flaw during the World Series. A male co-host's lack of passion about sports verges on unforgivable. Unmasculine.

My low point in terms of cross-cultural blunders came during an interview with Arnold Palmer, who asked what kind of golfer I was. I replied, "You wouldn't even want me to carry your clubs—I'm a putz." The New York–born executive producer's voice coldly informed me, via my earpiece, that "putz" is the Yiddish word for penis, and ordered me to apologize to the audience immediately. I decided to handle it a little differently. Issuing a lengthy, serious apology would derail the whole interview and possibly make my gaffe seem even more offensive. So I waited until the end of the segment to apologize, and said, "I'm a putz for saying 'putz.'"

A dry sense of humour had worked well on other shows, particularly the overnight broadcast *World News Now*, so I asked the executive producer, Shelley Lewis, if I could borrow a producer and a friend from that show to help me enhance my performance. She agreed, and Victor Dorff joined me at five in the morning in my dressing room to look over the day's content with an eye toward creating the "moments" that might help lift the show. After a month of that, Shelley pulled me aside one day and told me Victor wasn't helping me. I wasn't sure what she meant by that, but let's just say it didn't bolster my self-esteem. I had to tell Victor myself that his services were no longer required, and I added, "You should get as far away from me as you can. I'm going down and don't want to take you with me."

I never knew if Lisa was being picked apart in the same way; I assumed that Shelley was shielding her somewhat. Whatever the case, it was clear to me that ABC News executives were running for cover and I was being set up to take the fall. When the *TV Guide* article finally ran, months after the photo session on the day of Cathy's diagnosis and at the height of the press pile-on about the show's troubles, it was headlined "The Toughest Year of His Life." The article correctly noted that ratings were in free-fall, the show lacked focus and the hosts lacked chemistry, and mentioned that Aaron Brown was the latest name being floated as my replacement. There was no mention of a replacement for Lisa, though she didn't escape criticism altogether. According to unnamed sources, the writer reported, "McRee is freezing Newman out, on- and off-camera." For the record, she denied it, calling me "a wonderful journalist," while Westin praised my "superb reporting skills" and Shelley vouched for me as "smart and charming and quick on his feet." However, as the article also reported, Westin would not confirm that I would remain anchor of *GMA*.

"I just want the uncertainty to end. It's not healthy for anyone on the program," I'd told the journalist, sounding very much like a host who's already got one foot out the door. And I did. I wanted to stop pretending to be a QB, or Matt Lauer, or Optimal Kevin. I wanted a job where I could be myself and people would value what I had to offer. It's one thing to feel desperately unhappy when you're searching for the cure for cancer or fighting for freedom. It's quite another when you're hosting cooking segments. As I told *TV Guide*, "I don't mean to belittle what I do, but it's just TV. It's not my real life. What matters to me are the people I love."

Forrest Sawyer, Connie Chung and several other high-profile anchors had already pulled me aside, saying, "What you need to focus on now is trying to control your landing." All of them had experienced public failure to some degree, and their advice was to accept the inevitability of it rather than trying to fight it, and to focus on what would come next. Barbara Walters urged me to do the best work of my career and make sure it was the most serious work so far. She said it was how she'd bounced back from career disappointments and resurrected herself as a journalist. Ted Koppel, the host of *Nightline*, kindly walked across the room at an event and threw me a lifeline, saying, "You can work for me when the time comes." Peter Jennings was also supportive, and told me he'd make a place for me. I felt lucky that some key people still had faith in me.

I had been requesting a meeting with David Westin for several weeks, with no response. Then, one December morning in the car on the way to work, I read a column in the *New York Post* suggesting I was a lightweight as a journalist. To me, the story read like a plant, something that had been handed to the paper by the network, and I was alarmed. There had been no shortage of speculation and bad reviews, but until that point no one had ever challenged my intellect or journalistic credentials. If those were trashed, I'd never work again. So after the show wrapped for the day, I marched up to Westin's office and asked to see him immediately. When I was told he was unavailable, I announced that I would sit outside his door, for the rest of the day if necessary, until he was free. And I did. By the time he agreed to see me I was pretty worked up. I don't remember exactly what either of us said, but at the end of the meeting we were both very clear that there was no future for me at *GMA* and I didn't want there to be one, either. Right afterwards, I had a previously scheduled meeting with the network president, Bob Iger, who's now CEO of Disney. Bob was gracious and understanding, and I asked him for one thing that would allow me to bow out gracefully: passage to a job at *Nightline*, which Ted had already told me was mine for the asking. Bob thanked me for my work and said he would discuss it with Westin.

The end came exactly the way it had all began, with a phone call at home one night. I could tell David Westin was tense on the other end of the line, and mercifully, he got right to the point. Shelley, Lisa and I were all being dropped from the show. Lisa was already on her way home to L.A., but I was expected to host with Elizabeth Vargas the next morning and for a few weeks thereafter, until the new team was in place. He told me he'd introduce me to them the next day. I was frankly surprised he was still willing to trust me with hosting, knowing I'd been toasted. I decided to take it as a compliment: he knew I was too professional to have a meltdown on air.

I saw this as an opportunity to shape my departure, save my career and show what I was really made of. The next morning I asked for five minutes before air to address the studio and control-room staff. By then anyone who'd read a newspaper already knew Lisa and I had been fired. I thanked everyone for their support over the past eight months, and told them that I didn't want a single viewer sensing anything was amiss at *GMA*. We needed to provide stability during this transitional period, and I intended to provide it.

After that first post-Lisa show I was summoned to Westin's office and there sat Charlie Gibson and Diane Sawyer. It was the first time I had any idea who'd be taking over, and I was relieved:

the network was throwing its biggest stars at the problem, so they obviously knew it was the biggest kind of problem, one that went far beyond having a Canadian host with pale eyelashes. Charlie looked a little sheepish but was gracious as always, and Diane was very comforting and warm. I expressed concern about how traumatized the staff was after all the upheaval, and ABC vice-president Phyllis McGrady, who had helped engineer the change, kindly said that the sign of a great host is caring about your crew. They were trying to take some of the sting out of what had happened, and I was grateful they cared enough to try. When I was told that I would be joining *Nightline* for a short while, I felt tremendous relief.

Shortly after that meeting, Charlie and Diane walked into the offices of *GMA*, to surprised gasps and delighted applause. ABC issued a press release minutes later announcing their appointment, which became front-page news. Just as had happened in Canada with *Midday* at the CBC, I had to keep the seat warm until my replacement was ready to take over, but this time I was thankful. Those three weeks convinced me that I wasn't solely responsible for the show's crash and burn. The shows I did with Elizabeth were some of the best of my tenure. We trusted one another and quickly developed good chemistry; I was more relaxed and in charge, feeling part of a supportive team and knowing the end was near. It took being fired for me to grow into the job.

On my final Friday, I talked about the highlights coming up on Monday, when I'd be long gone. The producers had booked Joan Lunden, Charlie's former co-host, who was going to talk about "life after *GMA*." I saw the opportunity. I paused after reading the teaser, and added, "Maybe I'll stick around to ask some questions, too." The crew laughed out loud, and I signed off with a quick thank-you to viewers. Despite everything, there were still millions of them.

CHAPTER EIGHT

BEING A NOBODY
ALEX

THE SUMMER BEFORE GRADE SEVEN, I knew something was wrong in my family. One day my mother's joy and spirit seemed to vanish. I remember asking her if she was okay, and she told me she was fine, though her smile seemed forced. A couple of days later my parents called a family meeting, and as we trooped into their bedroom, Erica and I found my mother with her head down, staring at the bedspread as though it was suddenly very interesting. It was clear we weren't about to hear good news.

A lot of kids at school were dealing with divorced or divorcing parents, but I knew my parents would never do that. Fighting, drinking, affairs—none of that was ever a part of my childhood. I grew up with absolute certainty that my mom and dad would be together for the rest of their lives. They were clearly in love but also just obviously really liked and respected one another. They'd both suffered when their own parents had split up; I'd seen how tense and unpleasant it still was for everyone else when either set of grandparents had to be in the same room. I knew they'd never put me and Erica through that. But I knew what we were about to hear was serious. The mood in the room was grave.

The moment my mother said the words "multiple sclerosis" I knew exactly what she was talking about. One of her friends from Montreal had the disease. She was partially paralyzed, and when we visited her and her family, she'd roll out in a wheelchair; her children had to help her do basic things. My mother was always a little sombre leaving their house, and she'd explained to me and Erica how difficult things were for her friend, who'd once been so athletic and active, and how brave she was.

The idea that my mom had the same disease terrified me. My mind immediately raced to catastrophic scenarios: my mom in a wheelchair, no longer able to draw. Or drive. Or hug me back. I could tell by the look on Erica's face that she was thinking along the same lines. MS wouldn't just change our mother's life. It would change ours, too.

Our parents quickly countered our worst fears and did their best to reassure us. They were getting a second opinion. There was medication that would help. Scientists were working to find more treatments, even a cure. My mom's case was mild.

But the changes in her were not mild. She was weaker, more fragile, taking naps during the day and avoiding the sun because people with MS tend to overheat more easily. A matter-of-fact greyness replaced her customary joie de vivre. She'd been the steady centre point of our family, but after her diagnosis she turned inward. Sometimes I'd come into the kitchen and she'd be injecting herself with the medication that was supposed to help but seemed to make her feel even worse. Maybe she wanted to normalize this new part of her daily routine, and maybe she also wanted us to see that she had some control over the disease and was fighting back. But watching her stab herself with a needle made me squeamish and I usually left the room. I wanted my mom back.

One day that fall we took a family trip to Camelbeach Mountain Waterpark in Pennsylvania, and for the first time in a long time, my mother laughed, I mean *really* laughed, so hard she had to wipe tears from her eyes. Floating down the lazy river in inner tubes, we'd spotted a kid stuck under a man-made waterfall, flailing and sputtering as the force of the water spun his tube around and around. It looked like something you'd see in a cartoon, and my mom and I just lost it, too helpless with laughter to help the kid escape the current. I felt a surge of hope that this was the turning point, and now my mom would be her old self again. But once we'd hopped out of our inner tubes, she'd scurried to an umbrella to get out of the sun, spent.

Grade seven was the first year I didn't hate school. I didn't love it, either, but I was getting better grades and had a sense of purpose: I was going to be a scientist. My dad knew he wanted to be a journalist from the time he was twelve years old; now that I was the same age, I thought I should have a dream, too, one that would motivate and shape me the way my father's had motivated and shaped him. Nothing intimidated the guy or threw him off track. When he encountered an obstacle, he just focused harder, worked longer and kept tackling it until he won. He'd sleep in the day and work all night, go to a war zone or cover a tragedy, whatever it took—and he never crumbled or showed weakness. He wasn't a quitter, and one of the things he told me and Erica all the time was never to run away from something. "If you're going to leave, just make sure you're not running," he'd say.

So I didn't run after I took a career aptitude test at school and "scientist" came back close to the bottom of the list of professions to which I'd be well suited. I'd scored high on mechanical ability and three-dimensional problem solving, but had bombed the math portion. Apparently, I'd make a wonderful dental hygienist, electrician or animator. After a brief period of despair, I picked myself up and decided that I wasn't going to change my life plan because of some stupid test. I didn't like math or particularly care about English—my view was that I shouldn't have to work at it, since I already spoke the language—or history or social studies, but I loved the beauty and certainty and precision of science. In my other classes I tended to sit mutely, praying the teacher wouldn't call on me. In science, there was no shutting me up. Clearly, it was my calling. Once I'd settled the question in my own mind, it was easier to overlook the indignities of school and see it as a stepping stone to a brilliant career.

The main reason I was happier at school, though, was that finally, I had a group of friends. All underdogs, we'd found each other on the sidelines at gym or eating alone in the cafeteria. The composition of the core group was something a politically correct casting agent might cook up: there was the fat kid, the one Asian kid in the grade, the un-girlie girl, the boy who liked *The Princess Bride*, the obsessive kid with thick glasses, and Frank and me, who lived for computers and Pokémon. Occasionally other kids, refugees from some kind of social disgrace, would drift down to our clique for awhile then fight their way back to the mainstream or at least closer to it, and pretend they didn't know us anymore. There were also a few floaters, kids with a near-miraculous ability to migrate from one social group to the next and be accepted by all, who occasionally sat with us at the far end of the cafeteria or joined us under the big tree where we gathered before the first bell. For the first time in my life, I wanted to get to school early every morning.

We were at the very bottom of the social ladder, but that was fine with me. I was happy simply to feel I belonged somewhere, anywhere. I was interested in the cool kids in the same way I was interested in exotic reptiles: they were colourful and entertaining, but it was best to observe them from a safe distance. Even from afar, it was evident that the income split in Summit created much clearer social divides in middle school than it had in elementary school. The popular kids from the wrong side of the tracks were now the daring ones who openly flouted authority. They were responsible for the bomb threat that put the school in lockdown until police uncovered the prank. The popular kids from the rich part of town were enthralled with designer clothes and wanted to run the school, not destroy it.

Both groups obsessed over who was going out with whom, and who might or might not have had sex. Apparently one trend-setting boy in our grade had actually done so—on school property, no less. Rumour had it that a girl had given him a blow job in the auditorium, and the scandal was big enough that even we caught wind of it. Maybe because our clique was co-ed, we never talked about sex or objectified girls. Even if everyone else had, though, I wouldn't have joined in. My dad had taught me to hold the door, show respect, be a gentleman. My mom had taught me girls aren't pieces of meat. Frankly, the auditorium scene struck me as gross. The guy in question wasn't exactly a paragon of hygiene. I felt sorry for the girl.

I had a crush on a girl myself, Rhiannon, but my imagination didn't stray beyond being liked back and maybe kissing her. The chances of this happening were non-existent, of course, because every guy in our grade had a crush on Rhiannon. She seemed older, wiser and distinctly unimpressed by the posturing of twelve- and thirteen-year-old boys. The year before she'd been in the choir with me and Frank—the main redeeming feature of that particular organization as far as we were concerned—and she was the kind of girl who'd acknowledge us in the hallway. She seemed not to care what anyone thought of her, and I liked the way she brushed off the cool kids as though they were dirt.

It didn't occur to me to try to get closer to her. I was quite happy to like her from afar, and I would have been mortified if she'd figured out that I liked her. For years, most of my friends had been girls, but I had no clue how to interact with a girl on a romantic level.

The closest I'd come had been in gym class, when, for a hormonally chaotic week or so, we square danced. I'm not sure why this was still part of the curriculum a hundred years after the last un-ironic hoedown, but it was. The teacher would be calling out "do-si-do" and we'd all be rolling our eyes, but there was an undeniable charge in the air because you were holding hands with a member of the opposite sex. During one dance—I think it was the Virginia reel—each couple had to link arms and, one

by one, promenade past a gauntlet of other clapping couples. I
wanted to be in the spotlight, yet felt horribly self-conscious on
the few occasions I found myself there. Waiting for my turn, my
heart hammered with dread and my palms became slick with
sweat. I didn't want everyone looking at me. But when I was
awkwardly dancing past my classmates, cheeks flushed with
embarrassment, I felt a small blaze of pride. I was thinking,
"Remember me? You haven't crushed me yet. I'm still here!"

Maybe because I'd been the target of so many jokes, I didn't
have much of a sense of humour about myself. I was overly sensitive and quick to take offence—problematic traits now that I
actually had friends. If kids in my group started snatching spicy
fries off my tray in the cafeteria, for instance, I didn't react well.
Spicy fries were the rage that year, almost a status symbol
because demand always outstripped supply, and I had to budget
carefully to afford them. When a friend grabbed a few, I felt
attacked, not teased. Instead of laughing it off or telling him to
get his hands off my fries, I felt I'd been grievously wronged and
then nursed a grudge.

I knew that my defensiveness made me ridiculous, but I didn't
know how to let things roll off my back. The previous year my
parents had sent me to a therapist to help me deal with the
emotional fallout of being bullied, but it hadn't helped. I was
reluctant to go, partly because I didn't want to admit to my
father that I could use some help, and partly because I thought
it was a waste of time. Why not just send me to a new school,
instead? My parents didn't think that was a good idea, though,
so each week I'd gone to see a therapist I'll call Aaron. A genial,

soft-spoken guy with jet-black hair and an office full of toys, Aaron was more about listening than offering advice. Because he knew I liked building with Lego, he asked me to bring a new creation to each appointment, which I did, though some of the things I built were so absurdly complex and flimsy that transporting them became a major ordeal. After I'd shown him my latest invention, he'd ask how being bullied was making me feel, why I thought it was happening, and so forth.

It was pleasant to be the focus of someone's attention but he didn't give me any insight into my problems. I felt I was talking to him more for my parents' benefit than my own, so that he could explain to them what was wrong with me. At the end of every session I'd go sit in the waiting room and he'd talk to my mother behind closed doors; knowing that whatever I said would go right back to her wasn't conducive to soul-baring. After four or five months I stopped going.

My second experience of a therapeutic nature came in grade seven when, in the middle of a class, I was summoned by the school counsellor. As I walked down the hall to her office I was freaking out, trying to figure out what I'd done wrong, but couldn't think of anything. She sat me down in this weird little windowless room and got right to the point. "I want to talk about your mother," she said, oozing sympathy. Everyone knew about my mom's MS diagnosis, since it had been in all the papers. I hated the fact that private family matters were public, and had no intention of talking about them with this counsellor.

The truth was, my parents were getting third, fourth and fifth opinions, and even the doctors who thought my mother had

MS said she might not manifest symptoms for years; one said that maybe she didn't have the disease at all, and the lesions in her brain could just be scars from a very high fever when she was a child. I'd seized on that, and allowed myself to hope. After all, my mother was still mobile and she didn't seem to be getting worse, though she was on red alert for symptoms of the disease. Whatever she had, it didn't seem the same as what her friend had. I'm sure every kid whose parent is seriously ill is in denial, but this was a little different: I started to believe that my mother had wilted not because she was sick, but because a doctor had told her she was.

A similar thing had happened to me when I found out I had mono, right around the time she found out she had MS. Before I had the blood tests, I felt tired but also felt that maybe the real problem was that I hated school. As soon as the blood tests came back confirming that I'd had mono—my body had fought off the virus by that point—I retroactively embraced illness. I hadn't just been tired; I'd been floored by fatigue, barely able to function. I wondered if this was what was going on with my mom, who was similar to me in many ways.

There was no way I was going to admit any of this to a stranger, though, so I just told the school counsellor, "She's okay and I'm okay. Don't worry about me." She smiled indulgently, and continued to probe. "You're not worried? Is everything okay at home?" I told her everything was fine, but she persisted. "It would be normal to be concerned about having a mother in a wheelchair. Have you thought about what that will be like for you?" The vibe was weirdly confrontational, given that she said she wanted to help me, and finally she scored a direct hit: "You're scared she's going to die, aren't you?" On cue I started crying, but they were tears of rage. I saw the look of quiet triumph on her face as she pushed a box of tissues toward me, and wondered what she was getting out of the encounter. Was she looking for a juicy anecdote about a famous guy's family or was she just the most inept counsellor on the planet?

For the rest of the day, I was distraught. Maybe I should have been upset because there was a possibility my mother was going to die, but I wasn't. I was upset because I felt I'd been mentally assaulted by a faculty member. When I got home I told my parents what had happened and I'm not sure who was more furious, my mom or my dad. Something I love about my father: he doesn't hem and haw when there's a problem. He takes action. He called the school immediately. I didn't hear what he said but I didn't need to—I knew he'd be polite but also cold and cutting, the way he always was when he was really angry and expected someone to do something about it.

I braced for a similar reaction, this time directed at me, when I was suspended a few months later. The day began with a group of guys harassing me for wearing "the wrong brand of jeans." Apparently my fashion crime had racial overtones—they insisted only black kids were allowed to wear these particular jeans, a fact my mother was likely unaware of when she purchased them. For her, I'm sure the main attraction was that they were on sale. These guys didn't intimidate me, though their ringleader towered over some of our teachers, but later that day, they decided to ramp it up.

We were running around the school track, accompanied by the shrieking of our ex-Marine gym teacher, when the ringleader and one of his cronies started jogging right behind me. I picked up the pace. So did they. I ran a little faster, scared now. They matched me, then the sidekick passed me, sticking out his foot to trip me, while the big guy shoved me, hard, from behind. I hit the gravel face-first and they bolted past, laughing. When I limped to the sidelines, picking bits of gravel out of my cheek, the gym teacher went insane. "Get back out there! I'll fail you if you don't start running!" He was practically foaming at the mouth, but I stayed put, watching the other kids huff and puff their way around the track. No way was I going back out there. Walking down the hall afterwards, I spotted the ringleader drinking from a water fountain, not a henchman in sight. I saw my chance: his back was to me, he was vulnerable. I body-checked him, hard. "What the fuck?" he yelled. I laughed and kept walking. There! I'd made him feel the way he'd made me feel on the track. We were even.

Only, we weren't. After the next class he and his posse cornered me at the top of a staircase, pushing and shoving, jeering about my jeans again. I tried to stand my ground, pushing back, and fortunately I had an ally: Frank, who had the "right" skin colour for the jeans, threw a punch, quite possibly the first of his life, and knocked down one of the loudest kids. Next thing I knew, a hand was on my back and I was tumbling down the staircase, completely out of control. As soon as I thwacked my head at the bottom and there was blood, the ringleader hightailed it to the principal's office and said I'd instigated the attack, whereupon I was suspended for fighting. My mother was outraged on my behalf. Her attitude was, "My poor baby, you haven't done anything wrong, how dare they punish you?" When my dad got home, I heard her talking quietly to him, dreading the moment when I'd experience the icy blast of his disapproval head-on.

But instead he bounded into the room all smiles. Elated, actually. It wasn't, "Are you okay?" It was, "Good for you!" He pumped me for details as though I were a prizefighter, and made it clear he thought it was about time that I'd stood up for myself. Others must have thought so, too, because a few days later, I was named the school's student of the week. Some of the teachers knew very well I hadn't started the fight, and decided to make a point to the administration. That show of solidarity was the crowning achievement of my career in middle school.

One day when I walked into the cafeteria, my old nemesis Neil blocked my path. A couple of members of his entourage were lined up behind him, and he had a knowing grin on his round, red face. "So I heard your dad is a failure," he crowed, then waited, expectantly. But I didn't react. I had no idea what he was talking about. "He got *fired*," Neil snarled. "I guess you'll be deported back to Canada now. Good riddance. No one here likes you anyways." The comments stung but I didn't rise to the bait. I knew he was lying. My dad hadn't been fired from *GMA*. He'd decided he'd rather do an evening show, so he left. He was always changing jobs. "Failure"? Please. He was still on TV— the very definition of success, to a kid. I shrugged off Neil's idiocy and got in the food line.

Later, when other kids approached me and said anything about my dad, I ignored them. They were obviously getting their misinformation from Neil, who'd been torturing me for years. If

I'd read one of the newspapers that was tossed at the end of our driveway every morning I would have known the truth, but I didn't figure it out, not for three years. My parents' spin control was so artful that both Erica and I were under the impression that *Nightline* was a step up, a promotion of sorts.

Our dad seemed less tense, happier somehow, so we had no reason to believe otherwise. *Nightline* filmed in Washington, DC, so he worked there during the week and came home on weekends. It was great not to have to tiptoe around during the day or worry about waking him, and he seemed to have a lot more energy. He was always doing something on Saturday and Sunday: sprucing up the yard, buying a new barbecue and, on one memorable occasion, showing us around Washington. We tore around the city to the Lincoln Memorial, the Vietnam Veterans Memorial, the Smithsonian—a history buff, Dad could always explain what we were seeing and why. At the Air and Space Museum, he made sure I saw certain exhibits, like the model of the Russian space station *Mir*, which I'd been reading about and studying in school. A few months earlier he'd taken me to John Glenn's space launch, and we'd got to go behind the scenes at NASA and sit in a real simulator that astronauts use. I'd felt like the luckiest kid alive and I felt that again in the museum, looking at all these rockets and planes dangling from the ceiling, with my dad there to explain it all to me. It was astounding, really, the depth of his knowledge, and I wasn't the only one who thought so. The whole nation listened to him. People admired him.

All of which is to say that both Erica and I were a little shocked when we finally realized that our dad really had lost his job at *GMA*—and a little hurt that we were the last to find out. I'm sure his intention was to protect us, so we wouldn't worry about him or our family's future. But even now, it bothers me to think that Neil, of all people, knew something about my father years before I did.

As I write these words, I'm still not sure what really happened at *GMA*. My father has never discussed it with me. He's a person who looks forward, not back, and both my parents believed in shielding me and Erica from adult worries and cares. They didn't anticipate, I guess, that we'd wind up filling in the blanks with our own theories—or that these theories might create more harm than the truth would have.

In the absence of knowledge, I created a narrative that shaped—and misshaped—how I saw my parents and, ultimately, how I saw myself. Perhaps I'm wrong, but I think it would have helped me to know, when I was in seventh grade, that my dad had failed at something. In my eyes, he was unassailable and invulnerable, good at everything. It's hard to relate to a superhero, and hard, also, to feel like anything other than a disappointment by comparison. It never crossed my mind that my dad had ever felt humiliated, or foolish, or like a loser. That was the kind of stuff someone like me worried about. Silently. I didn't want anyone else to know, least of all my father, who couldn't possibly understand.

CHAPTER NINE

THE SIXTEENTH MINUTE
KEVIN

I'VE LIVED MY ADULT LIFE surrounded by men who run toward trouble when they think they can make a difference. Cameramen, firemen, soldiers, cops—I have a lot of friends who are calm and collected under fire. I'd always looked up to them, not sure how strong I've been in a crisis. That incident at the traffic light in Baghdad made me realize I could be courageous. And I think I have been, later in life: covering the war in Afghanistan, for instance, and taking real risks with my career, including substantial pay cuts, to do the kind of work I really want to do.

But as my career at *GMA* blew up, I did not feel courageous. If hiding out at home for a few weeks had been an option, that's what I would have done. Humiliation felt more dangerous to me than actual danger ever had. I could (and did) rationalize what was happening: the show had been in trouble when I started, it was poorly run, I wasn't being coached or mentored— just made over. At the end of this litany, though, I still felt the same. I hadn't measured up.

My sense of my own masculinity allowed no room for mistakes, failure or emotional vulnerability. It was, in other words, still tenuous, linked so strongly to what other people thought of me that a TV executive could confer it on me by offering me a big job—or take it away by ordering me to act more like a quarterback. In my own mind, manliness boiled down to a mess of clichés about not showing weakness or fear, especially when you felt weak or fearful. Masculinity was all in the eye of the beholder, ratified by other people's perceptions of me rather than how I felt about myself.

Once I learned I was being replaced at *GMA*, I started to realize that the quest for approval was what had got me into trouble in the first place. It was why I'd taken a job I thought I was wrong for: I'd put more stock in other people's opinions than in my own judgement. The money had been attractive (very), but what I'd really been after was the prospect of approval, writ large, in the form of Nielsen ratings and smiles on the faces of network executives. Knowing that they didn't think I was good enough ate away at me in a way that being broke never had. That's why I'd tap danced to please managers I hadn't trusted and, in some cases, hadn't even respected. And because their focus had been my ability to play to type, whether the type was football player or heartthrob, the experience had felt like a referendum on my masculinity.

Ultimately, it was. That experience helped me to recognize that my problem wasn't a lack of testosterone. My problem was that I had let other people define for me what kind of person I was, or should be. I wasn't my own man. And I would not be happy until I was.

Even at the best of times, there's a strange decompression period in those first few silent, empty moments after a TV show goes off air. You've received no audience reaction, good or bad, though you've been performing for two hours, so you feel drained, not pumped. You slump back in your chair, blankly, while the crew quietly moves the cameras back into their storage positions and people in the control room rise from their chairs and stretch, throwing that day's script in the garbage and wandering off to the bathroom, now that they finally can. It's completely anti-climactic.

Before my last broadcast as co-host of *GMA*, I knew those post-wrap moments would be something else, too: strained and tense. There wouldn't be goodbye cakes or speeches. No one would know quite what to do. Many of the crew had been having trouble making eye contact for several weeks, not because they didn't respect me, but because the "dead man walking" factor made the situation exquisitely awkward for all of us.

Having Cathy and the kids join me on the set as soon as the red light went out made the situation easier for everyone, not just me. *See, he's got a loving family, they'll take care of him.* They'd waited in the wings while we were still on air—Cathy knew that if I saw them, it might trigger emotions I was fighting to hide from viewers—then the kids bounded on set, full of smiles and energy, and Cathy (not for the first or last time) whispered in my ear how proud she was of me for getting through it. Erica jumped into my lap, Alex scored Elizabeth Vargas's big cushy chair, and my family just hung out and kept me occupied during those first few emotionally delicate moments.

Both kids knew I'd lost my job. I hadn't told them—didn't even get a chance. The schoolyard grapevine took care of it. They'd been teased because their dad had been fired; it must have been the topic of conversation at multiple dinner tables in Summit after the news was in the papers. Sitting with them on my last day, I felt bathed in love, and I remember telling myself, "This is the best luck, to have these two. I'm going to focus on them now."

But I'm not a Pollyanna. Along with love and gratitude, I also felt anger, the cold, steely kind that has been building for months and can no longer be swallowed. Right on cue, the *GMA* hairstylist appeared. I was still sitting in the same chair where, just minutes before, I'd broadcast my goodbyes. Erica slipped off my lap, and the hairdresser put a smock on me and proceeded to cut my hair. Short. Then shorter. Cathy looked a little puzzled by this public shearing—why the sudden, urgent need for a haircut?—and so did the crew. Someone turned a camera on me so people in the control room, a fair distance away, could see what was happening on the studio floor. I don't know if anyone up there was watching, but I like to think they were—even now, years later, when I recognize that what I did was probably a little childish. But at that moment, chopping off my focus-grouped, side-parted hair seemed necessary and urgent. The fact that I viewed a haircut as a brave move tells you everything you need to know about my experience in morning television.

I didn't want to be Optimal Kevin, didn't want to be told to impersonate someone else. I was no longer going to ignore my own instincts. I wasn't sure exactly what I should do next, but I knew that the only person I could count on, professionally, was me. I had to take control of my career or it wouldn't be rescued.

Freshly shorn, I asked ABC for three weeks' vacation. I still had more than two years left on my contract, but there were emotions I had been holding at bay for a very long time, and I needed space and time to let them bubble up and reveal themselves. I was a little afraid of how powerful they might be. I wasn't sure if I was going to have a breakdown or what. I just knew that I needed to let whatever was going to happen, happen.

So, despite having just vowed to myself that my family was now going to be my number one priority, I asked Cathy if it would be all right with her if I took a road trip by myself. Did I feel guilty? Self-indulgent? Like a deserter? All of the above. However, Cathy's MS was not progressing. She was fatigued, but holding steady in terms of her overall health. I'd become an honourary ambassador for the National Multiple Sclerosis Society, helping to raise awareness and money, but I was beginning to doubt that Cathy actually had the disease. She seemed to need the certainty of the diagnosis, but I'd started to focus on the neurologists' uncertainty and disagreement about the results of her MRIs. The only thing that would prove she had full-blown MS would be an actual attack. We were in limbo, waiting for something awful to happen, but I was starting to hope that maybe nothing ever would. At any rate, I was pretty certain that I could safely vanish for a few days.

Cathy understood, as she always has. She'd likely been worried about my mental health for some time, the same way I'd been worried about her physical health. "Where will you go?"

she asked. I explained that I only knew where I needed to start from: home.

So, with her blessing, I loaded up my BMW Z3 (my one extravagant gift to myself during those high-flying years) and headed toward the Delaware Water Gap, then up the New York Thruway to Buffalo, where the familiar highways of my youth led to Toronto. It was about a ten-hour drive in all, enough time to play music, loud, and let my mind wander. I knew my first stop had to be to see my mother, Sheila, who'd be worried about me. But I also stopped on the road to call my dad, George, to ask if he would meet me for lunch the next day. In the twenty-five years since his marriage to my mother had broken up, I'd never asked to see him one-on-one. As a teenager, I'd seen him with my sisters every other week for the visits outlined in the divorce settlement, and also at Christmas and for a week or two during the summer, at his cottage.

Our relationship was cordial but distant. He didn't really know me and seemed to have little curiosity about my life and how I viewed the world. It was his approval, I finally saw, that I'd always been after. I had questions I'd wanted to ask for years, and the emotional numbness I felt post-*GMA* made me brave enough to ask them. I didn't fear his answers anymore. The worst had already happened, both in terms of my career and the uncertainty over Cathy's health.

That it took me until I was almost forty to have a frank conversation with my father probably says more about my reluctance than his willingness. Growing up, I had been too afraid of his judgement. After he left our family and immersed himself in his new relationship with his girlfriend and her family,

our relationship stopped evolving. I was fourteen years old, trying to step up and be the man of the house by protecting my
mother and doing the yard work and not being a source of more
trouble. I blamed my father for the divorce but I grieved the loss
of him—and beat up on myself for being the kind of kid he
could walk away from so easily. Now, as an adult, I needed to
hear what he had to say, even if it confirmed my fear that he'd
never really loved me. Or even cared about me.

We met just west of Toronto, at one of those mid-level chain
restaurants with booths and happy-hour cocktails. After exchang-
ing a few pleasantries and ordering lunch, I quickly broached the
subjects I'd wanted to raise for years. Why had his marriage to
my mother ended? Why had he so enthusiastically embraced his
new wife's family and seemingly left ours behind? What, really,
did he think of me?

He was not at all defensive, just puzzled that any of these
things still bothered a forty-year-old man. Still, he was prepared
to oblige me. He didn't go into a lot of detail about the end of his
marriage, and he was practical and unemotional answering
my other questions, too. He reminded me that he had provided
child support until my sisters and I were eighteen and that money
from his parents' will had funded our university education. From
his perspective, his responsibility to us was pretty much wrapped
up by the time we finished high school.

It hurt to hear him define the obligations of a father in purely
financial terms. But it freed me, too. The issue wasn't me or my
worth as a human being. My dad was a product of his own dis-
ciplined upbringing, and his reticence was likely the result of
his restrained relationship with his own father, which he rarely

spoke about. He did have an emotional side and he'd shown it when my sister died. I remembered how he'd wrapped his arms around Debbie and me as we'd looked at Kelly for the last time, how devastated he was. He did care for us, in his way.

I left the lunch knowing it was time to stop waiting for him to become someone he was incapable of being. Affectionate approval and affirmation weren't his style and never would be. Continuing to carry a chip on my shoulder about that would hold me back from becoming who I needed to be.

Back in the car, driving with no particular destination in mind, I thought about the power I'd given to authority figures at ABC, the lengths I'd gone to try to please them. Had I been seeking paternal approval from them, too? Looking for them to validate me in a way my father hadn't? Maybe. Probably.

One thing I knew for sure: I didn't ever want my own children to be in that situation, looking elsewhere for validation they should have received from me. But I had an uneasy feeling that it could happen. I was more like my father than I wanted to admit. Like him, I saw being a provider as my most important role. Like him, I believed a father should promote his children's independence and encourage them to feel self-sufficient. Yet I also wanted my kids to feel supported, loved and understood—and after that meeting with my father, I pledged to do better on all three fronts. Yes, I had always been affectionate with Erica and Alex, but how well did I really know them?

Alex, in particular, puzzled me. A lone wolf, introverted yet opinionated, he was sometimes tentative, other times steely in his determination to do things his own way. As his parent, this was sometimes maddening. But to a man who now regretted having been a pleaser, Alex's tough, uncompromising streak seemed admirable. He wasn't a badass—I still wished he'd stand up to boys who bullied him—but he didn't crave approval and he didn't seem to care much what other kids thought of him. I just needed to figure out a way to give him the guidance I'd longed for at his age.

Still longed for, to tell the truth. For years, I'd been too busy for self-reflection, but now with nothing else to do except think and allow myself to feel, the patterns were becoming clear. I gravitated towards friendships with men who seemed to have the being-a-man thing figured out, looking to them almost as coaches. Before I started at *GMA*, a senior executive who'd championed me at ABC said, "On most people, the camera adds ten pounds, but on you, it seems to subtract weight. You should bulk up a little." I did, with the help of Mike Bronco, a personal trainer in New Jersey, who became my friend. Bronco, as everyone called him, fascinated me because he was so completely comfortable in his own skin, more so than any man I'd ever met. He was the ultimate guy's guy: he'd built a log cabin with his bare hands and could fashion a fishing kit out of some reeds, a bird-bone hook and some fish-gut glue. But he didn't have the swaggering machismo that belies deep insecurity, nor was he arrogant or overbearing or inauthentic in any way. He didn't need to advertise his self-confidence because it was absolutely unshakeable. I admired that about him, along with his unwavering personal loyalty, Jersey-boy roughness, passion for the military and total devotion to his family. His starting place, the foundation of everything he was, was being a father and husband. His business was personal training, but what he was really teaching was how to be a good man.

I wanted to learn. I think a lot of men learn the way I did, from men who are not our fathers. As a man now approaching sixty, I feel lucky to be surrounded by many Broncos—friends who watch out for each other, invest in each other's success, and are determined to keep trying to do and be better. Very few of the men I'm close to are journalists, but we share the common ground of failures and fuckups, a hunger for physical activity and a taste for brutal text messages that make us laugh out loud.

I wanted Alex to have both: a dad who taught him about being a good man, and friends who kept him true to himself. I didn't want him to wait until he was nearly forty to try to have a real conversation with me, didn't want him to question whether I really cared for him. I knew I had work to do.

But I wasn't ready to return to New Jersey and my family. I still felt too raw. I realized that I'd been driving east, automatically seeking the familiar roads of my childhood, heading up to the lake where I'd spent every summer swimming, canoeing, exploring. My sacred place. The cottages had grown more opulent and the roads were straighter and better paved since I'd last travelled them, but the place remained as I remembered it, peaceful and still. I wanted this for my children: a place they viewed as theirs. I was going to buy a cottage on this same lake. I realized, too, that if I was thinking about the future and about what my family needed, I must be coming out of my funk.

From there I drove to Ottawa, where I'd spent many years as a parliamentary correspondent. It seemed to have grown up in my absence, even developed a nightlife. Continuing eastward I drove through Quebec and on to New Brunswick, and at some point I decided to aim for the tiny island province of Prince

Edward Island, where Cathy and I had vacationed with the kids for several happy summers. In the five years since we'd left the country, PEI had been connected to the mainland of Canada by an eight-mile bridge, an impressive structure I drove across to reach the Island's familiar roads, framed by red-tinged soil. I checked into a motel in Charlottetown and made my way to the nearest pub. It's what I'd done at every stop, not wanting to reach out to old friends, preferring to be the anonymous guy on a barstool, drinking beer. Usually a few too many.

No one recognized me with my nearly shaved head and patchy beard. For the first time in years I was invisible, and that felt like a gift. I listened to the conversations of everyday working men, occasionally joining in and telling them I was a writer named John (my real first name). I hardly knew what was going on in Canada anymore, but over those ten days I noticed something interesting. I was starting to feel more connected, both socially and geographically, than I had in a long time. I'd become used to being the "hidden Canadian" in New York, someone who could pass for American. There was something tremendously reassuring about not feeling like an outsider. I knew these people in a way I'd never fully known Americans or understood what motivated them. I felt I belonged.

Ten days of anonymity stripped me down to someone close to who I'd been before I became a TV host or husband or father. Just me. And it helped me make a big decision, one I hoped Cathy would agree with: I wanted to try to rebuild my career in Canada. I was lucky I had Canada to come back to. Most hosts who've been bounced from American morning television (and there are many more of us than there are of the other breed, the ones who succeed) have never regained their career trajectory. But in Canada, I wasn't viewed as a loser—at least I'd played in the big leagues. No other Canadian had ever hosted an American morning show, and I was one of very few who'd ever substituted for the anchor of a flagship evening newscast. My currency in Canada was higher than it was in the US. I needed to figure out a way to come home.

Heading south past the magnificent coastal scenery of New England, I thought about my family, how much more they mattered to me than any job ever could, and how much I owed them. My career had taken up way too much energy, time and mental real estate.

Back in New Jersey, with a bit of time left before I had to return to work, I tried to help Cathy with the everyday routines her fatigue was making more difficult. I drove the kids to school and picked them up afterwards, helped with food shopping, and tried to have the calm family life I had aspired to on my road trip. I knew I needed to establish a different routine or I'd risk falling back into old habits. Spending a week focused on my family forced me to recognize just how out of touch with my children I'd become. I'd known that Alex was being bullied again, but when I picked him up from school I could see it was worse than I'd imagined. He was always the first kid out of the least-used door in the school, which told me he was on the run from a real threat. When he slipped into the seat beside me for the ride home, there was relief in his eyes, and hurt, too. I spent more time with him at night trying to coax out of him what was going on, just how bad things were. He wouldn't say much. When I pressed, he'd shut down. I wasn't sure if he was protecting me or himself.

When he and another boy were suspended for fighting, I knew that Alex couldn't really have been at fault. The other kid was much larger, a troublemaker. Turned out he had cornered Alex in a stairwell and punched him, and Alex, for the first time, stood up for himself. But the school's policy was to suspend kids who fought, whether they were instigators or just trying to defend themselves. That night I went to Alex's bedroom, feeling crushed by what he'd been enduring, and also feeling horrible that I hadn't been there to help him. Mostly, though, I felt proud of him. I told him that while he might be embarrassed about the suspension, I was not—and it would send a clear message to his tormentors that he was going to fight back, which might deter them. I think it did. Later that week, his teachers sent an equally clear signal that they knew the score: they named Alex "Student of the Week." I e-mailed his homeroom teacher that Friday, thanking her for supporting my son in the best possible way.

Erica was enduring her own humiliation at the time, but it was online and therefore much less obvious to us. Those were the early days of chat rooms, and she was among the first generation to endure the anonymous and vicious bullying teenage girls reserve for each other. Overwhelmed with fear about what others might say about her if she logged off, Erica couldn't pull herself away from her computer. I tried imposing a complete ban, but that left her feeling defenceless and certain she was being attacked. Eventually we negotiated time limits, so Erica could calm down and focus on other things for awhile, knowing that eventually she'd be allowed to jump back into the digital viper pit her so-called friends were creating.

Watching my children going through so much emotional turmoil helped me put my own career humiliation into perspective. Yes, I felt bad. But I'd be all right. I had the strength that comes from experience and self-knowledge, including knowing my own weaknesses. They were being victimized in a much more serious way than I had been at their age, and it was happening before they fully knew who they were and they were therefore less able to combat it. I'd been too preoccupied to notice—and they'd been so worried about Cathy's health that they hadn't wanted to burden her. They'd been protecting us while they felt their own lives were disintegrating. It was a sharp, sobering reminder of my responsibilities and also of my ignorance. I needed to know my children better, to protect them better, to love them better.

And so I returned to work, this time in Washington, DC, with a different perspective. Going forward, I vowed to focus only on the quality of my work, not whether I was rising or falling in the eyes of others. It was important to me to do well, but my job was not the ultimate test of my worth—that would happen at home, with my family.

The environment at *Nightline* was the antithesis of *GMA*. Ted Koppel and his executive producer Tom Bettag had created a small and passionate unit dedicated to providing the context for a deeper understanding of current events. Everyone at *Nightline* was driving toward the same goal: meaningful features that would open viewers' eyes to uncomfortable truths. It was as close to journalistic heaven as I'd ever been. All of us, I soon learned, shared common ground: we'd all been screwed over somehow in our previous jobs, and felt so thankful to have found safe haven in a caring and intellectually serious environment that Ted and Tom didn't have to do much to get the best from us. My first assignment was to create a documentary on the killing of an unarmed black man in New York—a full-hour show, and we had just a few days to turn it around. I borrowed a few techniques that had worked for me at the CBC and threw myself into the story like it was my last chance to save my reputation. After the piece aired, Dan Rather called Ted and told him it was "spectacular." Ted kindly relayed that review from his CBS competitor to me. Hearing that others in my industry still had some respect for my work buoyed and healed me more than I would have believed possible.

My tenure at *Nightline* lasted only six months. Tom was upfront about why: his budget couldn't absorb my outsized anchor salary any longer, and the bean-counters at ABC News couldn't see a way to move the lines on their ledger. But that was the happiest six months I'd had to date in television news. Working on serious issues in a place where journalistic depth was expected as a matter of course had restored my faith in my own profession.

Next, I was assigned to a bigger-budget broadcast, *World News Tonight with Peter Jennings*. It meant a return to the ABC studios near Lincoln Center where, inevitably, I was going to run into people who knew all about my decline and fall at *GMA*. I wasn't looking forward to that.

But it turned out better than I'd feared. I was given one of the most prestigious office spaces, right next to the editorial hub of

World News Tonight, which, in the Kremlinesque pecking order at ABC, meant I still had status. Peter Jennings was warm and welcoming, and apparently the producers on his broadcast had competed to be assigned to me. In spite of my very public defeat, inside the ABC News offices at Columbus and 67th Street, I still had a reputation as a decent person and a good journalist.

No one there ever mentioned the *GMA* experience to me, but I'd also perfected a bluff, hearty manner that discouraged questions. I didn't want to come off as self-pitying or bitter. On several occasions, though, I found myself alone at an Irish bar at lunchtime, drinking. It was pathetic, sure. But also, briefly, anaesthetizing and therefore consoling.

I was paired with Joanne Levine, a very talented producer, and we were assigned to the "Closer Look" feature unit; it was one of Peter's favoured segments, and it tended to keep me out of the daily grind of chasing breaking stories. Peter further helped resuscitate my career by inviting me to fill in for him when he was away—an honour in the network news world and, in this case, an act not just of generosity but courage. Instead of distancing himself from my failure, he invested in my future success. It was what everyone at ABC News hoped for, because if Peter didn't respect you, you wouldn't be there long.

My work at *WNT* was noticed by critics, this time favourably. Ratings didn't drop when I substituted for Peter, the way they usually do with a substitute. I earned two Emmy Awards and shared in the news division's Peabody Award for its Millennium Broadcast, and was given more high-profile opportunities of the sort I could only have dreamed of several years before. Two years after crashing and burning on morning TV, the network wanted to extend my contract, giving me another shot at the brass ring.

My hours were more predictable, and work and life were in better balance than they'd been since *Midday*. I was able to go out to dinner with my wife and I made it to all of Erica's dance recitals; I taught Alex how to make little movies in the backyard (and how to stay calm when actors forget their lines). Life was, in many ways, very good.

But I wanted more. I wanted to be a better man, and that wasn't going to happen if I stayed at ABC. At a relatively young age, I had reached my career peak. What was the point of striving to get back there? Even before my slide, I'd been unhappy. The environment seemed conducive to unhappiness. Even Peter, brilliant as he was, didn't seem particularly happy. He had his game face on every day; after a broadcast, he'd agonize that he hadn't used the right word or asked the best question. Once I'd bumped into him in the lobby and casually asked how everything was going, and he'd unloaded: ABC was asking him to take a pay cut, they didn't respect the contribution he was making to the network, he felt like a pawn in a corporate game. I could hear the hurt in his voice. That was instructive. If things like that happened to a guy like him, my ride was never going to be smooth.

Peter's office was surprisingly modest given his importance to ABC News. The only evidence of his status was the door leading to a small private bathroom. Unlike most of us, he didn't display his many awards in his office, which was in any event too cramped to hold them all. Instead, there were books—his passion for Lebanon was well represented on the bookshelf under his window—and a clutch of substantial Inuit stone carvings, acquired on his regular summer trips back to Canada. There weren't pictures of the luminaries he'd interviewed, just photos of his son and daughter canoeing, travelling, hanging out with their famous father. In those shots, he looked happier, more open and more alive than I'd ever seen him.

The guy I knew was mercurial, unpredictable, and sitting across from him on this particular day in early 2001, I was nervous. I expected him to be disappointed in me. It had happened before on a few occasions: without warning, he'd dismissed my writing or reporting with withering scorn. I'd learned to rehearse my lines before any lengthy encounter so I wouldn't be reduced to spluttering helplessly if the conversation went south. I was afraid this one would, just as soon as I told him I was leaving ABC News.

I wanted to make the most of these years while Cathy was still mobile and our kids were still at home. I also wanted to risk a leadership role again, under conditions where I felt I had a better chance of success. Looking to be a bigger fish in a smaller, more familiar pond, I'd accepted a job in Vancouver; Global Television, my first employer, had finally acquired enough stations to broadcast coast-to-coast in Canada, and wanted to build a national newscast to compete with CBC's and CTV's. Secretly, I had been flying to Toronto to meet with Global's vice-president of news, Ken MacDonald, to discuss how to build an innovative and modern evening news program. I'd be anchor and executive editor, running the show—and, more important, the hours would be family friendly. Global wanted to base it in Vancouver, so, thanks to the Pacific time zone, I'd be home for dinner every evening.

There were drawbacks, of course. The salary was less than half what ABC News would pay me to stay, and moving would be a sacrifice for Cathy, who loved Summit and had many close friends there. Montreal, where her mother lived, was only an hour's flight away from New Jersey, which made visits easy; in Vancouver, we'd both be very far away from our parents. But Cathy was ready to embrace a fresh start, not just for my sake but for the kids', who seemed very ready for a change of scene socially. She also knew the day might come when I'd need to be around more to take care of her. It was hard to imagine how I could do that if I were still at ABC.

I'd decided to start my conversation with Peter with the headline "I want to go home." There was no sense burying the lede with one of the world's top journalists. I also wanted to frame my decision as coming from my heart, not my head—no one who was thinking logically about his journalistic career would turn down the chance to stay at ABC News. "I need predictable hours in order to be the kind of husband and father I want to be, and haven't been," I continued, sticking to my script. Softly, Peter asked whether my decision was driven by Cathy's MS diagnosis. I told him that was a big part of it, but also, I wanted my children to grow up knowing their father. I added that I loved New York, but in my heart, I felt Canadian, and I wanted to live and work where I felt I belonged.

Peter listened, saying nothing, then he did the one thing I was completely unprepared for. He cried. As his eyes filled with tears, he said he fully understood and supported my decision. He'd reached a point in life, he confided, where his family was his passion, in the way his career had once been, so how could he stand in the way of another father who was trying to find the same balance? The pull of Canada, too, he understood well. He'd never given up his citizenship (later, after 9/11, he pledged allegiance to the US as well, but remained a dual citizen). I think this was the Peter Jennings only his family and closest friends ever saw: gentle, sentimental, patient, understanding.

Knowing I had his blessing made it easier to let go of the past and start thinking about the future. Over the next few months, every time I got stuck in Manhattan traffic I let my mind roam ahead. No one had reinvented the format of network news for generations (it's still largely unchanged) and *Global National* was an opportunity to dream up new ways of doing things. They didn't want the same old, same old; success depended on creating something truly new. During those traffic jams I thought about ways to tell stories differently. I wanted to use new digital technology to change how we shot and edited the news, and to capitalize on iTunes as a distribution platform. I was excited by the prospect of hiring a young team and basing them in Vancouver, instead of Toronto, for a fresh perspective on the country and the world. The more I thought about it, the more energized I felt.

There would be obstacles, of course. Global wanted to create an American-style, dinner-hour national newscast, but the tradition in Canada was late-night national news viewing. We'd have to find a way to change long-established viewing habits. More problematic, Global's national infrastructure was nascent and weak, and its local news broadcasts were generally ratings losers.

But there was the promise of more creative freedom than I'd ever dreamed of. Best of all, it was a desk job, meaning little travel and a more typical Monday to Friday routine. All of us went to Vancouver to look for a house, one with hallways large enough for a wheelchair, in case Cathy's disease progressed. We found a beautiful place on the North Shore: wide halls and spacious rooms, tall cedars all around, and a small waterfall in front, so at night, we'd fall asleep to the sound of rushing water. All of us were excited about the house, the city, this new life we'd have.

In April, when I was leaving the *World News Tonight* newsroom for the last time, Peter stopped me, saying he had a going-away gift. A few people gathered to watch, and he carefully laid a perfectly folded American flag, one that had flown on the US Capitol dome, across my arms. It sent a jolt through my body, almost like an electric shock. "Did you know it would do that to me?" I asked. Peter smiled and said, "I wasn't sure, but I thought it might." He knew that after nearly seven years, I might feel Canadian, but I had learned to love America, too. That flag is one of the most meaningful gifts I've ever received.

Another is the long letter Charlie wrote me on *GMA* letterhead when he heard I was leaving. He wished me all the best, he wrote, but felt a "personal sense of loss and regret." He was sorry that he hadn't warned me not to take the *GMA* job "at a time when probably Walter Cronkite in his prime couldn't have saved it." In 1998, he explained, "I was convinced it was time for me to go, and that you were the right person to take over this broadcast. I still think I was right about both things. Would that you had not been saddled with the burdens that existed at the time. You were, I guess, presented with a hill too steep for anyone to climb." As Charlie wrote those words, he and Diane Sawyer were still struggling up that steep hill. It was a hellishly hard climb and while they quickly improved the ratings of *GMA* they never overtook *Today*. (That didn't happen until NBC's own clumsy anchor change, adding then subtracting Ann Curry, gave *Good Morning America* an opening in 2012.)

When reporters asked, my standard line was that I didn't regret hosting *Good Morning America* because it had been a rare opportunity and I'd learned many invaluable lessons from it. Charlie knew this was horseshit. I could have learned those same lessons in much less public and painful ways, and I wish I had. It took me years to get over the scars and writing about them now, I realize they will always be with me. It meant a lot to me that Charlie wished I hadn't gone through that particular trial by fire, and that I still had his support and respect.

There wasn't much time for a going-away party, but my producer Joanne kindly arranged a farewell dinner for me and Cathy, and asked who I'd like to invite. I gave her a list of a dozen names of women and men I'd worked with, all people I felt had been overlooked by management because of their race and/or gender. ABC News executives were enamoured of Ivy League grads and people with good connections, and tended to promote them higher, faster. I was an obvious exception, and so was Peter, but I wanted to celebrate people who hadn't been so lucky. We had a wonderful last evening together at a restaurant on the Upper West Side, and after we said goodnight, Cathy and I walked hand in hand down the leafy streets near Central Park. On my first day in the city I felt I'd arrived on a movie set—the street names and scenes were so familiar. I'd never stopped feeling that way. As our American adventure came to a close, I felt blessed that I'd spent seven years working in New York.

But I was ready to start a completely new chapter, one where I measured success using my own yardstick, not anyone else's. For the first time, I was thinking strategically about my career, trying to tailor a job to fit my strengths rather than trying to tailor my personality to fit a job—or trying to tailor my life to achieve someone else's definition of success. I had my own definition now.

I was forty years old. I wanted to set a different pattern for my next decade. Ambition had returned to me, but it was tempered now by realism as well as a keen appreciation of the cost of success. And failure.

For better or worse, I was now my own man.

CHAPTER TEN

THE SIXTEENTH YEAR
ALEX

IN THE SUMMER OF 2001, my dad had a brainstorm: I needed to listen to music. When he embarks on a project—and he always has a project—his enthusiasm knows no bounds. We weren't just going to start listening to top forty stations on the car radio every once in awhile. We were going to master the whole pop culture thing that very afternoon! He hit on this while we were visiting his mother, and I was all for anything that would get me out of the house. Twenty minutes later we were driving to the mall. This was back when every mall still had a record store, and he marched into one, headed over to the top-ten rack, and started pulling down CDs. My father had never heard of any of this stuff, either. "What are teenagers listening to?" he asked a clerk. This was the heyday of Destiny's Child and Britney Spears, so my dad clarified: we wanted stuff that *guys* were listening to. We left the store with a bulging sack of CDs. Blink 182, Dave Matthews Band, Creed, and Sum 41 had all made the cut.

Back at my grandma's house I popped the Creed CD into my brand new Discman, listened to the first three tracks and knew it wasn't for me. Next up, Blink 182. I picked a random track and suddenly my headphones were filled with punk rock and a male voice singing what sure sounded like "ejaculate into a sock." That got my attention. The track "Happy Holidays, You Bastard" was very short and as soon as it was over, I listened to it again. Yes, I'd heard right, and the second time around I picked up quite a few more words and images, none of them gentlemanly. I realized I was turned on by the lyrics even though I couldn't quite figure out why. I sure wasn't going to ask my dad. Later, when he wanted to know how the music project was going, I just told him that some of the CDs he got me were pretty good.

This was the summer before high school, and he must have been thinking about how to help me get ready for the leap. It was going to be bigger for me than for most kids because we were moving again—clear across the continent this time, to Vancouver. My parents had told me they thought it would be a good idea to enroll in a martial arts class once we got there. Maybe this idea had been floated in the past and I'd rejected it, but after the incident in the stairwell, I was all for it. I wanted to be able to defend myself at my new school. I assumed there would be bullies. There always had been everywhere else.

That prospect didn't dampen my enthusiasm about the move, though. It was another chance to reinvent myself, and after seven years in New Jersey, I was ready. When my parents took us to Vancouver early that summer to introduce us to the city, I got even more excited. It was both more urban and more scenic than Summit, with forests, mountains, ocean and gleaming skyscrapers. There were ski hills. Beaches. A laid-back vibe. We were moving to paradise, apparently.

I thought the rest of my family felt the way I did—that we were on the verge of an especially shiny new adventure—but one afternoon while we were house hunting, my dad had a meltdown in the car. Crying. Actually, crying isn't the right word, because he didn't seem sad. He seemed to be fearful and in pain, sick with worry that we wouldn't find a house. He thought he was failing us in some monumental way that went way beyond real estate. Erica and I had never seen him like that before and we both froze in the back seat, unsure what to do. We'd seen him stressed out and sad and angry but we'd never seen him fearful, weak or at a loss. It was a little scary. He was supposed to be in charge—if he didn't know what to do, we were all screwed.

I had no idea why my father was distressed. It didn't seem like he had anything to be upset about, frankly. He'd jumped from one success to the next, and now he had this amazing opportunity to create and anchor an evening news broadcast in a ridiculously beautiful place. What could possibly be wrong? My mom calmed him down and later in the day he apologized, saying he'd been overwhelmed by needing to find a house quickly. But the incident has stuck in my mind all these years because I'd never seen my father emotionally naked before. For the first time, I realized he had depths and cares I was completely unaware of, and a side I knew nothing about.

Two days before we left Summit my dad did the kind of awesome thing you always hope your parents will do: he took me and my band of misfit friends to the same Pennsylvania water park we'd visited as a family, for a going-away party. We had an amazing time, though toward the end of the day, when we were all sun-burned and waterlogged, adolescent solemnity set in and prom-ises to stay in touch ensued. I couldn't hold on to the mood for more than a few minutes, though. I was focused on the future, not the past. The next day, while movers bustled around loading our belongings into the moving truck, I sat across the street, under a tree in Kim's yard. She was weeping, and I'm afraid I didn't exactly rise to the occasion. My attitude was, "See ya! Have a nice life." It was my ninth move in fourteen years.

From my parents' perspective we were going home, but I didn't feel that way because I didn't really feel Canadian. My main attachment to Canada was to my grandmothers, especially Gallo, and to our cottage in Ontario, which we had bought in 1999. That summer we'd been eating at a little sandwich place near my grandfather's cottage when Erica and I noticed a bulletin board with property listings. We ran over to look at them, and then our parents were reading over our shoulders, and next thing we knew, the purpose of our trip wasn't seeing Grandpa but finding a cot-tage for ourselves. It was almost unbelievable that my parents indulged this whim my sister and I had had, and wound up buy-ing a place. When we walked into the fourth cottage, all of us were just, "This is the one." It was big, at least twice the size of our house, with a huge stone fireplace, endless windows over-looking the lake and a cozy rustic feeling. As it was set partway up a densely wooded hill, you couldn't see the cottages on either side until you were out on the dock. It was perfect. It didn't seem weird to me that we were buying property in Ontario though we lived in New Jersey. Nor did it occur to me until right this minute that perhaps Erica and I didn't really drive the purchase—more likely, it was part of a larger plan our parents had about moving back to Canada. It's funny how your own childhood narrative solidifies into fact, sometimes so quickly that you never sense there might be another side to the story.

To me the cottage was yet another wonderful thing we got out of *Good Morning America*. Thanks to my father's stint on that show, I'd been able to hold a baby lion and go to a shuttle launch, we'd taken family trips to Europe and, best of all, we'd wound up with a place on the same clear northern lake as my grandfather. His cottage was two bays over, though, so the lake felt both familiar and new to me. I had a lot of independence there because my parents trusted me to be sensible (one upside of nerdiness). There was a little Zodiac I was allowed to zip around in, plus a real motorboat my dad said I'd be able to drive someday.

My dad loved the lake as much as I did, and it was the one place where he truly unwound. Though he always had some kind of cottage improvement project going, he slowed down, stopped checking his watch and phone, and relaxed. For those few weeks every summer, it was easy to get his attention and hold it. Erica and I made sure that we monopolized his time, clamouring for boat rides and trips to town for frozen yogurt, and insisting that he jump off the dock with us and swim out to our raft, anchored in the lake.

The summer before we moved to Vancouver, though, I was more wary of his attention. I didn't want him studying me too closely, because I wasn't sure what he would see. That year I'd become more interested in art, and sketching was starting to become a compulsion, the way Lego had been for years. I drew a lot of things, from spaceships to people, sometimes even nudes. Then a lot of nudes. Male nudes. Afterwards, alarmed and ashamed about what someone else would think if they saw them, I'd rip my drawings into tiny pieces. I was confused about why I was drawing naked men, just as I was confused by my reaction to the Blink 182 CD. The impulse was sexual, obviously, but I didn't know what it meant.

My parents and especially my mother had always talked openly with me about sex. Shortly after we got to Summit, I'd helpfully explained to all the other kids on the street how babies are made, and when they went home and shared this fascinating news with their own families, my parents received a number of angry calls. Compared to my friends' parents, who tended to be conservative and über-Christian, mine were progressive. They weren't telling either me or Erica to save ourselves for marriage (though I do think my dad, who is more traditional than my mom, was secretly in favour of that option). And they didn't present sex as some super-serious, potentially scary act. They told us it could be beautiful and fun so long as you were with someone you really cared about, and they couldn't say enough good things about condoms. In any discussions about the mechanics of sex, though, they always described it as something that happened between a man and a woman. I have memories of my mom telling my sister and me when we were pretty little that it was okay to be gay, and if we were, she'd love us just the same. But no one ever explained how a gay person would have sex, nor did I wonder about that.

I didn't know any actual gay people. Insofar as I ever thought about homosexuality, I thought entirely in terms of stereotypes:

drag queens or limp-wristed guys. I didn't relate to or identify with those stereotypes at all, therefore I knew I wasn't gay. Sex ed in grade eight confirmed it. There were just a few vague paragraphs about homosexuality in our textbook, but one phrase made an indelible impression: "Men are attracted to the musky smell of other men's rear ends." All right, I'm likely mis-remembering "rear ends," but I know for sure "musky smell" was in there because it grossed me out. Odour, dirt, germs—I'm my mother's child. None of that appealed to me in the slightest. Therefore, I couldn't possibly be gay.

In retrospect, certain incidents stand out to me as indicators of my sexual identity, but at the time, they were not aha moments. They were just stray threads in the fabric of my childhood, which acquired a discernible pattern only after the fact. The first occurred in grade six on a school field trip to Washington, DC. My trip "buddy" and I talked and laughed on the bus, shared a snack or two, and then as we approached Capitol Hill, I put on my baseball hat—the wrong way, he told me, casually reaching over to adjust the bill, tucking my hair behind my ear. For him, I'm sure the moment had no relevance: just a bro helping a bro. But no boy had ever touched me in a caring way before and his touch was electric, though I had no idea why. I wasn't actually attracted to him, then or later.

The following summer there'd been another moment. All the kids at the cottage were playing a nighttime variation of hide-and-seek: half of us hid in the forest surrounding the lake while everyone else tried to find us, armed with flashlights. It was thrilling and terrifying, crashing through the dark woods looking for a good hiding place while a pack of hunters pounded along not far behind. When one guy flung himself into a narrow ditch and motioned for me to follow, I jumped right in. It was a tight fit. I had to lie down beside him and press up against his back—and suddenly, I lost all interest in getting back to home base safely. I didn't want to leave. But the thought that went through my mind wasn't "Oh my God, I must be homosexual!" It was "This feels great!" I didn't question the feeling or what it signified.

I didn't think it signified a thing. Until grade six, I hadn't even liked boys enough to want to be friends with them. My crushes were on girls, always had been. Along with her sketchbooks of family cartoons, my mother kept a journal where she wrote down funny things all of us said, which is how I know that in kindergarten I came home one day and said, "I made a new friend today and guess what? I'm in love. Don't tell anyone! She's beautiful. She has blonde hair, teddy bear earrings and a nice mouth . . . I just looked at her in circle time and winked at her. She winked back. That's when I fell in love with her. It's crazy. I don't know what's wrong with me, but when I'm with her . . . I don't love Erica anymore." (My mother may have embroidered this quote to make it more adorable, but I did not.)

So why, in the summer after grade eight, was I compulsively drawing pictures of naked men? I had no idea, but I didn't want anyone, especially my father, to find out.

Several times during those first few months in Vancouver my parents mentioned how good it felt not to have to pretend to fit in anymore. I'd picked up on it only once when we lived in Summit: my dad, who'd never had any interest in televised sports, had bought a big-screen TV and invited all the dads in the neigh-bourhood over to watch football. I'd thought that was phony, and had judged him as charitably as teenagers usually judge their par-ents. But now it came out that both my parents had been faking stuff in Summit. I was floored. I thought I was the only person in my family who'd ever felt like an outsider, but apparently not. It turned out that Mom and Dad had only made us go to church because everyone else in Summit did. Now that we were in Vancouver and neighbourhood busybodies weren't keeping tabs, they said Erica and I could decide for ourselves how to explore and express our spirituality. Church attendance was, in other words, optional. Let's just say that I started sleeping in a lot more often on Sundays.

Unlike my parents, I'd never pretended in order to try to fit in anywhere. In Summit, I'd known it wouldn't work, so why bother? In Vancouver, however, I did want to fit in, and decided my best shot was to act as if I'd always been accepted. No one had to know that I'd been at the bottom of the food chain at my old school, and they wouldn't, so long as I acted "as if." In Summit, most kids thought they were just as awesome and gifted as their parents had always told them they were, and I tried to project some of that same brash confidence at my new school. The more American I acted, the more confident I seemed, and the more forceful and outspoken I actually became. It was incredible, really, how wrapping myself in the US flag seemed to make my shyness and weakness invisible.

I played up the fact that I'd lived close to New York, which helped make me intriguing for the first time in my life; a lot of the kids at school were obsessed with hip hop and New York ghetto culture. This was West Vancouver though, a community not known for its racial diversity, and it was comical watching these privileged white kids climbing out of their mom's and dad's Porsches with their jeans hanging off their butts, trying to look and sound gangsta. In the US I'd gone to school with a lot of black and Hispanic kids, including some tough ones who'd shove you down a flight of stairs for wearing jeans they considered "black only." They'd have made mincemeat out of these west coast posers. *I* was tougher than they were, for goodness' sake.

No one in the school intimidated me, and for the first few months, I ping-ponged between cliques at will. Ignorance of the social pecking order helped. I didn't know the unwritten rules about who was allowed to talk to whom, the way I had in Summit, so I talked to everybody, including the popular kids. It turned out to be easier than I'd ever imagined. All you needed to do was act as if you had the right.

I made friends easily, like Buzz, who had a houseful of little brothers obsessed with Lego the way I'd been. We'd play Halo on his Xbox for hours, taking breaks only to torment his siblings or prowl around the neighbourhood on our bikes. I made friends with some of the kids who lived in palatial houses with maids, hot tubs and ocean views. There were pool parties, sometimes catered, and a mind-numbing level of wealth. One kid had a basement entirely devoted to miniature trains, like something out of a movie. Another had his own assistant, and a two-storey bedroom that was easily as big as our whole house in Summit. I seemed to be the only person in the school who wasn't going to be getting a car for his sixteenth birthday.

Although my social prospects were considerably brighter than they had been in Summit, I proceeded with my parents' martial arts plan. I wanted to become a guy no one would dream of messing with. Thai kickboxing and judo turned out to be among the rare physical activities I was actually good at. I could kick higher than most kids, and I was faster and more flexible. I'd train and spar until I was so tired that I barely had the energy to bike home, and got in the habit of biking on the railway tracks, where it was flatter. It was one of the first times I purposely and repeatedly broke one of my parents' rules, and I'm sure they would have grounded me for life had they found out. But I no longer felt like a kid bad things happened to as a matter of course. The world no longer seemed so dangerous to me.

We'd been living in Vancouver for six months, long enough that the novelty had worn off, when I woke one morning to the sound of knocking on my bedroom door. The door opened slowly, and my father softly called my name then came and sat on the edge of my bed. "You're not going to school today," was his opening line. "Gallo passed away in her sleep." I heard the words but didn't process them. Gently, he told me what he knew: Esmond, Gallo's partner, had come to her apartment and found her in her bed. She had died peacefully.

Several months earlier, Gallo had come to Vancouver. After a blissful week of introducing her to our new house and neighbourhood, I'd hugged her goodbye on our driveway. She was the person in the world who saw me most clearly yet still believed I could do no wrong, and I loved her fiercely. She'd held on to me tightly for an extra few seconds, and as I'd breathed in her perfume I'd had a strange thought: I might never see her again. I'd brushed it off. Ridiculous. Gallo had recently retired and was bursting with optimism about the future, all the amazing things she was going to do, all the places she'd go. She gave me a little wave out the car window, then was off to the airport.

Now, in the living room, my sister and mother were hugging each other on the couch, and my mother's face was puffy from crying. She'd adored her mother. We all had. I sat down beside them but I didn't cry. I couldn't. I just kept telling myself, stupidly, "She wasn't even that old." I couldn't access my emotions, much less express them. A few days later my father asked me whether I'd cried, and I shook my head. No. I'm sure he was concerned that I was internalizing her death, but there was nothing I could do. My feelings would not come out.

The subsequent days were a blur. My mother went to Montreal ahead of the rest of us to begin sorting through Gallo's apartment, which was piled to the ceiling with stuff. She was a bit of a hoarder. When we got there, my mother was working away in the guest room, and I wandered into the kitchen. There on the table was a blister pack of Gravol and Gallo's reading glasses. Apparently the onset of a heart attack sometimes involves nausea. I could picture her final hours, reading a book at the table, then putting it face down, pages spread, and reaching for the Gravol, thinking she'd feel better if she lay down. Later, for years, I had nightmares about this scene; in my dreams, I was helpless, unable to call out, unable to warn her.

My mother said we could take something small from Gallo's apartment to remember her by, and I searched for something that embodied her spirit. In the medicine cabinet, I found it.

Her perfume bottle. I carefully dripped perfume into the small porcelain container shaped like an apple that had always sat on my grandmother's bedside table. I still have that apple, though it lost its scent long ago, likely because in the months and years following my grandmother's death, I opened it, carefully, many times, to feel she was near me again. I can't say that I've ever gotten over the loss.

Shortly after moving to Vancouver my dad took all of us to see the *Global National* studio, which was in Burnaby, about forty minutes from our house. I was surprised by how long the drive was, but he just shrugged. He wanted Erica and me to go to good schools. Commuting wasn't that big a deal.

TV studios didn't impress me, generally. I'd seen too many of them. But there was one impressive novelty at *Global National*: my dad was clearly the boss, in control of everything. Before he came back to Canada, the network hadn't even existed, nor had the studio, or the evening news broadcast itself. He'd had to build from the ground up, and he seemed rejuvenated by the effort. I still didn't know why he felt he needed to reinvent himself, but I knew that being an anchor was considered a step up from being a reporter, and for the first time, he wasn't sharing the stage with a co-anchor. He was on his own, in charge of a team of reporters, and clearly loving it.

He seemed absolutely sure of himself, the commander of an empire, which is what I wanted to be when I grew up, too. To me, that was the distilled essence of manhood: you owned your life and were completely in control of it. The paragon of masculinity, as far as I was concerned, was my dad's friend Mike Bronco, who ran a gym in New Jersey and was the most self-sufficient person I'd ever met. He'd taught me how to fire a rifle, write with a quill pen and navigate with a compass. He was unacquainted with self-doubt and didn't yearn for anything he couldn't make or build himself. My dad was very different but he was also a survivor; you could drop him down in the middle of a war zone and in two hours he'd have found a cold beer and lined up an interview with a rebel leader. Like Mike, he spoke with conviction and projected unshakeable confidence. Each of them seemed at home in a world he'd created for himself. I wanted to feel that way, too, and I began thinking consciously about how to toughen myself up, get stronger.

Lifting weights would help, but there was no way I was going to start doing it in a gym. I didn't want anyone to see me struggling. So my dad, who'd always worked out, took me to a fitness supply store and got me a bench and a set of weights, and set me up in our garage. At first, I was very secretive. My body didn't reflect who I wanted to be, and if I saw anyone peeking in the little window in the door between the kitchen and the garage, I'd freak out. Eventually I got smart and taped a piece of paper over the window, and eventually, too, picking up heavy dumbbells then putting them down again started to have a noticeable effect on my arms. My father bought me the first of many protein shakes, and after a year in the garage, when I finally had the confidence to let him see me in action, he gave me some pointers. It was the first time we'd bonded over something physical, and though not a sport like basketball, lifting weights was still masculine. Eventually we even went to the gym together sometimes. I liked that, liked knowing what to do and liked feeling that my father was proud of me, proud enough to be seen working out with me.

As soon as I started to look more muscular, people treated me differently—or maybe I carried myself with more confidence, and that's what they responded to, I'm not sure. Looking the part, however, didn't mean I felt tough. I never progressed past a brown belt in judo because, near the end of one sparring match in my second year, I got over-confident and wound up getting punched in the head by a black belt. I knew it was the purpose of the exercise, but I just felt, "Why did someone do this to me?" My lower lip started to quiver and I had to walk away for a moment because I was afraid I was going to cry. I loved the principles and the movements of judo, but I wasn't into the idea of inflicting harm and was even less enthusiastic about being harmed. So I quit, though I didn't tell my parents why. I had the perfect excuse: signs had recently been posted in the martial arts studio asking us to kindly refrain from vomiting on the exercise mats—kids had apparently started doing this after exercising too intensely, and the proprietors wanted us to vomit in the bathroom in the future. My parents were all too aware of my phobia, and bought my argument that I couldn't work out in a place where I'd have to bear witness to ritual vomiting.

Besides, if I cut out judo, I'd have more time to study math. It was clear to me that unless I got a whole lot better at it, I'd never make it as a nuclear physicist. I was fascinated by atoms and the mysteries of quantum physics, and when I was fifteen and sixteen, spent hours hunting down scientific information on the internet and reading books by people like Stephen Hawking. I liked teaching myself new things and found I retained information better than I did in the classroom, but the more I learned about science, the more obvious it became that my lack of mathematical aptitude was a serious problem. Inspired by my dad's self-discipline and determination, I kept at it, toiling away with the help of a math tutor who had mind-blowingly bad breath. Whatever. I had a dream. I tried not to inhale when he exhaled.

Aside from science, my favourite class was Japanese. It's a really difficult language but I wanted to learn it because I was drawn to the culture, especially the aesthetic. I'd been watching anime for years, starting with Pokémon, and I admired the tidy beauty and intricate graphics of Japanese cartoons. A little later, when my school offered an elective in animation, I signed up for it immediately and discovered that I was good at it, good enough that I fell in with the artsy crowd and became known for art at high school in the same way that I'd been known for trading Pokémon cards in middle school. I created a little character called Page Alien, and drew comic book after comic book of his adventures. In grade eleven, my friend Carrie and I made an animated short together that won a provincial prize, and my dad encouraged me to think about animation as a career. My mom told me dreamily that she could see me falling in love with a nice Japanese girl and becoming a famous animator in Tokyo.

I hoped she was right, especially about falling in love with a girl. I was really starting to worry about myself. One day when I was in grade ten my dad had come home from work and proceeded directly to my bedroom, which was a little unusual. Without much preamble he passed me a paper bag with a magazine inside. The *Sports Illustrated* swimsuit issue. "Don't tell your mother," he said, but he didn't sound as though he were proudly ushering me into the inner sanctum of maledom. He was grinning sheepishly and seemed embarrassed. My father never objectified women. He'd never ogle a busty woman or make an off-colour remark, and he certainly didn't have a hidden stash of porno mags, like my friends' dads. Buying the *SI* swimsuit issue was completely out of character, so much so that I wondered if he was giving it to me because he was worried that I wasn't interested enough in girls. I thanked him, and tried to look excited. Then I did what any teenager does with contraband: I hid it. I wasn't particularly interested, was the truth.

Like many teenagers in North America, I'd stumbled across internet porn, and I'd been alarmed by my reaction to images of men. I told myself that my hormones were raging, so anything sexual would be a turn-on. Actually, I reasoned, it would be more abnormal if I *didn't* respond. Nevertheless, I didn't want to like looking at naked guys, so I resisted the urge to seek out gay porn. I told myself I was only allowed to look at girls. This had one benefit: unlike most boys my age, I wasn't a big consumer of porn, period.

Nevertheless, as my hormones kicked into high gear, sexual thoughts about guys popped into my head more and more insistently. *Am I gay?* At sixteen it was a question, not a conviction. But even thinking it made me feel panicky and ashamed. I couldn't figure out why, the more masculine I looked, the less masculine I felt. It was like my brain was sabotaging all the hard work I was doing in the garage, and I started to get compulsive, lifting heavier and heavier weights, as though by bulking up I could crowd my thoughts and feelings out of existence.

I'd noticed how my father had winced and changed the channel when, on some TV program we were all watching together, two actors had moved in to kiss one another. The very suggestion of two men touching clearly pained him. And he was a model of tolerance compared to the sixteen-year-olds I knew. Teenage boys police the borders of masculinity vigilantly. "Homo" and "fag" are the insults that trump all other insults and gay is, at that age, the worst thing you can possibly be—even at a relatively enlightened school, even in an era of political correctness.

I wanted to feel the way a guy was supposed to feel. I grew increasingly paranoid that people might somehow figure out that I didn't. Maybe they already had. As my voice deepened and my body developed, a steady drumbeat of anxiety punctuated my waking thoughts: Am I standing correctly or is my back arched too much? Are my clothes masculine enough? Is this music the kind I should be listening to? Why am I looking at the guy instead of the girl in the Calvin Klein ad? Did anyone notice? I was terrified of doing or saying something that would give me away—and terrified, too, of what I seemed to be becoming. I was afraid there was the equivalent of a light switch in my psyche, one that could instantly transform me into a screaming queen complete with sequins and a pink boa, and I might accidentally flip it if I continued thinking about guys.

Heterosexuality was, to me, the *sine qua non* of masculinity. I couldn't see how I'd ever be successful at anything in life if I failed this first, most basic test of manhood.

So I did what anyone who was afraid he might be gay would do. I set out to prove I wasn't. I hoped that dating a girl would awaken the "right" kinds of feelings. And I had an eye on the PR benefits, too: no one would think I was gay if I had a girlfriend.

It was with this highly romantic mindset that I began seeing Karen in grade eleven. At the beginning, everything was great. The buzz hit the school and if people had been discussing my sexuality, they stopped, or so I thought. I was relieved about that, but, as the relationship proceeded, increasingly apprehensive about my own lack of sexual interest in her. She was smart, easy to talk to, pretty—what the hell was wrong with me? I genuinely liked her. But the fireworks my father had told me about were not happening.

Karen and I would go out to dinner, chat and hang with friends—nothing deeply emotional, except for my feeling of dread as the end of the evening drew nearer. Each time she leaned across the car for a goodnight kiss, I'd tense up, bracing myself for the moment when our lips would lock. Hers were soft and gentle, just as I had imagined a girl's lips to be. But the hoped-for surge of desire, that natural, instinctive response any seventeen-year-old male is supposed to feel in this situation, never materialized. So before anything more intimate could happen, I'd pull away, invent some excuse to go home and boot her out of the car unceremoniously. Maybe, I told myself lamely, I'm just not into kissing.

I took some solace in the fact that I felt protective of her. I empathized with her in a way I never had with anyone else, and got angry on her behalf, too, the way I'd seen my father get angry on my mother's behalf. Karen's family wasn't always nice to her, in my opinion. The first time I was invited over for dinner there was an array of dishes, including vegetarian options, because

Karen had been a vegetarian for many years. In my home, conversation was the focal point of a meal, but in Karen's home, the silence was punctuated only by the sound of chewing and the occasional rapid-fire exchange of small talk, which died out as quickly as it had started. Towards the end of dinner, Karen turned pale and put down her cutlery. "Mom, was there meat in here?" she asked. Before her mother could answer, Karen's grandmother embarked on a rant: growing girls need to eat meat, and if sneaking it into their food was the only way, well, she'd just have to keep on doing it. Karen bolted upstairs to be sick and I stayed at the table, hating her grandmother and wondering why her parents hadn't leapt to Karen's defence. I never ate dinner at her house again.

When she came over to my house, we'd draw the blinds and lie on my bed, watching movies. She cuddled up next me, but nothing more happened. She had nice breasts, ones I knew I should want to touch, but they drew my attention only when they obstructed my view of the screen. Karen must have thought I was the most gentlemanly guy on the planet, and actually, I was pretty square compared to a lot of our friends. I was always the designated driver at a party, for instance, because I didn't drink or smoke pot. Some of our friends got plastered every weekend, chugging Kahlúa and anything else they could find in their parents' liquor cabinets, but the notion of losing control or getting sick was a total turnoff for me. So I was always the one taking care of the girl who'd smoked too much weed or urging water on the guy who was bombed out of his mind. Maybe Karen figured that I was far too chivalrous to make a move on her.

But a girl on the periphery of our group thought differently.

Rachel's disdain for me reminded me of my old nemesis Neil, and on the few occasions when she deigned to speak to me, she was cutting and sarcastic. One day at lunch, Karen stepped away from the table and Rachel looked me right in the eye and said, her voice dripping with disgust, "You aren't fooling anyone. It's obvious you're gay." The blood probably drained from my face. How had she seen through my cover? "It's the way you hold your glass," she smirked. "You put your pinky underneath the base. So *gay*." When Karen returned to the table I clung to her, even made a show of kissing her neck, hoping that a little PDA might affirm my masculinity for anyone who was watching.

Sometimes a group of us would go to the park near Karen's house late at night and play Truth or Dare. We were sixteen and seventeen, far from childhood innocence, and as the game progressed it always got more overtly sexual. After a certain point, I'd only choose Dare, and I wound up doing some really stupid things, like marching across the freeway in my boxers. But that was better than choosing Truth, and having to answer the questions I feared: Do you want to have sex with Karen? Do you ever think about sex with guys? Are you gay?

In 2004, my dad took me to Japan for spring break. I was excited to go to this place I'd been learning so much about, and I appreciated the fact that he was trying to cater to my interests. But I was in a bad mood almost the whole time we were there. My normal morning crankiness was multiplied exponentially by jet lag and by the fact that my dad's snoring kept me up at night. He'd wake up, bright-eyed and bushy-tailed, flatly denying that he'd made a peep all night long. Finally one night when the familiar freight train-like rumbling started up on his side of the tiny room, I got out my video recorder and filmed him. End of debate.

I'd never been alone with my father for a whole week, and it was also the first time we were going somewhere he'd never been. He was clearly trying to pass the baton and let me be the tour guide, but I was horribly shy and unsure of myself, and afraid of making a mistake in front of him. My Japanese was pretty basic, and at one point we were in a tech store and I hit a language barrier there was no climbing over. I needed to find someone who spoke English, but I didn't want my father to witness this ignominy so I banished him to the hallway then timidly asked whether anyone in the store could speak English.

My dad is a good traveller, upbeat and positive even in a country he's too tall for, where he bashes his head on every doorway. A lot of my friends were embarrassed to be seen in public with their parents and would scurry ahead or lag behind, praying no one noticed the family resemblance. I never felt that way about either of my parents, but in Tokyo, I didn't feel particularly connected to my father and I felt bad about it, especially because he'd clearly gone out of his way to make the trip special. Through a colleague he'd arranged for me to tour Studio Ghibli, one of Japan's leading animation companies, where I got to flip through the head animator's book and see all the work he'd done on films I admired. It was a dream come true for anyone who wanted to be an animator, which I did by this point (my math marks were so abysmal that science was officially out of the question). It seemed like my dad was courting me, almost, trying to impress me, and he'd arranged one surprise after another: taking the bullet train from Tokyo to Kyoto, visiting amazing parks and temples he'd researched.

I think he'd hoped it would be a bonding experience, but maybe there was just too much distance between us to cover. The closest we came was the night in Tokyo when my father suggested having a drink in the hotel bar where Bill Murray's character spends most of his time in *Lost in Translation*. We walked over to the Park Hyatt, took the elevator up to the 52nd floor, and when the doors opened you had this incredible panoramic view of the city through the windows. I walked out, mesmerized, then realized I was on my own. My dad was still in the elevator, looking a little queasy. "I'm sorry," he said. "I can't do it." I'd forgotten he was afraid of heights, and I guess he'd tried to forget, too, hoping to pull off a big cinematic moment for my benefit. We went back down the elevator and had tea in an interior arboretum where, instead of windows, there were all kinds of flowers. I felt close to him then, having seen his momentary vulnerability and how he'd been unable to master it.

But it didn't inspire me to talk about my own feelings of vulnerability. There was no way I could tell my father I was afraid of something so much worse than heights: my own thoughts and feelings, my sexuality. He'd be disgusted. Once I'd heard him talk about being on a business trip somewhere, sitting in a hotel hot tub minding his own business, when another guy had tried to grope him. My father had felt violated and outraged, but mostly insulted that anyone could have mistaken him for *that* kind of man. I wanted my father to be proud of me. I wanted to be a man in his eyes, and there was only one way. I had to be sure he didn't see the real me.

———

As usual, the summer before my senior year, we left Vancouver to spend a few months at the cottage. When Karen and I said our goodbyes, she gave me a photo of herself with a love note on the back, to remind me of her until the fall. I told her I'd be busy, wouldn't have much time to write, and that wasn't entirely untrue. I'd lined up a job for myself at the local golf course, with the intention of earning as much money as I could because I wanted to buy a car. Most kids worked at the general store and my dad had helped line up a job for me there, but then, without his help, I'd landed the golf course gig. For whatever reason, it was considered more prestigious, a fact I reminded myself of a thousand times the day the septic tank exploded and I was instructed to clean it up. Alone. I knew my dad was proud of me for finding a job on my own, and I wanted to show him that working hard, just like he always had, was something I could definitely do.

Cleaning golf clubs and docking boats wasn't mentally stimulating, but it did keep my mind off thoughts of my girlfriend back home—or, to be more accurate, it kept my mind off thoughts of not thinking the right way about my girlfriend back home. Karen was the person I liked best in the world. And I was hoping I'd never have to have sex with her.

I worked as many extra shifts as I could that summer, not least because it was harder to distract myself when I wasn't working. Trying to suppress sexual thoughts about guys was enough to make me go mad. I'd equate the feeling to being at the bottom of a deep tank filled with water. You hold your breath for as long as possible, but at some point you begin to lose control. Air is running out. You need to find a way to get some oxygen in your lungs or you're going to drown. The idea that I was gay went against everything I wanted to believe about myself—and yet I felt like I was suffocating when I tried not to think gay thoughts.

I'm sure if our cottage had had internet access I would have logged countless furtive hours online, exploring gay sites. But this was in the days before wireless, so I went back to sketching, male nudes, all different scenarios. Any exhilaration and relief I felt while freely expressing my curiosity was followed by near hysteria. What could I do with the evidence? Where the hell could I hide it? I retrofitted my nightstand with a lock, and shoved my drawings in there.

One rainy day, alone in the living room, I was flipping through a poor selection of satellite TV channels when suddenly a gay sex scene flashed on the screen. It was *Queer as Folk*, a Showtime program I'd never seen before. I instantly changed the channel, worried that my parents might have heard the moaning in the next room. Then, heart racing, I cranked down the volume, checked over my shoulder about ten times and flipped back to the show. I couldn't believe what I was seeing. The scene was intensely graphic—I'd had no idea that watching two guys do this stuff was allowed on TV, cable channel or not. I watched for a few minutes, entranced, then lost my nerve and turned off the TV. The thought of my father catching me watching that show was sickening.

All that summer, I hardly slept. The sexual divide in society is clearly delineated: blue/pink, prince/princess. Just imagining crossing it stirred up a mental storm that kept me tossing and turning most nights, writhing in pain. I didn't want to be gay. I didn't want to be an outcast from mainstream society. The experience of being bullied had taught me what that felt like, and I wanted no part of it, ever again. I just wanted to be normal.

I couldn't risk telling anyone else what I was feeling, or asking for help or guidance. If I couldn't accept the possibility of being gay, how could anyone else possibly accept it?

Questions chased each other through my brain all night long. Who am I? What is my purpose on earth? If it's to procreate, and I'm gay, then what's the point of living? During that summer, I spent a lot of time thinking about killing myself. What would the best method be? Pills? No, I probably couldn't keep them down. Drowning, I finally decided, was the ticket. It was a sure thing, and there was a deep, dark lake right outside the door. I could just tie an anchor around my leg and jump off the dock. No, the boat would be better. Take it out to the middle of the lake, where I couldn't chicken out. I'd be deep in thought, considering which knot would work best, then I'd snap out of it, telling myself, No. I'm not going to kill myself because I am *not* gay. That's not my plan, it's not the vision I have for myself.

It took everything in my power to hide this emotional turbulence from my family, and it probably leaked through in ways that confused them. I was confused, too, still hoping, despite all the evidence, that perhaps I wasn't really gay after all. If I were, surely I'd no longer be questioning my sexuality. I'd just *know*. I remember wishing for a wet dream as though it were the ultimate polygraph: if I dreamed about Karen or some other girl, then I *couldn't* be gay. My subconscious would have settled the question once and for all.

I needed irrefutable proof. It didn't feel as though the answer resided within me, or I'd already have it. The answer, I became convinced, was something I needed to seek out and uncover.

CHAPTER ELEVEN

TESTS

KEVIN

AT *GLOBAL NATIONAL* I had the chance to build something from nothing, and I was determined not to preside over another debacle. I threw myself into creating a new kind of newscast with a fervour that probably struck observers as delusional. The network was brand new and its owners, the Asper family, weren't known as big spenders. The patriarch had once famously quipped that his employees were in "the business of selling soap"—attracting advertising dollars, that is, not revolutionizing journalism. I thought if we could build a great newscast with solid ratings, they'd see the wisdom of investing more in it. In the meantime, we'd have to manage on a shoestring budget, relative to the other two national networks' flagship newscasts.

I was convinced we could beat CTV and CBC if we created something distinctive. ESPN had revolutionized sports coverage by injecting personality, humour and sharp insight into its broadcasts, and I wanted to do something similar to network news. In rehearsals, I tried to set a relaxed and personal tone.

Instead of preaching the news, we'd share it with viewers, and we'd do it using cutting-edge digital equipment and graphic-rich explanations. Offering an opportunity to think outside the box turned out to be all that was needed to assemble a talented team of reporters, photojournalists and production staff. They were young but creative and hard-working. I was optimistic but I warned my managers to be realistic: it would take years for the broadcast to reach its full potential. This was a marathon, not a sprint.

On my seventh day on the job, I was in the shower when Cathy called out, horror in her voice: a second plane had just flown into the World Trade Center. Like many people, that's when we knew it was no accident. It was just after six a.m., Vancouver time. I pulled on a suit and raced to the studio on nearly empty expressways, in such a hurry to get to the anchor chair that I forgot to wear underwear. For the next sixteen hours, on a set where the paint was barely dry, working with reporters and cameramen who were still learning each other's names, on a network that had only flipped the switch on national satellite feeds the week before, we started to cover what we knew already would be the biggest story of our lives. We didn't have months to find our way and cohere as a team. We had to mature, that day, and punch above our weight.

We got on the air faster than our more established Canadian competitors, and my familiarity with New York—and experience anchoring wall-to-wall coverage of breaking news events—gave us a significant editorial edge, just as my familiarity with the royal family had given ABC an advantage the night Diana died. On September 11, as we switched between the live video feeds American broadcasters were supplying, I recognized street corners and could name the officials surrounding Mayor Rudy Giuliani at press briefings. Commuting from New Jersey, I'd walked through the World Trade Center so often that I could rattle off the names of its underground shops from memory, as well as the names of some of the world's leading financial companies, located in the highest floors of the towers. Several of my neighbours in Summit had worked in those companies. As the day wore on, I had the sickening realization that there was no chance every one of them had made it out alive. But there was no time to let myself feel, no time to do anything except scramble for information and try to provide context. I took only one quick bathroom break that very long day because I didn't feel I could afford to move away from the anchor desk. We were braced for another catastrophe, wondering whether there were more American targets. Or Canadian ones: in a little-remembered sidebar to that day, Canadian fighter jets had to force an unresponsive Korean Air jumbo jet to land in Yukon after its pilots failed to respond to hails. Years later, then prime minister Jean Chrétien admitted he had given the order to shoot the jet down if the pilots wouldn't land.

Driving home that night, with majestic coastal mountains on one side and the endless ocean on the other, I was overcome by a flood of conflicting emotions: gratitude to be safe in this lovely corner of the earth, but mostly sorrow. I pulled over on the side of the highway. A city I'd worked in for seven years had been attacked, and thousands of people were dead, including men I'd chatted with at Summit's Fourth of July fireworks celebrations and fathers who'd sat beside me on the little wooden chairs outside the ballet studio, as we'd waited for our daughters' class to finish. On air, my game face had not slipped. But by the side of the highway, where no one could see, I wept.

Back at work the next day, I outlined what we needed to do, starting with throwing out our plans for the newscast. We had to be strategic, trying to anticipate events rather than simply reacting to them. The US, for instance, was clearly going to become more paranoid, with good reason. How would that play out in terms of cross-border trade and travel? Would it affect Canada's willingness to participate in any international military conflict? And what moves would our own leaders likely make to ensure national security? These were the kinds of issues we needed to investigate proactively in order to provide distinctive coverage. And we needed to get reporters and crews ready to go into war zones, as they would surely have to do.

Though CTV and CBC both had much larger teams of reporters, most of whom were highly experienced, I knew we could own this story if we were passionate about finding new ways to tell it. Our ratings-winning live coverage the previous day had given us an opening—and had also given our team a reason to believe in me and my ambition for our newscast. The immediacy and complexity of the challenge we faced, right out of the gate, helped our team bond. One huge benefit of newness: no one was burnt out or disillusioned yet, and there was no deadwood on our team. United by a sense of mission, most days, we outhustled the competition.

I drove the team, and myself, very hard. I wanted almost complete control over the script that would be loaded into the teleprompter, and I wanted to write as much of it as humanly possible. For one thing, speaking my own words eases my jitters. I've never met an anchor who's cavalier about going live, and I'm no exception. Even after thousands of live broadcasts, I still clear my throat, twice, while the opening graphics roll. I still worry about choking.

I'd also learned that editorial control is the surest path to success. I'd worked for half a dozen seasoned anchors in the US and Canada, and the more involved they were in shaping their shows, the more successful they were. No one was more hands on than Peter Jennings. Like most anchors, he wrote the introductions to the top stories in his newscast, but he also approved every word written by everyone else. It seemed excessive to me until the day a tape jammed in the machine midway through *World News Tonight* and, suddenly, a correspondent's report stopped abruptly and TV screens across North America went blank. But just for a second. Because he'd been deeply involved in editing the story, Peter was able to paraphrase the rest of the report, smoothly covering the glitch.

Leading a team and a newscast is all about improvising and rejigging. You plan out a show six hours before airtime, but segments are shortened or lengthened depending on how events unfold, and some stories are jettisoned altogether to make way for new ones. Extra seconds can't be added to a television show in the same way you can add pages to a newspaper. You're always nipping and tucking to fit things into a finite template, even while you're on air. During commercial breaks or when field items were running, I'd sit at the anchor desk and write against the clock, either because reporters hadn't accurately estimated the length of their reports, or because something had gone differently than producers in the control room had expected. I became a very fast writer and developed a weird ability: I can glance at a page and know precisely how many seconds it will take to read it on air. This paragraph's explanation of the process looks to be a forty-four-second read. It's a useful talent for a broadcaster, but no one else.

Like every anchor I ever worked alongside, I also spent a good portion of the day asking questions and playing devil's advocate, challenging reporters and producers to be sure they'd considered every angle and had the facts straight. It introduced a level of tension to the relationship—no one enjoys being grilled—but at *Global National* we couldn't afford to get things wrong. One big lawsuit would have crippled the operation.

And then there was managing up. The Asper family were not hands-off proprietors; after 9/11, for example, they had strong feelings about how we should be covering the Middle East. I'd always been shielded from these kinds of demands by an anchor or executive producer, but when the owners suggested I step back and allow their designates to choose the experts who appeared on the broadcast, I didn't have to think twice about how to respond. I let them know I'd resign before I'd agree to that. I wasn't bluffing. I remember telling the network president, who flew to BC so he could personally twist my arm, "It's a shame. My family loves Vancouver and I intend to stay in Canada. But I just won't do it." In the end a compromise was reached: our newscast was shortened by five minutes to make way for a "commentary" section delivered by editorialists who shared the owners' political views. I couldn't stop them from doing it. It was their network after all. However, I did insist on saying good-night and signing off before the commentary began, to create an editorial moat between news and opinion. The owners and I maintained a cordial respect for each other, and when the commentaries proved to be bad for ratings, they quietly disappeared.

Belatedly, I realized I'd left *GMA* with more than just scars. I had some new skills. I could now hold my ground when I thought managers were dead wrong. And all that ad-libbing had given me a greater sense of comfort with the camera and less fear about going off-script. I'd started *GMA* wanting to be myself, and at *Global National*, I was finally able to do that, on air and off.

Shortly after we launched, one of my roommates from university casually mentioned that he was glad I was back in a serious news role. Ken Bacchus was best man at my wedding and the friend who introduced me to the insanity of camping near the tire-warming track at drag races where, at hang-over-busting volume, drivers spin their tires with the brakes on. "Never liked you on those other shows," he said, in an offhand way. "Which ones?" I asked. Ken replied, "The morning and noon shows. Made you look like a wimp." It was like being told I'd been walking around for years with a huge piece of spinach in my teeth. I decided to focus on the underlying message: Be yourself. The camera doesn't lie.

In only a few years, we became the most-watched newscast in the country. Professional success changed a lot about me. Anxiety and stress took up much less mental real estate. I felt both more in control of my own life and more generous towards others; I relished the professional growth of our staff and enjoyed mentoring them then watching them soar, solo. And I came to love that adrenaline-fuelled moment after the newscast animation ran out, when I could tell more than a million people what had happened that day.

Even better, though, by six o'clock the newscast was completely over, and for the first time in my professional life, I had my evenings free. I'd finally manoeuvred to a place where work still dominated, but my family occupied a protected space. Best of all, we weren't spending that time shuttling from one medical appointment to the next. Shortly after we'd moved to Vancouver, Cathy had had another MRI, which revealed that there had been no significant changes to the lesions on her brain over the past few years. Her new neurologist believed she'd been misdiagnosed and that she didn't have MS after all. Cathy still tired easily, but the universe had smiled on us. If there are words adequate to describe our relief and joy, I don't know them.

For me, there was more cause for relief: I realized I'd had a more positive influence on my kids than I'd thought. I'd insisted they get jobs during the summer months at the cottage; even when the work was menial, both of them cared, tremendously, about doing it to the best of their ability. I was proud of their work ethic, and felt they'd learned something from watching me.

I wanted to be more to them than a distant role model, though. However, my initial attempts to become more involved in their lives didn't go over very well. After years as a parachute dad, dropping in to lay down the law then taking off again, I didn't have a lot of credibility. We had to get to know each other better.

It was easier with Erica. Whereas Alex was closed off, shying away or stiffening when I tried to put an arm around his shoulder, Erica was cuddly and affectionate. She was younger, of course, but I'd also parented her in an entirely different way. I'd had no preconceived notions about what a girl's life should be like, so I'd been better able to stand back and watch her personality emerge, rather than trying to mould her. I hadn't expected her to be good at all the things I'd wished I was good at as a child. My main expectation was that she not hide or shortchange her impressive intellect.

Nevertheless, when Erica was fourteen, Cathy had to point out to me that my words carried tremendous weight with our daughter, and I needed to choose them a little more carefully. At her new school, Erica had fallen in with a drama-infused pack of girls who alternately clung to her, then slammed her, which, over time, sliced away at her self-confidence. She hated conflict and just wanted everyone to get along, so instead of defending herself, she internalized the negativity. She was very hard on herself—too hard—so even a hint of disappointment from me when, say, she didn't study for a test, crushed her. I learned to focus on encouragement and praise, trying to help her strengthen her emotional boundaries so that when a friend crossed a line, she could protect herself accordingly. I started to feel good about myself as a parent, for the first time.

I was making less progress with Alex. True, he'd let me introduce him to martial arts, and I think he surprised himself with his own strength, agility and fighting spirit. He discovered he could be tough, and asked me to help him get started weightlifting, too. I was relieved that the bullying seemed to have stopped, and he had a group of friends, even a girlfriend. But at home, and especially with me, he'd become withdrawn and angry—why, I didn't know. I couldn't get him talking, either. Most of the time he was home, he was in his room, on his computer.

Thinking a father-son trip might be a bonding experience, I took Alex to Japan. He had a passion for Japanese culture, so I figured this was a chance for him to take the lead. I hoped he'd let me in a little, let me see what was going on in his head. It didn't happen. He remained a puzzle, full of contradictions: at home, he'd immersed himself in all things Japanese but in Japan he insisted on eating at Wendy's. Normally wilful and stubborn, there he seemed tentative, melancholy. We were sharing tiny hotel rooms, yet instead of familiarity this seemed to breed formality, on Alex's part. Had I become the stranger in my son's life that my own father had been in mine?

I remember thinking, on that trip, "Maybe it's just too late." Maybe the gap between us had widened to the point where it was no longer possible to close. But I wasn't going to stop trying.

Thanksgiving, 2004. Alex walked into the kitchen, shoulders slouched, refusing to look at me. Cathy, Erica and I were babbling away, but he sat down on a stool at the kitchen counter and said nothing. He didn't seem to be listening. But he didn't vanish to his room, either, as had become his habit.

By that point I'd learned that asking teenagers "What's wrong?" doesn't get you anywhere. They're tough interview subjects. You need to draw them out. So I asked Alex what book was he reading for English, that sort of thing—but he responded with halting monosyllables. Well, at least they weren't sullen, angry monosyllables. I decided not to push.

When we sat down at the table, Alex finally said, "If you have the time, I'd like to have a family meeting after dinner." Asking for a family meeting was basically code to brace for impending trauma. It was never "Good news everyone, I won the lottery!" It was "We're moving again" or "Mom is sick." And Cathy and I had always been the ones to call these meetings. Alex was clearly nervous. His hands were trembling slightly, and he still wouldn't look me in the eye. Was it drugs? Bullies? Oh God. Was his girlfriend pregnant? As conversation limped around the unnamed elephant on the table, I tried to calculate the correct response to each crisis. I wanted to get out in front of this thing, whatever it was.

Finally dinner was over and we moved to the TV room, where Erica sat down on the couch beside Alex, and Cathy took the seat facing them. The kids seemed to be a team, but Erica's demeanour was completely different than her brother's: calm, lighthearted, even. Strange. In what I hoped was my best, soothing interviewer voice, I asked, "Alex, what would you like to talk about?"

The emotional weather in the room changed immediately. Alex hugged his knees to his chest, and suddenly he was crying. A few moments of fraught silence passed. I needed to know what was going on. Now. Alex seemed to be holding himself so tightly because he was afraid of blowing apart; I thought the threat must be inside him, not something that was being done to him.

Could he be gay?

Why did I think that? Well, I'd wondered, off and on, for some time. Not because of the way Alex looked or acted, but because he had always set himself apart and had difficulty getting along with boys. When we were still living in Summit and he was being bullied, Cathy and I had taken him to a psychologist, hoping that therapy might help him cope. At one point the therapist spoke to us privately about the challenges facing a sensitive boy in our culture, and I remember saying, "Maybe Alex will grow up and be gay." I'm not sure I would have floated the idea if I hadn't thought the therapist himself was gay. He asked how I'd feel about that, and I said, "I'd just hope Alex would be all right and safe." During the intervening years the thought had returned to me occasionally, most recently in Japan. One day, I'd suggested he go wander around by himself for a bit. As he ambled off, I noticed how thrilled Japanese girls were when this blond boy walked past—and noticed also that he seemed to be entirely unaware of their interest. Sure, he had a girlfriend, but . . . Was he gay? It wasn't a raging debate in my head. It was just a question mark. I'd been certain of only one thing: I sure as hell shouldn't come right out and ask. If I was wrong, how could our relationship ever come back from that?

But now, seeing my son curled up in a fetal position, weeping, I wanted to ease his burden. If he only had to say one word, "yes," maybe it would help him start talking. I remember thinking to myself, "You'd better be right," and then I asked.

"Alex, does it have something to do with your sexuality?"

A wail came from deep inside him, a primal and barely human sound I'd heard only once before, in a refugee camp in Kosovo. You'd hear it late at night, this wave of sorrow and loss passing from one tent to the next.

Hearing that same sound coming from my child was terrible, and I lunged towards him, hugging him tighter than I ever had. He tried to break loose, furious, but I wouldn't let go. I thought that if he didn't feel my love and support now, in the most vulnerable moment of his life, he might doubt me forever.

And there was something else: I needed to hold on to him for my own reasons, to express the intense rush of relief I was experiencing. I'd been imagining he was going to tell us something catastrophic. But being gay? That was no big deal. We could all cope with that, no problem. I told Alex how much I loved him, how proud I was of him, how I would never let him go. He struggled a little longer, then gave up. I couldn't tell if he'd just resigned himself to being hugged, but it seemed like a good sign, a sign that we were starting a new chapter. He was going to let me in.

The next day we had a session with a professional photographer, scheduled months earlier; we wanted to give my parents and Cathy's father a family portrait as a Christmas gift. In the morning, Cathy, Alex and Erica wanted to cancel, but I insisted we go. If we didn't, I thought, Alex might view it as evidence that we no longer wanted him in the picture. Literally. But all of us were a little raw and uncertain. We got through the session, half-heartedly, and one of the photos still hangs on the wall at our cottage, a reminder of that strained moment in the life of our family. Erica, Cathy and I are laughing, apparently genuinely, while Alex is off to one side, half-smiling and separate, his left arm barely resting on my shoulder. You can tell he's trying, but a fault line has opened between us.

I'd expected that once relieved of the burden of his secret, Alex would feel liberated. Euphoric, even. Instead, he was dark, guarded, distant—but only with me. I couldn't figure it out. I'd told him I loved him and accepted him, yet he seemed angry at me. There was a new dynamic in our relationship: I was under surveillance. Alex was constantly studying me, waiting for me to say or do the wrong thing. Every word I spoke, every gesture I made, felt self-conscious. Our conversations were stilted, carefully focused on mundane details. For the first time, I didn't feel like myself around my son.

Cathy wasn't having the same difficulty, although she'd been the most surprised of all of us by Alex's announcement. Interestingly, given how close they were, she'd had no idea he was gay, though once, after our Japan trip, I'd raised the topic. Erica, it turned out, had already known; Alex had confided in her a few days before Thanksgiving. The three of them seemed to segue effortlessly to the new normal. The night Alex came out, they were already joking and laughing about Cathy's initial confusion. She has difficulty hearing in one ear, and when I'd grabbed Alex and held him tight, Cathy had asked, alarmed, "What's going on? What did he say?" Whereupon Erica had leaned forward and bellowed at the top of her lungs, "He said he's GAY!" Even Alex, whose eyes were still red from crying, smiled.

Subsequently, though Cathy wasn't walking on eggshells with Alex the way I was, she was, like me, worrying about him. Depression, isolation, harassment, discrimination, AIDS, sexual exploitation, physical danger—we'd never been concerned about any of these things when we'd assumed Alex was straight. Now we wanted to protect him, but weren't sure how. We didn't know any families with openly gay kids, and we could count the number of close, openly gay friends we had on one hand. One finger, actually: a journalist we'd been friends with since the 1980s. We really didn't know a thing about how to parent a gay child.

But if Alex didn't have a way to meet other gay kids, we thought he might wind up connecting with guys he met online, and I suspected they'd be older, even predatory. The anonymity of the internet scared the hell out of me. Alex was naive, still a child, really. I could too easily imagine him being victimized. I didn't know his mind, but knowing he was angry, I could also imagine him taking it out on himself. Taking risks. Getting hurt. Hurting himself.

Cathy found Gab Youth, a gay youth group in Vancouver where he could socialize without fear, and lined up a therapist who specialized in talking to gay kids. Meanwhile, I was online, checking out sites for gay kids. A theme, on all of them, was how intolerant and rejecting fathers are. There were posts from kids who'd been kicked out of their houses by their dads, disowned, to all intents and purposes, because they were gay. I knew if I didn't acclimate quickly, it could be the undoing of my relationship with Alex. It could also be the undoing of Alex. The online research I was doing indicated that gay kids are far more likely to attempt and to commit suicide than straight kids are.

I wanted to show my son nothing but acceptance and support. I knew that sexuality is genetically determined; I also knew in my heart that homosexuality was not a defect or disease but an orientation, in the same way that being left-handed is an orientation. It was perfectly clear to me that being gay wasn't a choice Alex had made. He was suffering, and his distress upset me deeply, not least because it was obvious that it wasn't caused by his attraction to men, but by the stigma attached to that attraction. It was completely unacceptable to me that my child was experiencing anguish about an aspect of himself that he had no control over, any more than he had control over the colour of his skin.

I experienced anguish, too. He had the same right to happiness that my daughter did, but it seemed to me that life for a gay man would be more difficult and also potentially more dangerous. I feared for Alex's health, his safety, his future happiness. I feared for myself, too; maybe he'd turn toward men who could understand and empathize with him in ways I never could, and I'd lose him altogether. What could I offer him that he couldn't get elsewhere, with less awkwardness? I was afraid he'd replace me.

I was going to do everything in my power to stop that from happening. I'd encourage him to be true to himself and live by his own principles, even if I didn't understand them. I wanted him to feel as unstoppable as any other seventeen-year-old, and on some level I knew that my acceptance and support meant more to him at this point than any other man's could, no matter what Alex was saying. Or not saying.

Finally, late one night, when Alex was settling into sleep, I knocked on his bedroom door. This is how I remember our conversation.

"Alex, we're drifting apart and I need it to stop. We haven't really connected since you came out. Can I say a few things?"

"Sure." Warily, braced for idiocy.

"I have a lot to learn and I hope you'll teach me. But I still have a lot to teach you, too. You may not think so, but I can be a resource to you."

"How?" Skeptically, now certain idiocy is imminent.

"Well, in relationships, for example. I love your mom and I've grown up with women. But I would never pretend to understand them fully. But guys? I *get* guys. I can help you there."

He laughed. I exhaled.

It was the beginning of us figuring out a role for me in Alex's new life as a gay man. Yet as weeks turned into months, Alex constantly tested me. Could he shock me? Drive me away? At the time, I felt anger must be motivating these tests, but now, I think Alex was actually looking for guidance. He wanted me to help him accept himself.

I'll never forget coming home with Cathy after a dinner out early in 2005. Surprise: Alex was already home, with a boyfriend. I'd known he was seeing someone, his first real relationship, but I hadn't expected to meet the young man so quickly and I was caught off guard. Cathy and I walked through the door and there were Alex and Jack, their arms twined round one another. It was different than any bro-to-bro hug I'd seen. Lingering, sensual, determined. Both of them had big grins on their faces but Alex's eyes were trained on me, coolly scanning for any twinge of discomfort. I remember coaching myself to smile broadly, and I mumbled something encouraging like, "You guys look cute together!" And then, before we had a chance to take our coats off, Alex kissed Jack, beard on beard. Also lingering, sensual, determined.

Okay then.

Smiling robotically, I headed for the kitchen. Alex and Jack followed, and sat at the counter. I asked Jack a few questions about his schooling and family, and he answered confidently and politely, but I was distracted by my own stream of consciousness: "This is what a dad's supposed to do: size the guy up, ensure he's not an asshole. Right?" My head was spinning. Just months before, Alex's girlfriend had been sitting at our kitchen counter.

Alex had had time to get used to the knowledge that he was gay. I had not, but no extensions would be granted. What soon became clear to me was that I was just fine with homosexuality—as long as it wasn't in my face. I'd never felt comfortable watching two guys kiss on a movie screen, much less in my own living room.

But our home had to be a safe place for Alex, who faced dangers that even his younger sister didn't. The mere sight of two boys together can provoke gay-bashers. For Alex, who was still not entirely out at school, there was also the risk of being outed on social media. There were very few places where he could act like a normal, hormonal teenager. Cathy and I decided he had to be able to do that at home where at least we'd know he was safe. That was worth occasionally having to lie in bed trying to forget what was under way downstairs—whether it was Alex or, later, Erica. It doesn't matter if they're gay or straight. You don't want to think too much about your kids having sex, period.

Bringing Jack home seemed like a breakthrough. Alex was in love, and wanted to share that with us. Even with me. He was a different person than he had been six months earlier. And so was I, at least in relation to him. The more assured he became, the more tentative I was as a father. The power balance between us, always heavily weighted toward my end, had shifted. I tried to focus on the positive: Alex wouldn't test me if he didn't care what I thought. He still wanted to be connected, but he was, like any man, trying to define the terms of engagement.

After a week-long family vacation in Mexico where Alex missed his boyfriend more than he enjoyed his time away, we were greeted at the airport arrivals level by Jack himself. We piled into an airport limo and headed home, with the boys across from me, Cathy and Erica. Kissing passionately. Non-stop. We had nowhere else to look except the rearview mirror, where the driver was shooting us disbelieving, disgusted glances. I wanted to tell the boys to cut it out, just as I would have told Erica and a boyfriend who'd put on such a display, but I was afraid Alex would interpret this as a rejection of same-sex kissing, not simply kissing. So I said nothing. I'd gone from being the disciplinarian in the family to the dad who couldn't say no.

Not long afterwards, this relationship crashed and burned, and Jack showed up at our door, threatening to jump off a bridge if Alex wouldn't take him back. I wound up driving him home, reminding him of all he had to live for, while Alex hid in his room and Cathy got on the phone to Jack's mother, to tell her what was going on. "See?" I wanted to say to Alex. "You still need my protection."

Shortly thereafter, he embarked on another serious relationship, with a guy who was a few years older. Ken had experienced far more rejection than Alex, and he was angry about it. He was a provocateur, and Alex was very taken with him. Alex was sweet and caring, but impressionable; the more time he spent with Ken, the angrier and edgier he became. To me Ken seemed like Rasputin, the Russian peasant who held a mystical sway over Tsarina Alexandra. I didn't like the guy, and it was clear the feeling was mutual. I was better at concealing it, though. Game face.

The summer after Alex's senior year, Ken came from Vancouver to spend a week with us at the cottage. One hot, hazy Saturday, he and Alex swam out to the raft that floats in front of our cottage, pulled themselves out of the water and proceeded to make out. Theatrically, with much pelvis-grinding on Ken's part. I knew my son: this performance was not his idea. The raft was crawling with dock spiders. He hadn't swum out there in years.

Cathy and I could see everything clearly from our kitchen, which meant that everyone else in the dozen or so other cottages ringing the bay could also see everything clearly. Before that moment, no one outside our immediate family had known Alex was gay. I hadn't had a chance to talk to my father yet, and in fact had been putting it off. My dad had become a churchgoer and Lorraine, his second wife, was a devout Catholic. I wasn't certain they'd be accepting, but now, I felt I had to tell them. Immediately. Their cottage is just a few bays over from ours, and they were friends with our closest neighbours. I didn't want them to hear through the grapevine that Alex had a boyfriend. I felt I owed it to them to tell them, but even more, I owed it to Alex. I wanted to shield him from the hurt of their disapproval and possibly even rejection. I hoped that with some time, they'd come around and see that Alex was still the grandson they'd always known and loved.

I ran down to the boat, Cathy close behind. In my view we were on deadline: any minute now, our neighbours might pick up the phone and call my dad. Cathy didn't feel the same sense of urgency, but she's always a good companion in a crisis, taking some of the edge off my anxiety and my need to start a conversation too directly, with the headline. We untied our powerboat from the dock cleats, trolled past Alex and Ken on the raft—it was intermission, apparently; they weren't even holding hands—and then I opened the throttle and tore across the lake, full speed, to my dad's place.

An unannounced visit was unusual, but my dad and Lorraine took it in stride, offering us a drink before we settled into the Adirondack chairs circling his firepit. After a few minutes of small talk, I got to the point: "We have something to tell you about Alex. A few months ago he told us he was gay."

They blinked and didn't say anything for what felt like a minute. Then it was, "Is he sure? How does he know?" I gave what became my stock answer: "Oh, he's sure. He knows he likes boys, not girls." I realized, as I said those words, that I'd turned a corner. I no longer cared about my dad's approval. If he chose to judge me for having raised a gay son, it wouldn't bother me. And if he chose not to accept Alex, our relationship would be over.

I felt something I'd never felt before with my dad: strong. Sure of myself. In that moment I realized, in a visceral way, how hard it must have been for Alex to tell me he was gay. Ever since he had, I'd been thinking of all the ways he might be victimized, and how much more difficult his life would be from now on, but he'd already proved his courage in a way I couldn't imagine doing at seventeen. Only in my forties did I know myself well enough to insist on living by my own policies. Alex was already well on his way to being his own man. I wanted to help him get there, to be the father he deserved.

As it happened, my father and Lorraine surprised me. They never stopped loving Alex, and however much they may have wrestled privately, they've only ever shown him acceptance. I'm proud of my dad for that, and that day, I was grateful for his calm, measured reaction.

But there was only one man's approval I really cared about anymore: my son's.

CHAPTER TWELVE

PROOFS

THE SUMMER BEFORE SENIOR YEAR, while I was still at our cottage, I heard a startling piece of gossip: back in Vancouver, my friend Holly had come out at a party, telling everyone in our circle that she was bisexual. She lived in a beautiful little village nestled in a valley, and I went to see her there as soon as I got home. Sitting by the harbour, watching ferries heading out to the islands off the coast, we talked for hours. I told her I thought I might be gay, and peppered her with questions: How had she known for sure, had she actually done anything sexual with another girl, did she think anyone else we knew was gay? There was the guy at school who danced like Beyoncé and lived to shop for shoes, of course, but he was so effeminate I felt I had nothing in common with him. Holly was understanding and also hilarious, able to knock me out of my dark mood, at least for an afternoon. We were instantly, deeply, bonded.

But unlike her, I didn't want to be out and proud. I didn't want to be gay, period. To me, it seemed like having a birth defect, something disfiguring that would set me apart from the rest of society and make my life more difficult. I still held out some hope that maybe I wasn't. I hadn't even kissed a guy—maybe it would leave me cold, the way kissing a girl had. Thinking about kissing a guy, however, didn't leave me cold. Unfortunately.

By the time school started again, I was waking up every day feeling depressed that I was stuck in this situation, not knowing who I really was. Some days, I felt I'd rather die than have to find out; other days, I was just so sick of the uncertainty and bored with my own waffling that I felt it would be better to know for sure, even if my worst fears about myself turned out to be true.

In the end, the need for certainty won out. Whereas before I'd avoided gay porn, fearing what it might stir up, now my mindset was scientific: I was conducting an investigation into my own sexuality. Even so, the first couple of times I logged on to my computer for this purpose I was so petrified I began trembling and quickly turned the computer off, instead. Eventually, my curiosity bested my shame. My tastes turned out to be vanilla, given the mind-boggling variety that was on offer, but that was no consolation. Watching two guys together was unnatural, perverted. Electrifying.

My proudest accomplishment during this time was that I finally did the right thing and broke up with Karen. My first attempt was pathetic, involving both the telephone and the line "It isn't you, it's me." My follow-up was better: we met up in person and I told her I thought I might be gay. She didn't argue. I'm sure it helped her make sense of what had been going on, and not going on, between us. We vowed to stay friends forever, and we kept our pledge about as long as seventeen-year-olds usually do when one party feels wronged and the other feels guilty.

I also confided in two other carefully chosen friends, both girls. But unlike Holly, who enjoyed the shock factor of talking openly about her sexuality, I was apologetic and tentative. It was always, "I *think* I *might* be gay" followed by, "Don't tell anyone." No one reacted badly. In fact, my friends seemed excited that our clique's soap opera had a new storyline. Overnight, I'd been recast as the tortured guy with a secret, and they circled the wagons protectively. It felt good to be embraced rather than rejected, even if what they were really embracing was another excuse for drama and urgent, whispered conversations. No one but Holly understood how afraid I was of my attraction to men.

I started spending hours in my bedroom, with the door locked, but I wasn't doing what you might think. I needed to reach out, to feel less isolated. Chat rooms were an important first step. My parents would have freaked if they'd known what I was up to. They'd cautioned Erica and me repeatedly about the dark perversions and predators lurking on the internet. But I found that gay chat rooms were full of all sorts of people. Of course there were a lot of guys who were there for just one thing, and their posts always began with a brisk demand: ASL. Age? Sex? Location? But there were also men who really were there to chat. Once I confessed that I wasn't out of the closet and wasn't even sure I should be, they'd segue quickly into mentor mode, providing brotherly advice.

The moment anyone suggested meeting up in the real world, however, I'd close the browser, heart pounding. I had my mother's talent for imagining catastrophe. The guy could be a gay-baiter, a serial killer. What if he tried to hurt me? Or out me? What if he had an STD?

An in-person encounter with someone I'd met online was out of the question, but I felt I had to test what was still just a hypothesis. I had only one other way to find a guy like me: gaydar, which I'd liken to an animal's heightened senses while hunting. Many gay guys, especially teens who aren't out, aren't at all effeminate; most heterosexuals would assume them to be straight. We find one another through subtle body language, through a gaze that's held a fraction of a second longer than normal.

At seventeen, my gaydar wasn't well developed, but it was accurate enough to lead me to suspect that one of the guys on the periphery of my circle of friends was not entirely straight. Along with the sexually charged jokes he cracked every now and again, there was just something slightly, subtly, different about him. One night, chatting on MSN, I decided to take a step forward. Online, where I didn't have to look in his eyes, I felt safer; I was inclined to trust him because he was older—in college already— and didn't live in Vancouver anymore. No one had to find out.

Gingerly, I told him I wasn't sure I'd had the right feelings about Karen, and that I'd even found myself thinking about guys occasionally. He told me it was perfectly normal to be curious, and egged me on to tell him more. It was the first time I'd ever communicated my uncertainty to a guy I actually knew, and the conversation was so important to me that I saved it, encrypted on my hard drive. It's not great literature, but I'll include a portion of it here, changing only the screen names in order to protect his privacy. I'll call him Andrew.

Andrew: sometimes u wanna have sex with a guy but fall in love with a girl, sometimes vice versa, sometimes u get gay fantasies but u r straight and sometimes its the other way around

Alex: I know it is confusing

u might love having sex with a guy but at the same time u might find gayness disgusting and kissing even worse

thats true.

so dont worry about it too much. just do what feels right . . . remember . . . no one will know what's on your mind so u can think of anything u want and enjoy it

thats true. wow, u r really helpful.

glad i can help. and if u ever get horny u can come see me in _____ (or when im in vancouver)

(sarcasm?)

nah . . .

ok man. I'll put it on my to do list.

so you do wanna do that? have sex with a guy?

only to experience and experiment.

well then i have something to look forward to when im in van

u would actually let me do something like that?

do u want to?

well in all experimentation I would. But it is just to see where my mind is wanting to go. am I freaking u out? just say so if I am.

nah. is that something u fantasize about? and u can be as open as u want with me

well, it is something I wouldn't mind trying to see if I like it. I may think it is the grossest thing, but then again I wouldn't know unless I tried. how embarrassing, u must think I'm so sick.

i don't. u will get some idea when i come to van in a few weeks

so u will help me find who I really am? b/c I'm sick of not knowing

(:

(:

I'm glad I talked rather than end my life. I think u pulled me out of this depressive slump. Letting it out makes everything so much better

man im glad i could help. what would u have done if i said
"go away u sick bastard"?

I'd be driving to the bridge.

When I logged off, I felt dazed. I'd told my secret to a guy, a quasi friend, not a stranger. And I might actually be with him. Soon.

Two weeks later, Andrew came to Vancouver. When I bumped into him with a group of people, he acted as if our online conversation had never taken place, so I didn't allude to it, either. Then I heard he'd asked my friend Emily out. Jealousy boiled up quickly. Was Emily his beard? Had he been toying with me online? Oh God. What if he told people what I'd said? What if he already had?

A lucky break: crossing paths between classes, Emily confessed she was nervous about the date. She was sixteen, Andrew was twenty-one. Was he expecting to hook up? She didn't want to go out with him alone, she decided, and asked me to come along. Fine with me. I wanted to see whether I had something to fear from him.

Date night. I arrived at the pizza place early and turning the corner, spotted a girl slumped messily on the sidewalk. Emily. She'd downed a bottle of schnapps, hoping to ease herself into a confidently sexy frame of mind. Judging by the way she was slurring her words, she'd overshot the mark by three-quarters of a bottle, at least. I pulled her up off the street and steered her inside, where, as we waited for Andrew, she slumped lower and lower in the booth.

When he arrived, he seemed unperturbed by his date's condition (barely conscious, by this point) and sat down beside me. I ordered water for Emily, who, as Andrew and I chatted, lolled back in the booth and began to snore gently. Slowly, Andrew was inching closer to me. Each time he did, I'd inch closer to the wall. I wasn't sure what was going on; our conversation wasn't charged or deep. It was just two friends catching up, while a third friend dozed drunkenly on the other side of the table. Then it happened. His hand landed on my knee. By this point I was pinned against the wall, and completely confused by the weirdness of the situation. I quickly thought up an excuse to leave, a valid one: I needed to take Emily home. "Do you mind giving me a ride, too?" Andrew asked, casually. I agreed, trying to sound just as casual.

After we got Emily safely home, I was alone with Andrew and nervous as hell. He, apparently, was not. As soon as I pulled out of her driveway he reminded me of our online chat, asking if I still had an urge to experiment. I said I did. He suggested that I pull over, then. I wasn't particularly attracted to him—he was a little full of himself, actually, and I was pretty sure I didn't even like him—but I didn't hesitate. I started looking for a place to park.

On the edge of a quiet neighbourhood, I found a wooded area and stopped the car. It was late, there was no one around, and I put on a CD I'd made. I didn't want to come off airy-fairy, so I made sure the music was masculine, no sappy pop or dance music like I might have listened to with Emily. We started talking. And talking. And talking. I was paralyzed by fear and indecision, and it was a good hour before Andrew finally unzipped his jeans in a businesslike fashion and indicated that the conversation portion of the evening was over.

To this day I'm not sure whether he was gay or bisexual, or just wanted to get off and didn't care how or with whom. His motives didn't matter to me, though, because I didn't like him. I was just using him as a litmus test of my own sexual nature. Even as I was trying to satisfy him, I was silently, clinically analyzing: "Do I like this? Which aspects?" The scene couldn't have been less romantic. There was no pretense of reciprocity, I didn't really know what I was doing and my mom's SUV was anything but ergonomic.

Nevertheless, the encounter was charged and exciting in a way it never had been with Karen. I didn't get any fulfillment, sexually, but the animal instincts that took hold that night provided a definitive answer to my question about myself. And so for a few moments, driving home, I felt some degree of peace. I knew who I was.

But I wasn't ready to tell the world. I developed a vague plan to tell my parents in a year or so, once I was safely far away at university. In the meantime, I'd hide in plain sight. In some ways, it would be easy. As my father's newscast became ever more popular, I'd turned into "Kevin Newman's son" at school. I still hated living in his shadow. But it did make me—the real me, the person who was not just an appendage—less visible. Sometimes, even, to him. On weekends, when he made scrambled eggs, he'd ask whether I wanted some. I don't eat eggs. The fact that he'd never noticed struck me as emblematic of our relationship. He didn't know me well, didn't see me clearly. Thank God.

There were, however, times when he saw me too clearly. If I got a bad grade, for instance, or was late finishing an assignment, he noticed. Why hadn't I worked harder? His disapproval carried extra weight with me because his opinion mattered so much to everyone else. Shame cuts deeper when the person looking down on you is someone everyone else looks up to.

I couldn't imagine a failure that would disappoint him more than failing to be masculine. I was already deficient in that regard—too sensitive and emotional, too shy. When he learned that I was attracted to guys, it would be the last straw. He'd be dismayed and quietly disgusted, too. Maybe having a gay son would be so embarrassing to him, both personally and professionally, that he'd want me to stay in the closet. Or maybe he'd kick me out of the house and cut me off financially. Or give me money so I'd go away.

I was more sure of my mother, certain at least that she would always love me, but maybe she wouldn't want the same kind of closeness we'd always had. Maybe she'd be embarrassed about me, too. As a pre-emptive strike, I pulled away from both of them, withdrawing behind a wall of silence. At the kitchen table in the morning, I strategically arranged cereal boxes around my bowl to keep Erica out, too. I started trying to train myself to think as though I didn't have a family, as though I was totally alone in the world. I felt lonely, but thought I deserved to be.

My attraction to men was natural and instinctive, something I couldn't control any more than I could control my need for food. But if I could have pushed a button and changed myself, I would have. In a heartbeat. Maybe if I'd fallen madly in love with a guy, I would have felt happier, and I definitely would have felt less isolated. But though Andrew and I had continued our furtive, one-sided encounters for a week, there was no love lost between us. I liked him quite a bit less as a person than I'd liked Karen, and the fact that he'd warned me not to tell anyone about us didn't exactly inspire pride.

The internal pressure of my secret started to feel unbearable, and soon there was external pressure, too. I'd told Holly about Andrew, and she'd told someone else. Andrew sent me a text that scared the bejesus out of me, threatening to hunt me down and hurt me if I'd talked, and at about the same time, one of the friends I'd used as a sounding board made some offhand comments about outing me at school. Her betrayal cut me to the core and also induced panic. I couldn't tell if she was just being casually cruel, or if she seriously intended to tell everyone; distracted by paranoia, I could barely focus on schoolwork or much of anything else. *Who knows? Why did that girl look at me in the cafeteria and laugh? Will that guy over there beat me up? Is Andrew going to turn up with an entourage and break both my legs?*

Fearing that I was about to be outed changed my calculations about telling my family. I couldn't wait until I was at university. I didn't want them to hear I was gay from anyone else, not least because I wanted to see their faces in that first, unguarded moment, to see what they really thought of me.

I briefly considered telling my mother, alone, but there was no point. My parents weren't capable of keeping secrets from each other. So I went to Erica first. She was non-threatening—the roof over my head didn't depend on her—and because she was three years younger, I figured she was less likely to judge me. This would be a dry run for the real test: telling my parents.

My sister went to a private school and one day, I picked her up after school. This was not a regular occurrence and as she climbed into the car, I could tell she was surprised, but I didn't volunteer an explanation. We drove along in silence, Erica staring out the window and plucking absentmindedly at her kilt, while I tried to think of how to begin. Finally I pulled over to the side of the road and started babbling: a girl at school knew something about me, a secret, and she was going to tell everyone and I didn't know what to do, how to stop her. Erica said, "Well, what's the secret? I'm sure it can't be that bad." And then I just lost it, crying harder than I ever had in my life, the kind of crying where you're breathing raggedly and can only gasp out a few words at a time. Like, "I think I'm gay."

Erica was unfazed, kind. She patted my shoulder and told me not to worry, everything would be okay, our parents would understand, no one would think any differently of me. I realized I'd wanted her to say, "I'll help you find help" or "I know some gay people, let's talk to them" or "Here's how to tell Mom and Dad." Crazy expectations. I mean, Erica is very smart but she was fourteen years old. She didn't know how to bridge the isolation and loneliness I felt, and I'm sure she was stunned to see me in a state of emotional distress. She had no idea what I felt, or why. For her, being gay was part of everyday life, very *Will & Grace*. But for me, it meant being a person I did not want to be. In some strange way, her breezy acceptance made me feel even more lonely. Another person's acceptance didn't make it any easier for me to accept myself.

But I did hope she was right about our parents' reaction. Despite the fact that I was now convinced that Andrew was having me followed, I decided to wait until Thanksgiving to tell them. It was one night when everyone would be home. But Thanksgiving dinner time came, everyone gathered, and . . . I just couldn't do it. I stalled, asking for a family meeting afterwards, which turns out to be an excellent way to introduce a sense of foreboding to a festive occasion. I remember thinking, as we passed the turkey and stuffing, that our family would never be the same again after this meal. I wasn't worried about Erica— she knew what I was going to say, and I could feel her silent, steady support. But I remembered the happy look on my mom's face when she'd said that she could picture me married to a Japanese girl, and remembered, too, the way my dad had flinched and changed the channel when we were watching TV and two men were about to kiss. My mother would probably accept me eventually, but my father was a public figure, and I could become a source of shame. Rather than defend me or deny that he was ashamed, it might be easier just to forget all about me.

As it happened, though, I never got to tell my family. We retreated to the TV room after dinner and I was summoning the strength to declare myself when my dad beat me to it, asking, "Does this have something to do with your sexuality?" Apparently, my father *did* know me. All along, when I thought I'd been passing, he'd known what I really was—had everyone else, too? Was I so obviously gay? I didn't feel relieved but humiliated. Exposed. There was anger, too: my father had put himself at the centre of my crisis, and was taking on the weight of it. He was anchoring my coming-out speech, for God's sake, taking the words right out of my mouth, as though I wasn't strong enough to say them myself. He held me, tightly, and I discovered that all those hours in the garage and in the martial arts studio had not paid off. I couldn't break free. He was so much stronger than I was, still.

We never talked about that family meeting afterwards, but the more I thought about it, the more resentful and suspicious I became. My father had told me he loved me just the same and supported me one hundred percent. So what? I'd seen him turn his personality on and off, and suspected that was what he was doing now: play-acting. Pretending to be tolerant. Why, if he'd suspected I was gay, hadn't he ever said anything gay-positive, the way my mother had? Why couldn't he watch two men together on TV? I knew how he really felt about gay guys: revolted. I didn't accept that he was accepting. It seemed like a trick.

My mother was very surprised that I was gay, but there was no duality to her personality, as far as I could tell. And she swung into action right away, running out to get a DVD of the first season of *Queer as Folk*. Someone had told her it was essentially a soap opera, only with gay characters, and she thought it would be a great way for both of us to get to know more about gay life. We settled down on the couch, pressed "play" and suddenly we were watching a very raunchy, graphic sex scene between a young guy and an older man. My mom froze, embarrassed to her core, and I could tell she didn't know whether to stay or go. Then she did exactly the right thing: she burst out laughing at the absurdity of the situation, then I started laughing, and we peeled through that first season together. I knew she wasn't going to turn away from whatever I might become, even if she wasn't entirely comfortable with it. She found me a youth group to go to and I remember my parents driving me to the skating rink where this group was having a party. It was a surreal reprise of being dropped off at kindergarten, and I was actually like a little kid, entering this new world of gay people for the first time. But in the end, I didn't feel I had much in common with the other kids. Most of them had been cast off by their families and were now basically homeless. Getting to know them made me wonder about my own security: Would my parents kick me out, too? Was there a limit to their acceptance?

For the next year, I tested them. A lot of people come roaring out of the closet, and throw themselves into the gay club scene, or drugs and alcohol, or a wild level of promiscuity. I threw myself into relationships, instead. It turned out that I didn't have many wild oats to sow, or the courage to sow them. I just didn't have the stomach for anonymous, potentially dangerous encounters. My mother had instilled a fear of STDs and psycho killers; my father had instilled a yearning for romance and commitment. Online I was able to feign a degree of unbridled lust, but in real life I was neurotic about safety and hungry for approval. And love.

I wanted a boyfriend, and within weeks of coming out to my parents, I was on dating sites, looking for one. When I found a promising candidate, I'd show his profile to my mother, partly to ease her anxiety and partly to get her opinion. When I went on my first date with Jack, my first boyfriend, she was excited for me; when I brought him home, she took photos of us, including one of us kissing. I wasn't sure whether she did stuff like this because she didn't want to lose her baby boy, or what. So I pushed the envelope with her, and my father, to see if I could make their true colours show. They could handle kissing—but what if Jack slept over? What if I took him to the prom?

My mother passed all these tests. In fact, when I first started dating Jack she dragged me to the drugstore and snapped up every box of non-latex condoms on the shelf—no exaggeration—possibly leaving the cashier with the impression that I was a budding porn star. My mom's attitude was, "You're allergic to latex, let's stock up!"

My father seemed to endorse the relationship, too, but I still didn't believe he really meant it. I remember breaking down when my mom told me that Gallo had once mentioned to my aunt that she wondered if I was gay. My dad's suspicions had made me angry, because I thought his were laced with disgust, but Gallo had had gay friends and I knew she would have accepted me completely. I hadn't been able to cry when she died but I made up for it now, devastated all over again because I felt she'd died without really knowing me.

As an adult, I can see how ridiculous that is. My grandmother did know me; being gay is just one aspect of my identity. But immediately after coming out, I was still figuring that out. Gallo was the only person I loved who, given the option to push a button to turn me straight, absolutely would not have pushed it—the way I would have, and my parents probably would have, too. She would have believed something I did not, at seventeen: that I was actually better off gay, because now I could be myself.

I needed someone to do more than hold up a poster at the Pride Parade and tolerate my sexuality. I needed it to be celebrated, precisely because I wasn't able to celebrate it myself. Which explains my second serious boyfriend, Ken, who wasn't really out and proud so much as he was out and belligerent. He was the kind of person who likes to try to get a rise out of people so he can rail against intolerance. He was big on public displays of affection, which struck me as bold and passionate, though eventually I realized that the emphasis was on the public display rather than the affection. I was just a prop in his drama.

I did learn something from him, though. Once we were on the bus, holding hands, and a woman hissed as she got off that we were disgusting. Ken looked right at her and said, very deliberately, "Fuck you." I echoed the sentiment, and felt good about rising up to fight the homophobia I sensed was bubbling just below the surface of everyday life. Even, I thought, in my own home.

Ken alarmed my father, and I enjoyed that. I liked having the power, for a change, even if it was borrowed power. I wanted my father to approve of me, and I felt he never would. So why not piss him off a little, instead? My idea of a good son was someone a father was proud of, someone who didn't get into trouble. I'd been the good kid to a fault. Didn't drink, or take drugs, or break the rules. But in my father's eyes, being a good son seemed to boil down to a single characteristic: being masculine. That's what he'd always been trying to force me to be, with the sports and Scouting, and that seemed to be the essence, in his mind, of what our bond should revolve around, but never had. To him, masculinity meant being physically and emotionally tough, confident, knowledgeable, a leader. To me, it seemed like something you were born with. Or not. Guys on the rugby team were masculine; guys in the artsy crowd, who were sensitive and emotional, were not. My dad was masculine. I was not. And never could be, now that I was gay.

CHAPTER THIRTEEN

ALL OUT

KEVIN

AFTER FIVE YEARS of more hard work than any of us had imagined, *Global National* had become the most-watched newscast in Canada and a profit centre for the network. Winning felt good. Very good.

It was also addictive. I didn't want to lose ever again, so I pushed. Sometimes too hard. But as advertising markets softened, it became clear that despite our success, our owners would never grant us a large enough infusion of cash to boost our broadcast budget beyond its underfunded start-up level. Our national team members weren't earning what they should have; technical problems continually bedevilled our broadcasts. I started to fray, too, and was short-tempered at times, especially when the creative freedom that had made it all seem worthwhile started to evaporate. A new management team hired an American news consultant who imported many of the conventions of network news I had struggled to avoid. I was left out of staffing and major editorial decisions and was later broadsided when a major advertiser was promised coverage I felt compromised the integrity of the newscast. My bosses now seemed to want an anchor who would simply read, not lead. By 2006, I was increasingly unhappy.

Then as luck would have it, I met two firefighters at a charity function who were raising money and rounding up supplies for an impoverished village in Nicaragua. They invited me to go there with them, to help out—and threw in the added lure that in our downtime, I could learn to surf. Ten days far away from office politics sounded like a fine idea, and the reality was even better. Travel encourages easy intimacy and the three of us fast-forwarded to the kind of bond that, under normal circumstances, takes a very long time to achieve. On an undeveloped beach where the gentle surf provides a consistently perfect break for beginning surfers like me, we stayed in huts that looked like something out of *Gilligan's Island*. The camp had been built by another Canadian, Don Montgomery, a former teacher and rugby coach, who insisted that all guests help out in nearby Jiquilillio. We spent a few days attempting to dig a well by hand at the village school, giving up only when it became clear there was no water table to hit. We also visited local hospitals to see what equipment was needed, so we could try to line it up back home; we met with soup kitchen workers supporting the community of people who subsisted by scavenging in the region's dump. Purposeful physical labour, good company, beer on the beach and hammock-sleeping took me to a level of relaxation I hadn't known in many years.

The surf camp had no mirrors and when, on our last night, we checked into a hotel near the airport, I was startled by my reflection in the bathroom mirror. I'd forgotten what I looked like when I was truly happy.

Back at work, I was drawn into increasingly frequent clashes over the content of the newscast and realized I had to make a choice: keep fighting and feel miserable, or retreat and try to be happy. It's hard for any founder to let go. When you build something up from an idea, it feels like a part of you. I was protective of our team but I couldn't control what was happening at corporate headquarters thousands of miles away in Toronto. Maybe it was time to try to care less and let *Global National* evolve on its own.

I didn't withdraw as gracefully as I would have liked. It suited my managers to portray me as a "problem anchor," and though usually I was fighting the good fight, for editorial independence, sometimes they were right. It went against the grain to care less. My motto had always been to care more.

For my entire adult life I had been using my work, and the recognition that came with it, as the main measure of my self-worth. Even as an assistant manager at McDonald's, I'd out-hustled everyone in the place, trying to stand out from the pack. If I couldn't be popular, if my divorced parents were distracted, well, at least at work I could excel.

Being a top performer brought me the attention and regard I hadn't been able to get any other way, so I kept it up. In my first job in TV, when I was in charge of making coffee, I tried to make sure it was hotter, fresher and tasted better than when anyone else made it. In my first on-air position as a sports reporter I arrived at the station at nine a.m. every day to be sure I got a good assignment and stayed past midnight to ensure the product, which aired on the late sportscast, was the best it could be.

For almost thirty years, and despite life-changing experiences like the one I had at *GMA*, I'd been treating friendships, fitness and even my family as less essential than the quest to ensure that my work stood out. It did stand out. I got noticed, and I liked that. I liked the work, too, liked witnessing history with my own eyes. In my twenties, it had been thrilling. In my thirties, my job had brought financial security. In my forties, it had allowed me to be creative and build a legacy.

Closing in on fifty, I finally understood that work is just work. It is not me. Whereas post-*GMA*, I wanted to be in control of my destiny professionally, now I mostly wanted to be happy. So, in 2010, I quit as anchor of *Global National*. The managers allowed me to say goodbye on air, then our whole team repaired to a bar where we partied hard and shared a heartfelt farewell. It was hard to leave these journalists and friends who'd believed in me and helped build the newscast. They knew me well, and had arranged the perfect parting gift: a Canadian flag that had flown on Parliament Hill, now displayed at our cottage alongside the American flag Peter Jennings gave me.

Of all the goodbyes in my career, this one was the most wrenching, and I wound up leaving the party early. Abruptly. It hurt too much. I'd been at *Global National* longer than I'd been anywhere; I felt I was stepping away not only from a newscast but from the ambition that had defined my life for three decades. Who would I be without it?

I took some time off, produced documentaries, explored the emerging digital media landscape, saw more of the kids. When they had time, that is. Alex was a creative director at an ad agency, a high flyer at twenty-six; Erica had just finished university and was working her way up at a film production company. Then I went back to work full-time in Ottawa for *W5*, CTV's respected investigative show, which proudly boasts of being the inspiration for *60 Minutes*. It was an opportunity to make the kind of lengthy features I love.

I was always looking for good stories and, in 2012, Cathy brought me one, sharing a link to a video a kid had posted on his own YouTube channel. On the screen, his shaggy hair poking out at angles under his New Jersey Devils ball cap, he had that shrugging cool demeanour of every teenage boy who's good at sports. Good-looking kid, the tall, broad-shouldered kind who plays goalie because he fills up a hockey net and isn't afraid to defend it. He was talking about his life in a voice deeper than you'd expect of a seventeen-year-old, completely at ease in front of a webcam, like everyone of his generation. But he didn't preen or spout off. He had something special: real clarity to his thinking—wisdom, even. He didn't look a thing like Alex, but something about his delivery, thoughtful yet ferocious, reminded me of my son. I watched him, wondering. *Who is this kid?*

Big93scott he called himself on his YouTube channel, but he didn't say where he lived or what his real name was. In the first three-minute video I watched, he was lamenting the death of a gay kid he'd read about in the paper, a fifteen-year-old who'd killed himself after coming out and being mercilessly bullied. Big93scott came off the way most hockey players do, tough and direct. That, he explained, was one reason he'd escaped bullying after he came out: people accepted him because "I didn't act or look or sound like anybody's preconceptions of what a gay person acts or looks or sounds like."

In the year leading up to his sixteenth birthday, he'd been posting a video every day, chronicling his own coming-out process for anyone who cared to see. That seemed breathtakingly, stupidly brave to me. Why declare you're gay online, to a bunch of strangers, before telling your friends? Wouldn't you want to control who knew something that could be used against you?

But for Big93scott, self-disclosure seemed to be the path to self-acceptance. At times he was goofy, the average above-average teenager and, at other times, bored with himself. There were also moments when he looked into the webcam from the safety of his bedroom, clearly terrified. Vulnerable. "I set the knife down on the counter. And I cried for what must have been an hour," he confided, remembering contemplating suicide at the age of thirteen. "I was so close to getting into the bathtub and cutting my wrists that day. I was so close that it scares me even today."

That hit me hard. Had Alex ever done that, felt that, before he came out? Or after? How much did I really know about what he had gone through? Now, I was sure, he was happy, living in Toronto's gay village with his boyfriend. When we went out for drinks in his area, we always seemed to bump into legions of friends. But how long had it taken for him to feel proud? Months? Years? I really didn't know.

Later that summer, Big93scott posted interviews with his parents and siblings. I was particularly struck by his older brother, Russell, a carpenter, slouched on the family sofa in baggy cargo shorts, T-shirt and ball cap. A guy's guy if ever there was one. Talking about his brother's potential boyfriends, Russell said,

"You will bring home a partner of the same sex. Will I accept him? Yes—if I like him. If I don't like him, I'll let you know. 'You have a dick of a boyfriend.'" The not-so-little brother jumped out from behind the camera for a hug, later posting this: "Without my family's acceptance I would not be making this video today. Without my family's acceptance, I would be dead." To his family, his sexuality was no big deal. To him, it had been a life-and-death matter.

I thought a coming out-story with a confident gay jock at its centre would be perfect for *W5*. In my pitch, I didn't volunteer that my own son was gay, but of course that's why I wanted to do the story. My goal wasn't just to sensitize the viewing public. I wanted to get one step closer to understanding my son.

Big93scott turned out to be Scott Heggart, an Ottawa boy who, by the time we met in late 2012, had come out to his team-mates and was visiting local high schools as an anti-bullying advocate. He was the only openly gay male playing hockey in North America, at any level. To date, no minor league player, no NHL pro, current or retired, has ever come out publicly. Scott had no role models in his sport. So he became one.

Digging into the context in which Scott Heggart came out, with a backdrop of high-profile teen suicides in my mind, was a revelation. Even today, when it seems another athlete, rock star or actress comes out every week, gay kids are still bullied to death and are far more likely to attempt and commit suicide than straight kids are. For the first time in my career, I did not want to stand by and report objectively. I wanted to advocate for every gay kid who wasn't out yet. I wanted to change the social order, so that no child ever again thought death was preferable to being gay.

Coincidentally, as I was working on the feature about the Heggarts I was also reading Douglas Brinkley's penetrating biography of Walter Cronkite (I was a tiny, no doubt forgotten, footnote in his life: one morning he startled me at three a.m., dropping into the studio with Roone Arledge, then president of ABC News, while I was co-anchoring ABC's overnight news broadcast; they looked to have been enjoying a boozy night together and were laughing uproariously, their arms slung around one another's shoulders like frat boys). I was surprised to read that in the sixties, Cronkite and *CBS Evening News* had enraged the network's Southern affiliates by openly supporting the Civil Rights Act. Cronkite believed journalists had a moral obligation to put aside their notions of neutrality and play a role in shaping Americans' acceptance of equal rights. It was the only humane course of action.

To me, that felt like permission from one of the giants of journalism to put aside my own notions of neutrality. I had come to believe gay rights are the civil rights issue of our time. I didn't want to dig up the obligatory interview with someone who'd provide "balance" by fulminating against Scott Heggart's presence in a locker room. Eight years after Alex came out, I came out, too, as the proud father of a gay son. "Watching how Scott Heggart handled his personal crisis," I told viewers, "makes me realize how brave my own son has been."

For me, that process of "coming out" as the father of a gay son has been gradual and not always easy. I rushed to tell my own parents about Alex because I wanted to protect him. If their first reactions were shock or disgust, I didn't want him to see that, or to hear any barbed comments or be asked any invasive questions. I was worried that any rejection could be the tipping point for depression, even suicidal thoughts. But my family responded better than I would have predicted. Though my mother was initially uncomfortable, her long-time partner, Andy, was unequivocally supportive of Alex, which probably helped my mom get her head around it. Like my father and his wife, they were never anything other than loving grandparents. Coming out on Alex's behalf with my family, then, was not difficult.

But coming out as the father of a gay son to people who had no first-hand relationship with Alex was a different matter. To do that, I had to defend homosexuality, not just my son's right to happiness. I've never been a homophobe. I supported gay rights and had always been perfectly comfortable working alongside gay colleagues. Live and let live, was my attitude. To each his own, etc. But these were abstract principles, and they'd never really been tested until my son tested me.

In the weeks after Alex came out, I'd felt sadness, at times, and even grief—reactions that embarrassed me so deeply that I couldn't talk about them with Cathy. My emotional responses weren't just politically incorrect, but shamefully self-involved. I felt a sense of loss, but what had I lost, really? My own narrative about the future: Alex would fall in love with a woman, they'd have kids, I'd morph into a doting grandfather. He was rewriting that story, drastically, and I had no idea how the new version would go, much less whether there would be an ending I'd consider happy.

I felt like a jerk. My son was going through a major transition. He needed me, so I had my game face on, broadcasting tolerance

and acceptance, but behind it, for many months, I was still wondering: What does my son's sexuality say about me? Did I fail as
a father? Was I not masculine enough? What will my friends
think of me?

I wasn't eager to find out. Though hateful banter has never
been a staple of my friendships, we're men of a certain age.
When we were growing up, homophobia was a perfectly accept-
able way for young guys to assert their own masculinity. I'd
experienced the sting of that a few times myself in high school,
where joining the drama club was a "faggy" thing to do. Even at
my university, which was large, acceptance was limited. The
campus gay club had had only a handful of members.

My closest buddies, my university roommates, are intelligent,
thoughtful men, not neanderthals. After Alex came out, I knew
I should tell them, but . . . I was waiting for the right time. Early
in 2005 the moment arrived, late one boozy night during our
semi-annual weekend at my cottage. High-volume debates about
politics and current events are the norm during these retreats,
so it wasn't out of the ordinary that conversation turned to
gay marriage. This was shortly after the same-sex marriage legal
victories in Canada, with made-for-TV visuals: male couples
kissing on courthouse steps, female couples posing together in
matching wedding gowns. Most of my friends agreed that some
form of civil union made sense, but a few of them were strongly
of the opinion that marriage is a church-sanctioned institution
reserved for heterosexuals. And as I remember it, everyone
resented having to witness the open displays of same-sex affection
that stations like mine were broadcasting.

I couldn't come down on them too hard. They were simply

voicing many of the thoughts I'd had myself, before I knew Alex was gay. I hesitated, knowing that if I said anything, it would kill the mood. But by telling them now, en masse, I figured I could avoid having multiple awkward conversations later. I attempted a casual approach: "Guys, by the way, my son is gay."

Suddenly everyone was silent and serious. Someone finally asked, "Is he sure?"

"He has sex with other boys. He's sure."

More awkward silence. Then, "Maybe he's just confused."

"No. He's struggled with it for years. He knows his own mind."

"How do you feel about it?" one of my friends asked.

I said, "I love Alex. I support him. But I'm still adjusting, to be honest."

A pause. "Well," someone said, "at least it's a lot easier these days."

Today, the subject rarely comes up in conversation. Old news, and if my friends have something to say about homosexuality, they probably do it when I'm not around. There's likely some "there but for the grace of God" pity, and quite possibly some residual discomfort. It's hard not to take that personally. But I understand, because homosexuality is outside my friends' comfort zone. I've secretly pitied those friends whose children have done things outside my own comfort zone, like embracing radical religion or starting families when they're young and unmarried.

Interestingly, some of the toughest, most masculine guys in my wider circle of friends have been the most open-hearted in their acceptance. I'm talking about soldiers, cops, firefighters, rugby players, men who've told me about working shoulder to shoulder in clutch circumstances with gay men, and learning to judge them not for their sexuality but for their abilities. They say they have no problem (I don't doubt that it took time) sharing showers, tents and bunks with gay colleagues, and even feel protective of them. It's human nature: the better you know someone, the easier it is to see past a label and judge him by the content of his character.

A lot of men don't get that opportunity, though. There is still social segregation between straight and gay men; you might work together in an office but rarely go out for lunch or have anything approaching a deep conversation. Most of my male friends aren't close to anyone who's gay, and therefore they can't see past homosexuality. It colours their view, as do the more aggressively sexual aspects of gay culture—frequently, the fringe is mistaken for the norm.

I understand this discomfort with the loudest, most flamboyant aspects of the culture because for a long time, I felt it myself. The year after Alex came out, we went to Pride Day in Vancouver. Cathy and I had made big posters we could hold up when Alex walked by, something that would advertise our family's pride in him. We thought it would be like any parade, with orderly floats and music, and encouraged Erica, then fourteen, to bring a friend. I was shocked, I have to admit. A group of self-professed "dykes on bikes" kicked off the event, gleefully revving their motorcycles. Topless. There was a lot of leather, guys in sparkly G-strings, someone handing out free condoms, drag queens everywhere, a marked obsession with crotches. Erica and her friend sat on the curb, eyes wide as saucers. Cathy was surprised but she bought in quickly, enjoying the wildness of the spectacle.

We waved the posters and cheered like crazy when Alex walked past. But did I feel comfortable? No, I did not.

I don't like admitting this, because it proves I wasn't the enlightened, progressive individual I'd always thought I was. And there was more proof. Long after I accepted my son's sexuality, I continued to disappoint myself. In a room of Alex's friends, I was hyper-aware they were gay and unable to get the thought out of my mind. I truly believe I'm unbiased when it comes to gender, race or religious affiliation; I experience no discomfort around people who are living with disabilities, or are visibly "different." Yet I struggled to feel and act normal when I was the only straight guy in the room. I was trying to feel pride, but what I felt was shame: not about Alex, but about myself.

Reporting Scott Heggart's story forced me to confront the conflict between what I knew intellectually to be true—a gay man is fully the equal of a straight man—and how I felt, viscerally, about homosexuality. Scott's videos helped me understand some of what Alex must have gone through, and helped me understand the tension that had simmered between us after he came out, too. He'd needed me to be even more accepting of his sexuality than he was. He'd needed reassurance from his father that it wasn't just okay to be gay, it was actually a good thing, something worth fighting for and defending. He'd needed to hear that from me because he wasn't sure of it himself.

Now, as a grown man, Alex didn't just want tolerance. He wanted my approval—not only of him, but of homosexuality itself and gay culture. Supporting him, in his eyes, meant more than standing on the sidelines making high-minded pronouncements about equal rights. He wanted me to stand right beside him, look squarely at his world, see it the way he saw it, and recognize that being gay wasn't a handicap he had to overcome. He needed me to go all out, to believe that he is actually better off because he is gay.

It wasn't enough for me to talk the talk, and tell him I accepted him and loved him. He needed me to walk the walk, too. That's what makes a man a man: having the courage of his convictions and the strength to push past fear so he can own his own life. The way Alex, and Scott Heggart, and every gay man must, in order to come out.

Bear-hugging Alex on that Thanksgiving Day in 2004, I had no idea how much I would have to evolve in order to become the father I wanted to be, to both my children. I thought my acceptance of Alex at that moment was all that mattered. But I'd underestimated the distance between us, or the ways he felt I'd failed him in the years leading up to that moment. By trying to help him be sporty, popular and all the other things I hadn't been myself, I'd made him feel inadequate. He didn't think I could possibly accept him as a gay kid because he hadn't felt I'd accepted him when I thought he was straight, either. I now know that he'd expected I might reject him altogether when he came out. This stunned me, far more than the revelation that he was gay. Forget career setbacks—this was true, catastrophic failure. My son did not believe my love for him was unconditional.

I did not want to lose my child. I knew there was a very real chance that once he was surrounded by people who shared his experiences, he might start thinking of them as his family, and leave us—or more likely, just me—behind. A lot of kids do that, for a lot of different reasons. In a way, I was lucky that with Alex, the signposts and the risks of alienation were so clear. I was also lucky that he didn't want to let me go, and kept daring me to do better. The starting point, and it took several years because I was afraid to admit it, was to acknowledge that homosexuality—specifically, one man's desire for another man—just didn't feel normal to me. Once, when another man had put his hand on my knee, I'd felt angry: How could he think I was gay? But also scared: Did I seem gay?

Anger and intolerance are products of ignorance, and like many heterosexual men of my generation, I was almost wholly ignorant of gay culture. I was midway through my twenties before I met a man who was openly gay. Although I had gay colleagues, men and women I trusted and respected, I'd never had a close friendship with anyone who was gay.

Only by admitting my ignorance to myself, examining it and educating myself—and allowing Alex to educate me—did I get past it. When my son came out, I'd feared that older gay men would be predatory; instead, they were fatherly and caring. I assumed Alex would embrace promiscuity, but actually he sought monogamy. His gay friends were lively, intelligent and creative—exactly the kind of people whose company I enjoy most. Why would spending time with them threaten my sense of masculinity? Was it really so fragile? In fact, I came to see, these guys were in some ways more masculine than I was: they had the courage of their convictions and the strength to insist on owning and defining their lives.

One thing Alex needed to accept about me was that I don't like overt demonstrations of sexuality, period. I don't care whether it's a man or woman, gay or straight—to me, there's just something cartoonish about advertising sexual availability. In a gay bar this means I wince at leather thongs, but in a strip club catering to straight men, I'd wince at sequined thongs.

The hopelessly square truth is that when love is part of sex, it's much easier for me to understand and celebrate. One man's desire for another man—a particular man, not every guy in the room—now strikes me as a pretty normal thing, and nothing to turn away from. When I notice same-sex couples holding hands, my primary feeling is relief that they are now free to show the rest of us how they feel about each other. What could be more normal than falling in love and wanting to hold hands and kiss in public? When I'm with Alex in the gay village in Toronto and a young man recognizes me as "that guy who does the news," he will occasionally ask if I will be in a picture with him. A few years ago, I might have worried about what would happen if a gossip columnist got hold of one of those selfies. Not now.

I realized how far I'd come when, in the summer of 2014, Cathy and I went to an outdoor dance party in a huge park on Pride Day. Alex had to work, but his boyfriend had invited us, and we joined a long, rambunctious lineup for the security screening wondering if we'd ever be able to find him, but we did. Pretty soon we were inside a quadrangle where club music was blasting from enormous speakers. As I lined up to buy liquor tickets, a guy complimented me on my chest. A few years ago I would have flushed, and might have been angered by the comment. This time I thanked him and told him that his chest was pretty solid, too. When he moved on to other body parts, I smiled and assured him I wasn't in his league. He figured it out, and laughed. Later, up on a giant screen, a slide show: shots of all the men who'd taken off their shirts in the mid-summer heat. Most of them appeared to have been lifting weights (and, in some cases, taking steroids, by the looks of things) for months to look their best. I'd never seen so many jacked men in one place, not even a gym.

The beat of the music was insistent, and after Alex's boyfriend bought me a beer, I began to move to the rhythm like everyone else. As the afternoon went on, more dancing and drinking loosened up the crowd. Shirts came off, including, eventually, mine (with Cathy rolling her eyes, especially when I dared some of Alex's friends to match my dance moves; wisely, they passed). When Alex's boyfriend whipped out his phone for a selfie, I threw my arm around his shoulder, and the image he caught is of two men, shirtless, smiling back at the universe. To me, that snapshot captures my evolution as a man and as a father, my understanding that pride in one's sexuality—in-your-face exhibitionism of that pride, even—is something to be celebrated, not feared or disdained. When I posted it on Facebook with the caption "Sharing in Pride with Alex's partner," my son was the first to comment: "I wish I had been there, too!" Given all that we have been through, together and apart, that felt good.

I didn't expect or want to be the father of a gay son, it's true. I had great expectations for Alex, and they didn't include being homosexual. But Alex has met—exceeded!—the dreams I dreamed for him while I was rocking him to sleep on my chest twenty-nine years ago. Today, he is athletic, adventurous, popular. He is also highly successful. And here's the thing: he became all those things largely *because* he is gay. It was his own bravery in coming out and living his truth that enabled him to thrive. If he'd stayed in the closet, he could not have become the man he is today. Being gay has given Alex the life I always dreamed of for him. It has also made him a man I not only love, but deeply admire.

Another surprise: I've changed for the better, too.

In December 2014, Cathy and I returned to New York to attend a *GMA* alumni party in the lobby bar of the Empire Hotel—the same place I'd called home those first terrifying months in New York. As Cathy and I hopped into a Yellow Cab and headed to the hotel, I was nervous. I wasn't sure many people would even remember me; ABC had written me and Lisa out of the show's official history. And then there was the way it had all ended, and reminders of the shadow that had existed over Cathy's health when we left. So much had happened since then to make me stronger and more confident, but for a few brief minutes the bruises felt tender again.

Almost as soon as we walked in the door, my apprehension shifted to excitement. It was so good to reconnect with these people I'd shared so many early morning hours with, and everyone was amazed to see Cathy looking so well and then genuinely thrilled to hear that she'd been misdiagnosed. People asked after our kids, and we had wonderful stories to share: Alex had won a gold medal in the Young Lions competition at Cannes, the most prestigious event in advertising, and Erica was thriving as a production assistant at an animation company. Both of them had serious boyfriends, men we liked. As the evening went on and people loosened up, a few of the studio crew pulled me aside and said how sorry they were about how *GMA* had ended for me, that they felt I was never given a fair shot. It felt good to be able to tell them I was just fine and, in retrospect, thankful it hadn't worked out. I had a better-balanced life. I was finally happy.

And then Charlie Gibson showed up. The respect in the room was palpable. He had been unrelentingly courteous to every person at that party during his eighteen years as co-host, and now enjoyed their uncomplicated, unstinting affection. Everyone wanted some face time with him, so I hung back. Near the end of the evening, though, he found me and Cathy in a corner booth and sat down with us. We talked about our children, his grandchildren, Cathy's health, his wife, Arlene. Charlie had retired in 2009, stepping down voluntarily just three years after starting his dream job, anchoring ABC's *World News*. I suspected that he'd also discovered that work is just work. But I asked anyway: What did he miss? "Nothing," he replied. "There is so much more to my life now. It's so much richer. How much more work do you really need?"

I knew exactly what he meant. All those years, I'd looked at work as the way to become a better man. More successful, more approved of, more respected. I got all of that, but it did not make me a better man. My family did. I think I avoided falling in love with celebrity, or becoming bitter when I failed, because my family grounded me.

Here's the part I never would have predicted twenty-nine years ago: my children have been the most important teachers in my life. They have tested my beliefs and challenged my will.

They have called me to account and made me look at the world differently. They have taught me to aim for true success, the kind that lasts and matters: being a good father.

I'll keep trying.

CHAPTER FOURTEEN

ALL IN
ALEX

IN JANUARY 2013, my dad came to me and said he'd been working on a story about a gay teen coming out of the closet—would it be okay if he mentioned in the story that this issue is personal for him, because he has a gay son? I was fine with it—I live openly as a gay man and have nothing to hide—but a little startled. My dad is old school when it comes to journalistic objectivity, and he doesn't think reporters should take sides on any issue they cover. He's threatened to quit jobs where he's been pressured to report on things in a certain way to please a station owner or major advertiser. Putting himself into the story was a huge step for him, then, and he had to get permission from the network to do it.

When the story was about to air on *W5*, he asked me whether I'd go on a morning show with him to help promote the episode. I couldn't remember ever seeing him so passionate about a particular story. He really wanted people to watch it. I can't say I was fully conscious when I arrived at the studio, hours before sunrise, but he looked to be wide awake. We bolted some coffee, makeup was swabbed on our faces, and as we were about to take our seats on the set my father told me he was a little nervous. "I'm used to doing the interviewing, not talking about myself," he said. Then he asked, "Sure you're okay with this?" Some kind of wild reversal had taken place: my dad wanted to know whether I was as ready to teach the world about homosexuality as he was. Right before we went live, he hurriedly pulled out his phone and took a selfie of the two of us waiting to be interviewed. Being on TV had long since stopped being exciting for him, but this was clearly a big moment, bigger than I'd realized.

Then the cameras were on and he was talking about teen suicide and how crucial it is for parents to support gay kids when they're coming out. The interviewer asked whether I'd been scared to come out. "Terrified," I said. "Inside I had built it up to be such a momentous thing, because it's very traumatic to cross those social divides in your head and understand that you, yourself, may be different from everyone else—let alone try to make your parents understand 'This is who I am.'"

It was the first time I'd been on TV with my father since the Christmas-cookie segment for *GMA*, fifteen years earlier, when I'd been weirded out by the way that, as soon as the cameras started rolling, my father seemed to become someone I didn't know. This time was different. He was *on*, yes, but still himself, just a little more animated than he had been in the makeup room.

Something else: he was making a big, public declaration that he accepted my sexuality. He was leveraging his job, which means so much to him, to advocate for gay kids everywhere.

For years, I'd tested him and, yes, judged him. I never doubted his commitment to equal rights or same-sex marriage; I knew his opposition to legal discrimination was heartfelt. What I doubted was whether he felt anything positive when he saw a same-sex couple holding hands, say, or kissing. He's good at projecting confidence and neutrality—it's what he does for a living. After I came out, I never again saw him flinch when two guys kissed on TV, but I figured he must still be cringing inside. I'd seen his instinctive, reflexive response. I knew how he really felt.

But I also knew that, at least outwardly, he was a lot more accepting than most fathers are. Many of my gay friends are estranged from their dads, or might as well be, given the discomfort on both sides. Actually, I don't know anyone, straight or gay, who's as close to his father as I am to mine. Sexuality aside, we have a lot in common. I'm as engaged in my work as he is in his, and he's a sounding board for me on anything to do with my career. We've given speeches together, talking about the interplay between advertising and media. We both have a sentimental side, and a sarcastic side, and can be cold and determined when there's work to be done. We both place a high value on loyalty and crave the security only a loving family can provide. My parents are the people I seek out when I'm down, but also when I'm bored and just want to hang out and have some fun. Both Erica and I consider our parents, and one another, among our very closest friends.

I'm lucky, I know. But I wanted something else from my father, and I got it, fittingly enough, on television, when he told the world how proud he was of me and urged others parents to embrace their gay kids and reassure them they could have happy, normal lives. He went all out.

In the same way that black people know the world is not colour-blind, gay people know that despite legal gains, homosexuality is still stigmatized. Some people are completely accepting and others are openly homophobic, but there's a large grey area in between, filled with people whose personal responses don't always match up with their progressive political beliefs.Understandably, then, coming out is still profoundly difficult, not just for kids but for their parents. When my dad's *W5* episode aired, the response was overwhelming. So many families were obviously strug-gling and felt isolated; kids and parents reached out to me and to my dad, grateful to know they were not alone, but also hun-gry for guidance. We had a brainstorm: What if we wrote a book for families, a kind of guide to the coming-out process? Of course I'd be the hero of the story, which struck me as a fine idea, but our concept was that all of us, including my mom and Erica, would contribute chapters. The idea of a family project, something we could all contribute to and work on together, was appealing to everyone, as was the public service angle. But I had another, more self-interested motive. I knew that if we wrote a book, I'd finally get to hear details I didn't know—like why on earth my dad had told my grandparents instead of let-ting me do it—and I'd also get to educate my family a little on what it feels like to be gay.

Then we started writing, and the book insisted on a different direction. Erica, who's the most graceful writer in our family, was the first to finish a chapter, and it was amazing. But, she announced cheerfully, she had absolutely nothing else to say because she hadn't struggled even for an instant to accept my sexuality (she was, however, still pissed that I'd cut up her blankie). My mother, meanwhile, was losing sleep because she couldn't think what to write. "Honestly, there was never any conflict for me, I was just so proud of you for coming out," she'd say, then, "Wait a sec, I've got something: How about a chapter on condoms? You are being safe, right, Alex? Alex?" Yes, Mom.

That left me and my dad. In 2013, in the dead of winter, we went to the cottage to hash out the territory we'd cover. At one point, I said I thought the divide between gay and straight men was unbridgeable and that he could never fully understand me. My dad said he thought he could, actually, because there were so many similarities between us. We smiled at one another, stubbornly. It was on. Just one rule: we decided that to get as close to an honest account as possible, we had to write our chapters completely separately, and not read one another's until the manuscript was done.

Now that it is, I'm glad we worked this way. If we'd tried to write together, we would have quarrelled over whose version of each story was right. Seeing both narratives side by side, it's clear that we're both right, we're both telling the truth. What's important is to hear one another's truth, really take it in and think about it, not argue with it.

When I started writing, my goal was to make my dad understand me better, and I think he does now. Until he read my chapters, he hadn't known how much pain I was in growing up; he hadn't known how I'd interpreted his behaviour. But there's been an unlooked-for and, to me, even more important benefit:

I understand him better, too. I never knew my dad had struggled, or felt trapped, or felt vulnerable and exposed in many of
the same ways I have in my life. I never knew he felt he'd failed,
either at work or as a father. These are the kind of secrets you
rarely discover about your parents until they die and, cleaning
out a cupboard, you happen upon a diary or a stash of letters.
When it's too late.

Knowing my father's side of the story has brought us closer.
It's also helped me reframe my own story. I thought he wanted
me to be just like him, but now I see that he actually wanted me
to be different: happier and more confident than he was as a boy.
He just went about it the wrong way given that I actually *was* just
like him: bad at team sports, bad at making friends. I thought he
was trying to change me because he couldn't accept me the way
I was. He thought he was trying to save me from his own sad
fate, eating lunch alone in the school cafeteria every day.

We were prisoners of our own narratives, confident that we
understood one another's motives and interpretations. Getting
it all out in the open has given both of us, I think, a new understanding not only of one another, but of ourselves.

A few years ago, walking around Toronto with my dad, we passed
two guys holding hands. He kept walking for a minute, then
stopped and said, "Those guys were holding hands and I didn't
care!" He sounded delighted, as though he'd just discovered the
fountain of youth or something. In that moment, the moral of the
story seemed clear: I'd been right about him all along—he really
was uncomfortable with homosexuality.

But now I know that I was wrong, too. I didn't account for my dad's formidable work ethic. As hard as he worked at his job, he worked just that hard to overcome his programming and open his mind. I didn't appreciate that, fully, until I read his story, and understood how hard he tried to do all the right things. He drove me to that first youth group meeting in Vancouver—then waited outside with my mom for the duration of the event, in case I decided I had to get the hell out of there. He researched how to support gay kids as intensively as he'd research for an on-air interview. He went to Pride parades and waved handmade posters. He let my boyfriends spend the night and vacation with us at the cottage. He even went to the Board of Education in Vancouver to find out what they'd do if I were bullied. Just in case.

It makes *me* flinch to see my teenage self through his eyes, making out on the raft with Ken, but now I get why my dad dashed around telling my grandparents I was gay. What I'd understood as a form of robbery, almost, because he'd taken my truth and broadcast it, I now view as an attempt to protect me. I didn't understand just how concerned for me and protective he was and still is. Picture my father, who's not a small individual, crouching behind a pillar at the airport when I flew home to Vancouver after my first semester at university. He knew Ken was coming to pick me up and feared a rerun of the raft episode, only this time, a motorcycle gang would show up and beat us to death. As it happened, Ken did present me with an enormous bouquet and latch on to me like a barnacle as soon as I came out of the gate, but no bystanders said or did anything—except my dad, who kept watch to be sure I was safe, then hightailed it home so he'd be there when I walked through the door. In our family, this became something of a joke, a story about my dad's goofy earnestness, but now I see it as a story about the purest kind of love.

Though he wasn't always successful, my dad did consciously, diligently, try to see the world through my eyes. Occasionally, his vision was even clearer than mine. When I got my first apartment in Toronto, for instance, he offered to help me get furniture and as soon as he noticed me looking at a single bed, he jumped in with, "You need a double, at least—guys take up a lot of room." For a long time, I dated a man who, as he stomped all over my heart, said things like, "Being gay is like not having an arm: you'd give anything to have that arm back, but if someone was making fun of you for having a stump, you'd defend yourself." My dad said he didn't think someone who didn't accept himself could ever give me the love I deserved, and encouraged me to hold out for fireworks. Later, when I fell in love with a nice guy, my father gamely accompanied us to gay bars where, poor man, he looked totally out of place. By the time I saw pictures of him dancing with my friends at Pride 2014, I no longer doubted the depth of my father's acceptance. I wasn't even there, but he was—and he looked completely comfortable. Better than that, actually: elated. As proud of me as I am of him.

I know he understands that my life is better because I am gay, but I'm not sure he really knows why. It has very little to do with sexuality, in the end. The gay community is tight-knit, and after years as a loner, I value the sense of belonging, the effortless camaraderie. Of course, there are also things I don't like: the cultural emphasis on youth and beauty, the lack of support for monogamy. But knowing that the whole community would close ranks and rise to protect me if my freedom were threatened? That makes my life better.

Because I'm gay, and I accept my sexuality, I know myself well—you have to, in order to be willing to transgress societal norms. Self-awareness has a powerful, positive effect on all areas of my life; it's easier to figure out what's right for me, regardless of what others think, and then have the courage to follow through. In my mid-twenties, for instance, I won a major advertising award and landed a dream job in New York. The big leagues. I knew I was supposed to love it, but I didn't. What I loved was my boyfriend, back in Toronto. I gave it a year, then moved home.

If there's a moral to be found here, it's this: if you want to be happy, you have to figure out who you are, then be true to yourself. Own your life. To do that, everyone, gay or straight, has to come out, first to themselves, and then to the world. My father did, and then he helped me come out, too. He helped me accept myself and he taught me everything I know about strength, determination and self-reliance. In the end, he is the hero of my story, if not his own.

Thank you, Dad. I love you.

ACKNOWLEDGEMENTS

Originally, this book was meant to be a memoir written by every member of our family—Erica and Alex, Cathy and me—in alternating voices. But as we actually tackled the writing, it became clear where the tension in our family story lay: between Alex and me. Cathy and Erica have always been loving, supportive, without judgement and totally invested in our well-being, whereas the hurdles Alex and I had to overcome to reach that point seemed larger and potentially more meaningful to explore for the readers we hoped to reach. So we started over, probing deep into our relationship as father and son, our self-worth as men, and how we both (at very different ages) had to move beyond fear to claim ourselves and each other.

We didn't make that radical change in direction alone. There has been someone else instrumental to this book whose name is not on the cover. Someone who guided the narrative, who helped us probe our memories and feelings, who edited our words, wrote what we could not get down: Kate Fillion. With the two of us writing in isolation, we needed her enormous talent to ensure our stories came together to create a whole. She conducted hundreds of hours of interviews to draw out our life experiences, gently challenged us, and tested the accuracy of the facts and our memories. At all times we felt safe in her hands and certain that without her help we would be lost in the story.

I first met Kate when she was booked on *Good Morning America* to discuss her first, bestselling book, *Lip Service*. I'd been told she lived in Canada, although she was born in the United States. I always made a point of meeting guests from Canada ahead of the broadcast, so I introduced myself to Kate who was sitting in the makeup chair at the time, looking pretty tense. We chatted for a bit and, as I remember it, I told her the interview would be over quickly and not to worry too much. Apparently that pep talk made an impression on her because seventeen years later when our publisher suggested to Kate she might want to help us with this project, she agreed. I was excited because I also admired Kate's work as an accomplished magazine and newspaper writer. I had produced a few short print columns in my life, but a book—especially such a personal one? Having Kate to lean on helped steady me. Alex and I have learned so much working alongside a writer of Kate's skill; both of us believe our collaboration with Kate has been among the most fulfilling and creative of our careers.

We're also grateful for the supportive and exemplary team at Random House Canada, who kept our confidence afloat through the twists and turns our story has taken. From the outset our publisher and editor, Anne Collins, believed in the conversation we were hoping to help build between fathers and their gay, lesbian, bisexual or transgendered children. She and her team instantly understood that this is the parenting and civil rights issue of our time, and that our story had social significance. When I shared with her that gay and lesbian children were much more likely than straight kids to attempt suicide because of the emotional challenges of the coming-out process, and that a father's acceptance was found to be key to saving them from that fate, Anne paused, let those facts sink in, and from that moment on was devoted to helping us tell the story. We're also grateful for associate editor Amanda Lewis's efforts to develop the story and create the book you hold in your hands.

Alex would like to acknowledge and thank QMUNITY Gab Youth in Vancouver, the organization which supported him in those tentative and overwhelming first months after coming out. I'd like to thank my agent, Michael Levine, who has cared for and helped shape so much of my career in Canada. And we would both like to thank *you* for being interested enough in what we've experienced, and had to say about it, to have read right to the very end.

Kevin and Alex Newman

ABOUT THE AUTHORS

As co-host of *Good Morning America*, founding anchor of Global National and currently anchor/correspondent at CTV News, KEVIN NEWMAN has been a familiar face to television viewers in Canada and the US for decades. As an EMMY Award-winning network news correspondent, he has travelled the world, and reported from hot spots such as Iraq and Afghanistan.

ALEX NEWMAN, art director at J. Walter Thompson Toronto, has won numerous awards, including the Gold Medal in the Cannes Young Lions competition, one of the advertising industry's highest honours. In 2014, he was named one of Canada's top 30 under 30 by *Marketing Magazine*.